National Sheepdog Champions
of Britain and Ireland

Adam Telfer with Old Hemp (left) and Brigg Moss (right)

National Sheepdog Champions of Britain and Ireland

E. B. CARPENTER

Farming Press

First published 1994

ISBN 0 85236 282 X

A catalogue record for this book is available
from the British Library

Published by Farming Press Books
Wharfedale Road, Ipswich IP1 4LG, United Kingdom

Distributed in North America
by Diamond Farm Enterprises,
Box 537, Alexandria Bay, NY 13607, USA

Cover design by Mark Beesley
Typeset by Galleon Typesetting, Ipswich
Printed and bound in Great Britain by
Butler and Tanner Ltd, Frome and London

Contents

Preface   vii

Foreword by Austin Bennett   ix

Development of the International Sheep Dog Society Trials   2

English National Winners   5

Scottish National Winners   97

Welsh National Winners   183

Irish National Winners   263

Appendices

   Further Reading   306

   International Sheep Dog Society Awards   307

   National and International Championship Courses   309

   Pedigree Charts Showing Breeding Lines of ISDS
      Supreme Champions   315

   National Champion Handlers and Dogs   322

Indexes

   General Index   328

   Dog Index   332

Preface

THERE are now, as in the past, many good collies working daily on the hills, moors and farms of the British Isles, performing fantastic tasks that shepherds take for granted, but the layman would class as little short of miraculous.

Trials are the public method of testing these dogs and assessing the success or failure of breeding plans, upon which rests the continuation of the breed's shepherding prowess.

Some of the dogs mentioned in these pages have found fame with a vast public, watching and marvelling at the magical partnership of shepherd and dog, in the BBC television series of *One Man and his Dog*. Some may wonder that no mention has been made of these awards. I have listed only awards won in International Sheep Dog Society Trials, as it would be too daunting a task to record the many, many successes in even the most important annual trials held in every part of Britain, that most of these dogs have attained.

Data is taken from the Society Stud Books, trial programmes and trophy award books.

I am extremely grateful to all who have supplied photographs, for without their generosity this book could not have been compiled. I thank the *Scottish Farmer*, Frank Moyes and Austin Bennett for allowing me to include their photographs.

My special thanks to Mr Caldwell for his excellent reproduction of the photographs, some of necessity taken from the old agricultural papers. My thanks, too, to my sister, Ruth Hirst, for typing copy and proofreading, to Austin Bennett for writing the foreword, and to Marjorie Quarton for her help with the Irish dogs.

I hope readers will enjoy the 'company' of these champions, and trust that breeders of future generations of these unique shepherding dogs will keep faith with the wise stockmen of the past to whom we are indebted for the development of the present-day border collie; with its all pervading desire to work; its physical ability to cope with long hours on difficult, rough terrain, in all weathers; its loyalty and companionship.

I would be grateful to receive photographs of any dogs not illustrated. Unfortunately, despite all my efforts, there are a number that I have been unable to obtain.

Barbara Carpenter

Foreword

THE working collie has been a symbol of rural Britain for a very long time. Revered for its dedication to duty and admired for its intelligence, it has come to represent the apogee of man's collaboration with dogs.

To the working shepherd, a collie has always been an essential aid to proper flock management. Of necessity, the requirements have been demanding: resilience, courage, stamina, initiative. The early dogs from which today's great breeding lines have developed were the survivors of objective elimination. A shepherd could only afford to keep a dog that pulled its weight and this prime attention to intrinsic work ability produced a gene pool from which great working collies continue to spring.

It is heartening to know that collies are still very much part of our agricultural scene and they remain the reason that sheep farming can be carried on at all in parts of the British Isles. But time is the big reshaper and, undoubtedly, contemporary farming methods have seen the dog's demise in some areas. Ironically, the border collie has never been more popular. Basking in the limelit reflections of TV champions, its prowess is universally admired from armchairs, not just habitually accepted on the farm. The intense competition generated by a huge growth in sheepdog trialling has placed extra, sometimes different, demands on an already superlative animal, and its broad array of attributes is increasingly utilised in pastimes unrelated to shepherding.

None of this is to say that the archetype will disappear; shepherds still need dogs. But, with so many demands and influences placed on this adaptable animal, it is important that we recall and consider the criteria of earlier days. In producing this companion volume to her previous work on the Supreme Champions, Barbara Carpenter has provided perfect material for such reflection. The collies here are of legendary ancestry. They have proved their ability to excel in competitive shepherding, but they have done so because the focus for their breeding has been efficiency in practical work.

Barbara Carpenter has an authoritative knowledge of the working border collie backed up by several decades of practical work with them. She has given a great deal to the sheepdog world in a number of ways but as much as anything, perhaps, we should be grateful for her realistion in print of these invaluable reference works. It is fortunate, indeed, that she did not finally buckle in her arduous struggle to assemble their contents. The border collie is a quite exceptional animal and its devotees all over the world will thank her for this feast of a compilation.

Austin Bennett

Dedicated to Eric Halsall in appreciation
of all he has done to aid the understanding of the border collie
and so hopefully raise its stature
in the eyes of those who use the dog in their daily work

National Sheepdog Champions
of Britain and Ireland

Development of
the International Sheep Dog Society Trials

1873–1906

Most shepherds have always been jealous of their collies' reputations, and eager to prove that their dog is better than their neighbour's, or at least as good – so it is a natural progression to begin to compete in sheep dog trials.

Local trials began with local shepherds gathering to show off their dogs, and there were many small trials in most sheep rearing areas of

James Thomson judged the first Wirral Sheep-dog Society trial in 1893. Twenty-four dogs competed and the winner was W. Rigby's Turk. J. Barcroft's Bob, a mainly white, half-bred Old English sheepdog was second and Mr Piggin's Ormskirk Charlie, third. This latter dog, a pure-bred collie of show strain, a son of the famous show champion Christopher, who was

*Mr Wm. Thomson, winner of the first
sheepdog trial (Bala, October, 1873)*

Britain in the years preceding the first 'International' trial of 1906.

It was at Bala, North Wales, in 1873, that Mr Lloyd-Price organised the first official sheepdog trial in Britain. The winner was a Scottish shepherd residing in Wales: Mr James Thomson with his dog Tweed.

sold for £1,000 to the USA, won many trials, among them was Longshaw in 1898. He twice won Dovedale, and on four successive years he won Llangollen. All this as well as being a bench champion and a devoted family companion. Some dog!

The International Sheep Dog Society took the

centenary trial of 1973 to Bala, on a course close to the original one; on the same estate and hosted by the grandson of Mr Lloyd-Price. The winner was a North Wales man, Mr Glyn Jones of Bodfari and his dog Gel 63023.

At this centenary trial, the first ever sheepdog trial trophy, which was won at Rhiwlas by James Thomson in 1876, was displayed on the trophy table. It was presented in 1984 to the Supreme Champion, and has since, annually graced the trophy cabinets of succeeding Supreme Champions.

James Thomson's widow died in 1955, in her 103rd year, and the cup was given to the International Sheep Dog Society by her daughter.

Scotland's first official trial, held at Carnwath in the early 1870s, was won by James Gardner and Spy. James was a well-respected man, renowned for his great love and understanding of his sheepdogs and his skill as a shepherd. Sadly, he died at an early age, as the result of an accident while demolishing a farm building. It was said that: 'his dogs mourned his departure with all the pathos of loving and broken-hearted children.' One of his sons became a well-known journalist, writing on agricultural matters under the nom de plume 'Ralph Fleesh'.

One of Scotland's oldest trials was New Cumnock, which started in 1893, and at one time was held in greater esteem than the early 'International' trials, organised by the newly formed International Sheep Dog Society. New Cumnock was a testing, six-hundred-yard hill course, and hundreds of spectators attended the annual trials.

David Wilson, father of the great sheepdog handler, J. M. Wilson, competed at the early New Cumnock trials. Alex Millar won the trial in 1900 with five-year-old Bruce, a dog that became well known in the Border country, and is said to have been bred from a very good strain of local sheepdogs.

Two trials were held in England during 1876 within a couple of months of each other. The first, in a London park, was organised by Mr Lloyd-Price. Apparently it was not successful: many of the wild Welsh wether sheep, specially transported from Wales for this trial, escaped from the trial field and were never recovered! The other trial, held in real sheep country at Byrness in Redesdale, Northumberland, was won by Walter Telfer, known as 'Wat of the Rookin'. His son, Adam, was to become the famous breeder of Old Hemp 9, the dog which became known as 'father' of the modern border collie.

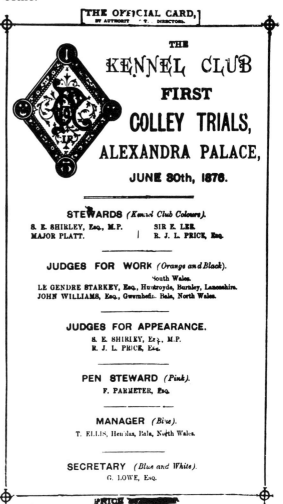

THE OFFICIAL CARD,
BY AUTHORITY OF THE DIRECTORS.

THE

KENNEL CLUB

FIRST

COLLEY TRIALS,

ALEXANDRA PALACE,

JUNE 30th, 1876.

STEWARDS (*Kennel Club Colours*).
S. E. SHIRLEY, Esq., M.P.   SIR E. LEE
MAJOR PLATT.   R. J. L. PRICE, Esq.

JUDGES FOR WORK (*Orange and Black*).
South Wales.
LE GENDRE STARKEY, Esq., Huntroyde, Burnley, Lancashire.
JOHN WILLIAMS, Esq., Gwernhefin, Bala, North Wales.

JUDGES FOR APPEARANCE.
S. E. SHIRLEY, Esq., M.P.
R. J. L. PRICE, Esq.

PEN STEWARD (*Pink*).
F. PARMETER, Esq.

MANAGER (*Blue*).
T. ELLIS, Henblas, Bala, North Wales.

SECRETARY (*Blue and White*).
G. LOWE, Esq.

PRICE

1906 – Present

The International Sheep Dog Society was formed in 1906, at Haddington, by Scottish sheepdog enthusiasts, and although it was international in name, the members were mostly Scottish. The annual Society trials were all held in Scotland, except for two in northern England, until the 1914–18 War, during which the Society ceased its activities.

Commencing again in 1919 with the enthusiastic honorary secretary, Mr James A. Reid, an Airdrie solicitor, the Society went from strength to strength, the annual trials being held alternately in Scotland and England until 1922. Increasing interest resulted in the Cricceith Sheepdog Society (in Wales) sending Captain Whittaker, supported by the Hon E. L. Mostyn – later Lord Mostyn – and Mr Jones-Jarrett, to the 1921 International trial, with an invitation to visit Wales. The directors unanimously decided to accept, and the 1922 International Trial was hosted by Wales at Cricceith, where William Wallace, of Otterburn, won the Supreme Championship with Meg 306.

Pre-war trials had been one day events with some 30–40 dogs competing; farmers and shepherds competed in one class. But from 1919 separate classes were instituted, and the trials became two day affairs. Shepherds felt they could compete together on equal terms with the farmers. General interest in the Society was increased by the formation of a registration system and a stud book.

With Wales taking part it was decided in 1922 that the annual National trials should take place in each of the three countries, England, Scotland and Wales, with a team of twelve dogs, from each country, going forward to the International trial, now extended to three days, and to be held alternately in each of the three countries.

The outbreak of World War II on 3 September 1939 caused the cancellation of the International that year, although the three Nationals had been run in the summer, and no further ISDS trials were held until 1946.

During the war years a few trials were organised by local committees to raise funds for the war effort.

In 1961 Northern Ireland became integrated with the International Society, a National trial taking place at Glenarm, from which three dogs went forward to compete at the International. Then in 1965 the Republic of Eire and Northern Ireland amalgamated their trials and held an Irish National, four dogs then competing at the International, making a total of forty dogs from the four countries.

In 1973 the Society produced a badge, its motif being Wiston Cap, in characteristic pose.

Ladies' membership badges were discontinued from 1975, and the Blue Riband award was re-introduced at the International that year. There seems to be no record of the years when it was previously awarded. It is a blue material sash, inscribed in gold with the words 'I.S.D.S. Supreme Champion' and the year in which it is won. Fitted with a clasp, it is fastened round the winning dog's neck.

The next change came in 1976 when the individual shepherds' class was abolished, farmers and shepherds once again competing in a combined class, the championship trophies being awarded to the respective highest-pointed farmers' dog and the highest-pointed shepherds' dog in the National trials, and in the International Qualifying trial.

Each National trial is now confined to running a maximum of one hundred and fifty dogs, plus nine brace partnerships, which have all qualified on points won in affiliated trials.

Fifteen dogs from England, Scotland and Wales, and ten from Ireland now compete in the International qualifying trial, the fifteen highest-pointed dogs, irrespective of country, going forward to the Supreme Championship course.

The Irish team 'came of age' in 1993 when one hundred and fifty dogs were entered for the Irish National. The team consisted of fifteen singles dogs and two brace competitors.

This made a total of sixty dogs in the International Qualifying trial, and eight brace competitors.

English National Winners

Born –/10/18   Black & white   E. Priestley, Hathersage

Awards

English National Champion 1922
English National Champion 1923

LADDIE 42, W. Rutherford	┌MOSS, P. Elliott	
	└QUEEN, J. K. Burns	
FLY 165, T. Hunter	┌DON, A. Hamilton	┌DON, W. Burns └TRIM 37, T. Armstrong
	└MAID 945, A. Hamilton	┌HEMP 153, Dickson └FLO 62, A. Hamilton

HEMP 153   *International Farmers' Champion 1924*

The Priestleys

The first two English Nationals were won by Ernest Priestley's Moss 233, a son of T. Hunter's Fly 165. Ernest Priestley, head shepherd on the Longshaw Estate, is renowned as the originator of one of England's oldest trials – Longshaw. He made a wager with Ellis Ashton, head keeper of the Duke of Rutland's Longshaw estate, and suggested a trial between the estate shepherds and their dogs, offering a fat wether as first prize. Sam White, landlord of the Grouse Inn, agreed to compete, and next day he and Ernest Priestley competed in the rough field opposite the Inn, Sam's dog Gyp being the winner. The next evening the fat wether was enjoyed by all at the supper in the Fox House Inn

This was in 1894, and in 1898 an 'official' trial was organised in the Wooden Pole field. A tall pole still stands in this exposed field – originally a guide post for the ancient packhorse route over the moors.

The weather was so bad, with heavy snow storms, that the trial was abandoned and was run the following day in a more sheltered field. This trial was won by Mr Piggin's show champion, the famous Ormskirk Charlie. Sam White's Gyp came second in the local class, and in 1900 she was sixth.

A painting of Gyp used to hang in the Grouse Inn, the venue for many Longshaw committee meetings, but when the bar room was extended, the picture was given to the Longshaw Society, on condition that it would be placed on display at the annual trials, among the magnificent trophies. Sadly it was not to be seen in 1990 when I visited Longshaw Trials, now a mini International, run over three full days, amid breathtaking moorland scenery, in an overpowering aura of history: the Fox House Inn and the Grouse Inn, both concerned with the society's meetings and dinners over all these years still stand. The competitors' family names, now well known – Elliott, Ollerenshaw, Saxon, Eyre, Sowerby, Priestley, Denniff, Shaw and Stevens – still appear in the programme; young men carrying on their forefathers' shepherding expertise.

Ernest Priestley's Hemp 1006, a son of Hemp 153, won the English National in 1930. He and his litter brother Lad 859, were out of Jet 607, who was a daughter of Moss 233 and Jed 358, a daughter of T. Hunter's Sweep 164. Jed and Jet were formerly owned by T. Capstick, who wrote the first little sheepdog training book, and who trained many of the successful trial dogs of the 1920s. Sadly, Ernest Priestley was killed in 1936 in an accident on his motorbike and sidecar, en route to a trial. His dogs were unharmed.

Ashton Priestley continued the family tradition of sheepdog handling, winning the Supreme Championship with Pat 4203, in 1951. He handled Lad 859 and Wylie 1184 to win the International Brace Championship in 1930, and in 1933 Lad and Hemp 1006 won the English Brace Class for him. These three dogs were litter mates from Hemp 153 and Jet 607. In 1937 Ashton ran old Hemp in his last trial, and the old dog excelled himself, gaining full points. Overcome, Ashton hugged the old dog in joy. He won the English Nationals in 1955 and 1960 with Jim 10071 and Sweep 11115 respectively, and Pat and Mac 8133 were English Brace Champions in 1952. Ashton took Pat and several other dogs to America where he gave many excellent demonstrations and exhibitions.

His son Malcolm is a successful handler and his daughter Margaret is married to Raymond MacPherson MBE who has twice won the Supreme Championship with Zac 66166, in 1975 and 1979.

Raymond MacPherson

Raymond MacPherson began trialling at the age of eleven, and was a Scottish team member on three occasions, winning the 1957 Scottish Brace Championship with Bill 13243 and Lark 9679, who was a sister to Whitehope Nap. Residing in England since 1965, he has been a regular member of the English team, winning the 1971 English National with Nap 43986, and twice winning the Supreme Championship with Zac, a grandson of the 1968 Supreme Champion, Bosworth Coon 34186.

John Templeton and Raymond MacPherson competed in the World Championship Trial in America in 1973, the latter winning the championship with Nap 43986, a grandson of J. M. Wilson's Whitehope Nap 8685, a strong-willed, powerful dog who left a legacy of powerful workers, and is in the breeding of many of the successful trial dogs of today.

The World Championship trial ended in a tragic motel fire in which John Templeton's Fleet and some American dogs died, but his Cap 50543, Supreme Champion in 1972, was saved with Nap. Cap was sold and remained in America. Raymond MacPherson again won the American World Championship in 1976 with Tweed 62901, a son of J. Gilchrist's Scottish National Champion, Spot 24981. Tweed, previously owned by Alan Jones, had been Welsh Driving Champion in 1972, and in 1980 he won the English Driving Championship with Raymond MacPherson, who was awarded the MBE in 1979 for his services to agriculture.

Margaret and Raymond MacPherson's only daughter, Nicola, is married to John Harrison, the 1990 English National Champion, who farms at Shap.

Ormskirk Charlie

Born –/7/18   Black, white & tan   A. Telfer, Stamfordham

Awards

International Supreme Champion 1921

	┌ RAP II, W. Wallace	┌ Not known └ Not known
GLEN 34, W.Wallace		
	└ LASSIE, R. Scott	┌ Not known └ Not known
	┌ DON I 17, T. Armstrong	┌ DON, W. Burns └ TRIM 37, T. Armstrong
MADDIE I 38, J. A. Reid		
	└ MADDIE 8, W. B. Telfer	┌ GLEN, McKenzie └ LASSIE, H. Renwick

The Telfer Family

The pedigree of most National Champions can be traced back to the dogs registered in the Society's first stud book, and the majority can be traced to one particular dog – Old Hemp 9 – and the family founded on his blood lines.

Born in September 1893, he was bred by Adam Telfer from his strong-eyed, black-coated, rather reserved Meg, and by his black and tan, friendly, plain working Roy. Both dogs were bred from old 'Rookin' White' dogs of Northumberland. Their finest qualities were united in Hemp, whose quiet firm method of work impressed the neighbouring sheepmen, who bred their bitches to him. So many of his offspring inherited his quiet power that his fame spread, and he sired over two hundred puppies before his death in 1901. It was fortunate that his prepotency was recognised, for such was his lasting effect on the breed that Hemp is now known as the 'Father' of the modern Border Collie.

Adam Telfer and his sons, Adam and Walter, were all good successful handlers. In 1910 Adam won the Supreme Championship with Sweep 21, who was also third the following year. Sweep was a grandson of Hemp, out of Trim 37, a daughter of Tommy 16, also a grandson of Hemp. Sweep was bred by Thomas Armstrong, a neighbour and a great friend of the Telfer family, and he was transferred back to Thomas Armstrong, who won the 1912 Supreme Championship with Sweep again, and later exported him to New Zealand.

Adam won the Supreme Championship again in 1921 at Ayre with Haig 252. That same day his son John's wife gave birth to a baby girl, who was christened Jean Ayre Telfer, and it is she who has so generously lent these historic photos of these famous men and their equally famous dogs. Haig, in 1924, won the English National. He was descended from J. Scott's Kep 13, who though not in direct line from Old Hemp, was from Cleg, a granddaughter of Hemp's grandam, Pose.

Kep 13, International Supreme Champion in 1908 and 1910, bred back to his own dam, Cleg, headed a family line which blended well with the main Hemp line, and Kep became a noted stud dog of his time. He was considered the best working collie of his day and many of his offspring competed successfully in the Nationals and International trials. When working, Kep completely ignored rabbits and hares, but was delighted to accompany James Scott with the gun and was an excellent gun dog, retrieving game for him.

Adam Telfer won the International Farmers' Championship in 1919 with Toss 151, who was also third in the Supreme Championship. He was bred by Adam Telfer, both his parents, Yarrow and Fenwick Jed later being exported to James Lilico, New Zealand. Toss was a great-grandson of Tommy 16 who was bred by Wm. Wallace, Otterburn. Tommy was a most influential sire within the border collie breed. The two main blood lines of Hemp 9 and Kep 13, were combined when Tommy, a grandson of Hemp, was bred to J. Scott's Ancrum Jed, who was a daughter of Kep. This mating produced Tyne 145, Moss 22 and Trim 37, and each of these dogs headed a distinct family line.

Tommy founded two more specific lines when bred to A. Brown's Old Maid 1, and to G. P. Brown's Nell 205.

Many International Sheep Dog Society champions can be traced to these specific family lines.

Within the border collie breed there were many distinct smaller 'families'. These groups are now, of course, very interwoven because as travel over all areas of the British Isles has become easier, stud dogs can be transported to bitches in all parts of the country.

The Telfer family was much involved in the breeding and blending so successfully of these bloodlines, and their trials successes continued, with Adam junior and Walter in the 1924 English team, captained by Adam senior with Haig.

Walter won the International Supreme Championship with Midge 152, in 1919, and with Queen 533, in 1932; both dogs were from the Hemp line. Midge won the International Farmers' Championship in 1920 and 1921, and Queen, whose sire was litter brother to Midge, won the English National in 1926, 1927 and 1929. She was third in the 1925 International Supreme Championship and was International Farmers' Champion in 1927. Alex Millar's International Supreme Champion, Spot 303, was initially trained by Walter. Spot's sire was W. Telfer's Cap 237, a litter brother to Adam Telfer's Haig.

Adam junior, like his father, was well known in North country wrestling circles, but when twenty-one he was knocked down by a bolting horse, and the cartwheel crushed his hip. At my first International visit in 1947 at Cardiff, I recall seeing him, very lame and by then, an elderly man. He led a busy life: farmer, land agent, lay preacher, and secretary of the Northumberland NFU, and was a successful handler and popular trial judge.

Adam Telfer senior had another son, John, who was destined to remain at home, farming, though he too was a good dog handler, and won the only trial he ever competed in. Through John, this famous family name has continued – via his son, Walter, and grandson, John, who now has a baby son, named Adam Stewart Telfer, the great-great-grandson of Adam, breeder of Old Hemp.

Walter Telfer, winner of the first English Sheepdog trial (Byrnes, 1876)

(Left to right) Walter Telfer with Queen 533 and Sweep 532; Adam Telfer's young grandson, Walter; and Adam Telfer with Haig 252

11

Father of the modern border collie, Adam Telfer's Hemp 9

Adam Telfer with Sweep 21

"OLD HEMP"

To Adam Telfer Esq

Sir

On behalf of the Members of the International Sheep Dog Society, we, the undersigned Presidents of the Society for Scotland, England, and Wales respectively, desire to express the deep regret felt by all the members on learning of your intention to resign the office of English President of the Society held by you for five years (1919-1923), and we now take this, the first occasion on which the members have assembled in general meeting since your resignation, to express their appreciation and grateful acknowledgment of the invaluable services rendered by you towards the attainment of the objects for which the Society exists.

For over forty years you have rendered yeoman service to the cause as a breeder, trainer, and judge, and it gives one and all of us the greatest pleasure in offering you our heartiest congratulations on the success which has attained your strenuous endeavours to improve the Sheep Dogs of this and other countries, encourage and extend the trial movement, and generally elevate the shepherd and his dog to that public recognition and esteem which both so well deserve.

The number and quality of the Sheep Dogs with which your name has been associated in one capacity or another during so many years, and your work otherwise, suggest the reflection that an extreme fondness for man's great friend and helper must have been an impelling force in sustaining so much commendable perseverance on your part, which has added lustre to the laudable cause and in no small degree contributed to the great popularity which it now enjoys at home and in many other parts of the world, especially New Zealand, Australia, and Tasmania.

Although you have resigned the office of English President of the Society, in which you were maintained by the unanimous vote of the members for five years, and only relinquished by your own request, it is gratifying to every one to know that your ties with the Society are not altogether severed, but that, on the contrary, as a Honorary President and otherwise, you will continue to assist in directing its work and advancing the cause generally at home and abroad. Should this token of goodwill in any small degree tend to stimulate you in doing so, or enable you to reflect with greater pleasure on what you have already done, your many friends will feel that their object in offering you this testimonial has been happily achieved.

Yours faithfully,

James Johnston
Scottish President, 1924.

John Maughan
English President, 1924.

T. M. Whittaker
Welsh President, 1924.

James A. Reid.
Hon. Secretary & Treasurer

Ayr,
26th September, 1924.

Born –/4/20   Black & tan   J. B. Bagshaw, Rotherham

Awards

International Supreme Champion 1927
International Farmers' Champion 1926

HEMP II 307, S. E. Batty	┌SWEEP 21, T. Armstrong	┌SWEEP, J. Oliver └TRIM 37, T. Armstrong
	└OLD MEG 27, J. Renwick	┌MOSS, Blaynay └QUEEN, Crammond
JED II 250, J. B. Bagshaw	┌Not known	
	└Not known	

HEMP II 307   *International Supreme Champion 1920*
SWEEP 21   *International Supreme Champion 1910 & 1912*

1926	**QUEEN 533**	Lancaster
1927		Lancaster
1929		Hexham

Born –/4/25   Black & white   W. B. Telfer, Morpeth

Awards

International Farmers' Champion 1927
International Supreme Champion 1932

BEN 75, T. Glendinning
┌ DON II, T. Armstrong
└ NELL, T. Armstrong

MADDIE 69, J. Scott
┌ DON 17, T. Armstrong
│   ┌ DON, W. Burns
│   └ TRIM 37, T. Armstrong
└ JEAN, T. Dickson

DON 17 *International Supreme Champion 1911 & 1914*
Exported to New Zealand

JESS 818

Born –/8/24   Black & white   W. B. Bagshaw, Worksop

JAFF 379, T. Roberts	LEADER 666, T. Gilholm	KEP 13, J. Scott LASSIE 518, T. Gilholm
	LILLE 26, T. Gilholm	MOSS III 28, W. Wallace BENTY, T. Gilholm
FAN 1292, T. Roberts	BEN 249, G. P. Brown	DON 217, C. Hardisty FAN 208, G. P. Brown
	FLY 165, T. Hunter	DON, A. Hamilton MAID 945, A. Hamilton

JAFF 379 *International Supreme Champion 1924*
Welsh National Champion 1923 & 1924
KEP 13 *International Supreme Champion 1908 & 1909*

J. B. and W. B. Bagshaw at the 1934 Longshaw Trials

Born 1/3/26 Black & white E. Priestley, Hathersage

Awards
English Brace Champion 1933 with LAD 859

HEMP 153, T. Dickson	⌐**YARROW 23, A. Telfer**	⌐**TYNE 145, I. Herdman** └**NELL (MEG), J. Renwick**
	└**FENWICK JED 33, A. Telfer**	⌐**MOSS, A. Telfer** └**WYLIE, G. Snaith**
JET 607, E. Priestley	⌐**MOSS 233, E. Priestley**	⌐**LADDIE 42, W. Rutherford** └**FLY 165, T. Hunter**
	└**JED 358, E. Priestley**	⌐**SWEEP 164, T. Hunter** └**Not known**

HEMP 153 *International Farmers' Champion 1924*
MOSS 233 *English National Champion 1922 & 1923*
SWEEP 164 *International Shepherds' Champion 1923 & 1924*

Born 17/5/23   Black & white   J. B. Bagshaw, Rotherham

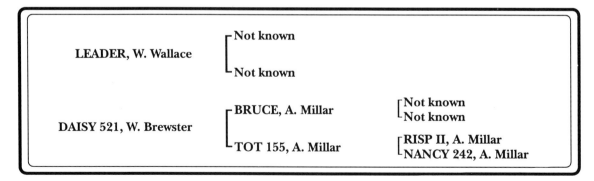

TOT 155   *Scottish National Champion 1924*

Born 24/7/30   Black & white   W. J. Wallace, Otterburn

Awards

International Supreme Champion 1938
International Brace Champion 1933 & 1934 with FLY 1657
International Aggregate Championship 1938
English Aggregate Championship 1938

MOSS IV 1009, W. Wallace
    NAP 434, A. E. Herdman
        GLEN, W. Wallace
        JED II, W. Cousin
    MEG 306, W. Wallace
        TIP, W. Amos
        NELL III, J. Hedley

MADDIE II, A. Heslop
    MOSS, Blancy
    MADDIE, A. Heslop

MEG 306   *International Supreme Champion, 1922*

19

FLY 1764

Born 8/4/31   Black & white   A. G. Liddle, Harrogate

Awards

English Brace Champion 1939 with BEN 2812

DAVE 660, T. Dickson	┌**HEMP 153, T. Dickson**	┌YARROW 23, A. Telfer └FENWICK JED 33, A. Telfer
	└NELL 167, D. Henderson	┌TOM, T. Gilholm └LILLE 26, T. Gilholm
NELL, J. Murray	┌Not known └Not known	

HEMP 153 *International Farmers' Champion 1924*

J. M. Renwick with Roy 2028 and Kep 1654

Born 1/3/29   Black & tan   J. Renwick, Alston

Awards
English Brace Champion 1934 with ROY 2028

	┌SWEEP 164, T. Hunter	┌LADDIE 42, W. Rutherford └FLY 165, T. Hunter
HEMP 89, J. Templeton		
	└KENT, Mrs Butter	┌Not known └Not known
	┌ARDLEY TOSS	┌Not known └Not known
DOT 488, J. Templeton		
	└MAID, T. Armstrong	┌Not known └Not known

SWEEP 164 *International Shepherds' Champion 1923 & 1924*

J. M. Renwick's Ben 2481

22

The Renwick Family

James Renwick's Kep 1654, winner of the 1935 and 1938 English Nationals, was a grandson of T. Hunter's Sweep 164, the 1923 and 1924 International Shepherds' Champion, and a popular stud dog, siring many successful trial dogs before being exported to New Zealand in 1926.

James Renwick won the 1934 English Brace Championship with Kep and Roy 2028, and the 1937 International Driving Championship with Ben 2481, who was the 1938 English Driving Champion.

He won the 1947 English and International Brace Championships with Glen 5107 and Heaplaw Moss 4420, the latter a son of Ben 2481. In 1947 Moss was reserve to Supreme Champion J. Gilchrist's Spot 3624, and also won the English Aggregate Championship.

The family moved to Corsebank, Sanquhar in 1948, and James then competed in the Scottish Nationals, winning the 1950 Scottish Brace Championship with Glen and Moss.

His brother, William Renwick, won the 1939 English National with Bet 2398, a granddaughter of J. B. Bagshaw's 1927 Supreme Champion, Lad 305. She was also great-granddaughter of S. E. Batty's 1920 Supreme Champion, Hemp II 307, and also of E. Priestley's Moss 233, winner of the first and second English Nationals of 1922 and 1923. Unfortunately, because of the outbreak of the 1939 War, the International was cancelled and Bet was deprived of her International cap.

Bet's grandsire, Lad, was a son of Batty's Hemp II, whose dam, Meg 27, was owned by John Renwick, father of James and William.

William Renwick was second with Mirk 12283, a son of J. M. Wilson's Moss 8754, in the 1958 Scottish National, won by W. Goodfellow and Laddie 8049.

Competing at Gullane in 1906, at the first International Trial, John Renwick's brother, Adam, gained third place, the Supreme Champion being R. Sandiland's Don 11, a son of J. Scott's Kep 13, Supreme Champion in 1908 and 1910. Sandiland's was a controversial victory, many considering that Adam Renwick's two-year-old, Don, should have been the winner on that historic day. Alex Coltherd was reserve to the champion, with Lassie. Adam Renwick's Don was sire of Andrew Brown's Old Maid, registered number one in the International Sheep Dog Society Stud Book.

J. M. Renwick's Moss 2393, Reserve to Supreme Champion 1947

Born –/2/34   Black & white   M. Hayton, Ilkley

Awards

International Farmers' Champion 1936
English Aggregate Championship 1936 & 1937

ROY, M. Hayton
┌ Not known

└ Not known

FLY II 2633, M. Hayton
┌ PAL GLEN 1854, M. Hayton
  ┌ DICK 1509, M. Hayton
  └ PATTIE 1515, A. Hayton

└ FLY 1008, M. Hayton
  ┌ ROCK 703, M. Hayton
  └ JED, H. Summerscales

PATTIE 1515   *International & English Shepherds' Champion 1934*
English Shepherds' Champion 1938
English Brace Champion 1935

Mark Hayton and his champion sheepdogs

Born –/1/35   Black & white   W. D. Renwick, Alston

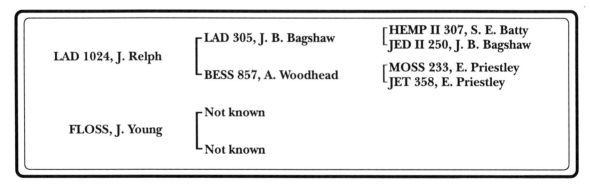

LAD 1024, J. Relph

LAD 305, J. B. Bagshaw
  HEMP II 307, S. E. Batty
  JED II 250, J. B. Bagshaw

BESS 857, A. Woodhead
  MOSS 233, E. Priestley
  JET 358, E. Priestley

FLOSS, J. Young

Not known

Not known

LAD 305   *International Supreme Champion 1927*
            International Farmers' Champion 1926
            English National Champion 1925
HEMP II 307   *International Supreme Champion 1920*
MOSS 233   *English National Champion 1922 & 1923*

No trials were held during the war years, 1940–45

1946   MAC 4418   Ilkley

Born –/9/40   Black & white   W. B. Bagshaw, Worksop

```
                              ┌ ROY, M. Hayton          ┌ Not known
                              │                         └ Not known
PAT 2219, M. Hayton          ┤
                              │                         ┌ PAL GLEN 1854, M. Hayton
                              └ FLY II 2633, M. Hayton  └ FLY 1008, M. Hayton

                              ┌ PAL GLEN 1854, M. Hayton ┌ DICK 1509, M. Hayton
                              │                          └ PATTIE 1515, A. Hayton
LASS 2849, Lawson            ┤
                              │                         ┌ Not known
                              └ JED, R. Duck            └ Not known
```

PAT 2219   *International Farmers' Champion 1936*
English National Champion 1937
English Aggregate Championship 1936 & 1937

PATTIE 1515   *International & English Shepherds' Champion 1934*
English Shepherds' Champion 1938
English Brace Champion 1935

Born 15/8/44   Black, tan & white   A. Hayton, Otley

Awards
International Brace Champion 1946 with PADDY 4364

PAT 2219, M. Hayton	ROY, M. Hayton	Not known Not known
	FLY II 2633, M. Hayton	PAL GLEN 1854, M. Hayton FLY 1008, M. Hayton
PADDY 4364, A. Hayton	JOCK 2029, A. Hayton	PAL GLEN 1854, M. Hayton MIDGE, J. Robinson
	NELL, M. Hayton	Not known Not known

PAT 2219   *International Farmers' Champion 1936*
English National Champion 1937
English Aggregate Championship 1936 & 1937
PADDY 4364   *International Brace Champion 1946*
JOCK 2029   *International Shepherds' Champion 1937*
English Shepherds' Champion 1935, 1936, 1937 & 1939
English Brace Champion 1935

Arthur Hayton's Pattie

Born –/11/44   Black, white & tan   J. Thorp, Nuneaton

Awards
English Brace Champion 1946 with JESS II 2852

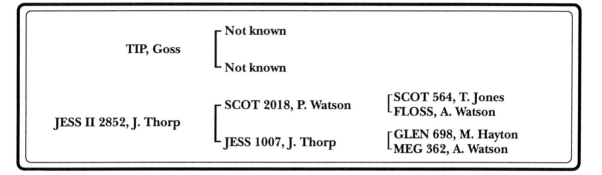

JESS II 2852, J. Thorp — SCOT 2018, P. Watson — SCOT 564, T. Jones / FLOSS, A. Watson
— JESS 1007, J. Thorp — GLEN 698, M. Hayton / MEG 362, A. Watson

TIP, Goss — Not known / Not known

JESS II 2852   *English Brace Champion 1946*
JESS 1007   *International Supreme Champion 1931*
        International Farmers' Champion 1932
        International Brace Champion 1936
        English Brace Champion 1931 & 1932
GLEN 698   *International Supreme Champion 1926*

Born 18/10/46   Black & white   Tim Longton, Quernmore

Awards

English Aggregate Championship 1949 & 1954
English Brace Champion 1955 with ROY 7729

CAP, H. Huddleston
┌ Not known
└ Not known

BUTE 4340, J. & D. Kay
┌ SPARK 3123, G. Allsop ┌ LADDIE, R.Isherwood
                        └ LASSIE, J. Jackson
└ MEG 4343, W. Jolly   ┌ TAM 1489, E. Powell
                       └ BETTY 2557, W. Jolly

1950
1956

MOSSIE 6235

Bakewell
Hereford

Born 1/6/48   Black & white   Tom Longton, Quernmore

Awards

International & English Brace Champion 1954 with BUTE 6236
Brace Aggregate Championship with Bute 6236 1954
English Driving Champion 1956
English Aggregate Championship 1953

GLEN 5837, W. Jolly	┌ **SPARK 3123, G. Allsop**	┌ **LADDIE, R. Isherwood** └ **LASSIE, J. Jackson**
	└ **MEG 4343, W. Jolly**	┌ **TAM 1489, E. Powell** └ **BETTY 2557, W. Jolly**
FAN 4442, T. Longton	┌ **KEN, F. Jennings**	┌ Not known └ Not known
	└ **NELL, G. Capstick**	┌ Not known └ Not known

FAN 4442   *J. H. Thorp Memorial Trophy 1956*
TAM 1489   *English Brace Champion 1938*

Born 25/8/46　Black, white & mottled　J. H. Holliday, Pateley Bridge

Awards
English Driving Champion 1950

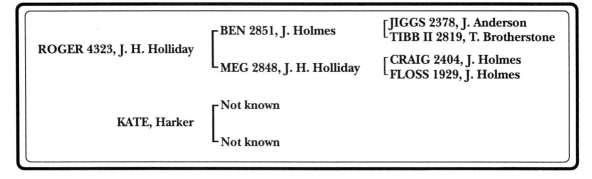

ROGER 4323, J. H. Holliday	BEN 2851, J. Holmes	JIGGS 2378, J. Anderson / TIBB II 2819, T. Brotherstone
	MEG 2848, J. H. Holliday	CRAIG 2404, J. Holmes / FLOSS 1929, J. Holmes
KATE, Harker	Not known	
	Not known	

Born 13/4/44   Black, white & mottled   C. Holmes, Ripponden

Awards
English Aggregate Championship 1952

MOSS 4354, R. H. Williams	⌐TAFF 2501, W. L. Parry	⌐JAFF II 2011, T. Roberts └RUBY 2505, W. L. Parry
	└FLY, J. Jones	⌐Not known └Not known
BET 4353, R. H. Williams	⌐COON 1608, Lord Mostyn	⌐MOSS 1318, G. Lauder └TRIM 73, P. Marshall
	└NELL 3867, T. A. Jones	⌐HEMP 1107, Craig └FLY 1266, T. Roberts

JAFF II 2011   *International Farmers' Champion 1938*
Welsh Aggregate Championship 1938

J. K. Gorst with Shep 6107 and Bet 6260

Born 28/5/48   Black, white & mottled   J. K. Gorst, Wennington

Awards

International Driving Champion 1953
English Driving Champion 1953 & 1954
J. H. Thorp Memorial Trophy 1953

	┌ GLEN 4339, H. Huddleston	┌ GLEN, W. Renwick └ QUEENIE, E. Huddleston
SHEP 6107, J. K. Gorst		
	└ BUTE 4340, D. Kay	┌ SPARK 3123, G. Allsop └ MEG 4343, W. Jolly
	┌ GLEN, W. Willan	┌ Not known └ Not known
MADDIE 4337, H. Huddleston		
	└ MADDIE 2656, H. Huddleston	┌ KEN 1194, T. Martindale └ MOSSIE, E. Huddleston

MADDIE 4337   *English Aggregate Championship 1948*

Born –/10/47 Black & white J. Denniff, Sheffield

SWEEP 3834, W. J. Hislop	⌐GLEN 3510, W. J. Hislop	⌐BEN 1572, A. Riddell └BEAT I, J. Guthrie
	└NELL 3514, W. J. Hislop	⌐CAP 3036, J. M. Wilson └MOSS 1827, McCaskie
FLY 4277, A. G. Hyslop	⌐TAM, G. Mc I. Hyslop	⌐Not known └Not known
	└MEG, A. G. Hyslop	⌐Not known └Not known

SWEEP 3834 *International Farmers' Champion 1946*
International & Scottish Driving Champion 1948
Scottish National Champion 1948

Born 24/4/52   Black & white   E. A. Priestley, Bamford

MOSS 7971, J. Jones	**CAP 7250, G. Williams**	MOSS 5666, J. Lumley SPY 5577, W. Jolly
	JUNO 4869, R. J. Davies	MOT, M. Jones MEG, J. Evans
MIDGE 7596, J. Jones	**MOSS 5176, J. M. Wilson**	MIRK 4438, J. M. Wilson NELL 3514, J. Kirk
	QUEEN 6859, T. H. Johnston	CAP 3036, J. M. Wilson FLOSS 4577, T. Johnston

MOSS 7971   *International Brace Champion 1957*
          Welsh Brace Champion 1956
          English National Champion 1958
          English Brace Champion 1958 & 1960
          International Brace Aggregate 1956 & 1957
          International Aggregate 1954
          Welsh Aggregate Championship 1954
JUNO 4869   *The Challis Shield 1957*
MOSS 5176   *International Aggregate Championship 1949*
          Scottish Aggregate Championship 1949 & 1951
MIRK 4438   *International Supreme Champion 1950*
          International Aggregate Championship 1950
          Scottish National Champion 1950
          Scottish Aggregate Trophy 1950

Born 6/6/51   Black & white   J. K. Gorst, Wennington

Awards
J. H. Thorp Memorial Trophy 1957 & 1959

SHEP 6107, J. K. Gorst	GLEN 4339, H. Huddleston	GLEN, W. Renwick QUEENIE, H. Huddleston
	BUTE 4340, D. Kay	SPARK 3123, G. Allsop MEG 4343, W. Jolly
MADDIE 4337, H. Huddleston	GLEN, W. Willan	Not known Not known
	MADDIE 2656, H. Huddleston	KEN 1194, T. Martindale MOSSIE, E. Huddleston

MADDIE 4337   *English Aggregate Championship 1948*

W. J. Evans with Tweed 9601 (left)
and Moss 7971 (right)

Born 2/10/50   Black & white   W. J. Evans, Tidenham

Awards

International Brace Champion with ROY 7696, 1957
Welsh Brace Champion with NELL 6879, 1956
English Brace Champion with TWEED 9601, 1958 & 1960
International Brace Aggregate Championship with NELL 6879, 1956 & ROY 7696, 1957
International Aggregate Championship 1954

CAP 7250, G. Williams	MOSS 5666, J. Lumley	HEMP 4504, W. J. Wallace SUSAN 4046, R. Gwilliam
	SPY 5577, W. Jolly	MOSS 4551, J. D. MacPherson SNIP 4341, W. Jolly
JUNO 4869, R. Davies	MOT, M. Jones	Not known Not known
	MEG, J. Evans	Not known Not known

JUNO 4869   *The Challis Shield 1957*
MOSS 4551   *English Driving Champion 1947 & 1948*

Born 9/10/52   Black, white & tan   W. J. Evans, Tidenham

Awards

International Supreme Champion 1958
English Driving Champion 1961
English Brace Champion with MOSS 7971, 1958 & 1960
International Aggregate Championship 1958
English Aggregate Championship 1958

```
                                    ┌MIRK 4438, J. M. Wilson      ┌SPOT 3369, J. MacDonald
MOSS 5176, J. M. Wilson  ┤                                        └CHRIS 4065, J. Cole
                                    │
                                    └NELL 3514, J. Kirk           ┌CAP 3036, J. M. Wilson
                                                                  └MOSS 1827, McCaskie

                                    ┌SPOT II 6775, W. Little      ┌GLEN 3957, S. Banks
TRIM 8859, R. Anderson   ┤                                        └TIB 4458, S. Banks
                                    │
                                    └PHIL 6132, W. Little         ┌MIRK 4438, J. M. Wilson
                                                                  └QUEEN 4205, J. M. Wilson
```

MOSS 5176   *International Aggregate Championship 1949*
              Scottish Aggregate Championship 1949 & 1951
MIRK 4438   *International Supreme Champion 1950*
              Scottish National Champion 1950
              International Aggregate Championship 1950
              Scottish Aggregate Championship 1950
SPOT II 6775 *Scottish National Champion 1954*

Born 14/7/53   Black & white   E. A. Priestley, Bamford

GLEN III 9191, J. Jones	┌**GLEN II 7738, J. Jones**	┌**SWEEP 4702, G. Pugh** └**QUEEN 6849, J. Ellis**
	└**MIDGE 7596, J. Jones**	┌**MOSS 5176, J. M. Wilson** └**QUEEN 6859, T. Johnston**
TEAMES 9454, R. Davies	┌**PATCH 6531, T. Roberts**	┌**SWEEP 4702, G. Pugh** └**JESS 5177, T. Roberts**
	└**JUNO 4869, R. Davies**	┌**MOT, M. Jones** └**MEG, J. Evans**

JUNO 4869   *The Challis Shield 1957*
SWEEP 4702   *Welsh Aggregate Championship 1948*
MOSS 5176   *International Aggregate Championship 1949*
Scottish Aggregate Championship 1949 & 1951

FARMERS GUARDIAN

Born 19/4/56   Black, tan & white   W. Hardisty, Cautley

Awards

J. H. Thorp Memorial Trophy 1961

LADDIE 8049, W. Goodfellow	BEN 5592, D. Dickson	TOSS 5009, Crozier BEAT, Robertson
	PHIL 6252, D. Dickson	GLEN 3940, J. M. Wilson MEG 4228, D. Dickson
MERRIE 6880, J. Warwick	MOSS 4551, J. D. McPherson	CAP 3036, J. M. Wilson JED 3086, F. Maclean
	SNIP 4341, W. Jolly	SPARK 3123, G. Allsop MEG 4343, W. Jolly

LADDIE 8049   *Scottish National Champion 1958*
MOSS 4551   *English Driving Champion 1947 & 1948*
GLEN 3940   *International Supreme Champion 1946 & 1948*
            International Farmers' Champion 1948
            Scottish National Champion 1946
            International Aggregate Championship 1946 & 1948
            Scottish Aggregate Championship 1946 & 1948

Born 22/4/56   Black, white & tan   W. J. Evans, Tidenham

Awards

International Farmers' Champion 1962
Captain Whittaker Outwork Cup 1963
English Farmers' Champion 1962
English Aggregate Championship 1962

ROY 7696, W. J. Evans	MAC 5498, J. Evans	JAFF 4313, R. Hughes MINN 3387, J. Williams
	MEG 6782, G. Jones	GLEN 2584, J. Jones MON 3417, T. Jones
NELL 6879, W. J. Evans	MOSS 6811, A. Jones	SPOT 3624, J. Gilchrist FAN 5486, J. Scott
	FLY N.R., R. Wood	Not known Not known

ROY 7696   *International Supreme Champion 1953*
International Brace Champion 1957
Welsh Brace Champion 1953
International Aggregate Championship 1953
Welsh Aggregate Championship 1953
Brace Aggregate Trophy 1957

NELL 6879   *International Farmers' Champion 1953*
Welsh Brace Champion 1951, 1953 & 1956
Welsh Aggregate Championship 1951
Brace Aggregate Championship 1956

MOSS 6811 *International Aggregate Championship 1952*
Welsh Brace Championship 1952
Welsh Aggregate Championship 1950 & 1952
JAFF 4313 *International & Welsh Driving Champion 1946, 1947 & 1949*
Welsh National Champion 1946 & 1948
Welsh Brace Champion 1946
SPOT 3624 *International Supreme Champion 1947*
International Brace champion 1948 & 1949
Scottish Shepherds' Champion 1947
Scottish Brace Champion 1948 & 1949
Scottish Driving Champion 1953
International Aggregate Championship 1947
Scottish Aggregate Trophy 1947
Scottish Shepherds' Aggregate Championship 1946 & 1947
MINN 3387 *The Challis Shield 1952*

W. J. Evans with Don 13392

W. J. Evans with (left to right) Ben 12953, Sandy, Tweed 9601, Roy 7696 and Moss 7971

Born 2/11/56   Black & white   W. J. Evans, Tidenham

Awards

English Farmers' Champion 1963
English Aggregate Championship 1961 & 1963

WHITEHOPE NAP 8685, J. M. Wilson	┌ GLEN 6123, W. McClure	┌ MARK 4991, J. Jones └ FLOSS 5058, J. Jones
	└ MEG 5141, W. McClure	┌ JIM N.R., Scott └ NELL 3514, J. Kirk
LASSIE 11468, W. Donald	┌ DAN 5739, A. G. Hyslop	┌ BRUCE 3728, Cameron └ SWIFT I 3932, Cullens
	└ FLY 4277, A. G. Hyslop	┌ TAM, G. McI. Hyslop └ MEG, A. G. Hyslop

WHITEHOPE NAP 8685   *Scottish National Champion 1955*

Scott's **JIM N. R.** was full brother to W. J. Hislop's **GLEN 3510**

Born 27/9/57   Black, white & tan   E. F. Morgan, Pershore

Awards

English Shepherds' Champion 1962, 1963, 1964 & 1967
J. H. Thorp Memorial Trophy 1964
English Shepherds' Aggregate Championship 1962 & 1963

	┌ SWEEP 3834, W. J. Hislop	┌ GLEN 3510, W. J. Hislop └ NELL 3514, J. Kirk
MOSS 6805, G. R. Redpath	└ JED 3403, J. Swinton	┌ JIGGS 2378, G. P. Brown └ FLY 2496, J. A. Hogg
	┌ MOSS 8754, J. M. Wilson	┌ MOSS 5176, J. M. Wilson └ NELL 5037, A. Hamilton
MEG 12094, H. Rutter	└ JUNE 8041, H. Rutter	┌ GARRY 3699, D. MacLeod └ NAN 6094, D. MacLeod

MOSS 6805   *International Supreme Champion 1956*
International Shepherds' Champion 1952
Scottish Shepherds' Champion 1952 & 1956
Scottish Driving Champion 1956

International Aggregate Championship 1956
Scottish Aggregate Trophy 1956

SWEEP 3834   *International Farmers' Champion 1946*
Scottish National Champion & Driving Champion 1948

MOSS 5176   *International Aggregate Championship 1949*
Scottish Aggregate Championship 1949 & 1951

GARRY 3699   *Scottish Shepherds' Champion 1946*
International Shepherds' Champion 1946
Scottish Shepherds' Aggregate Championship 1948

E. F. Morgan with Moss 14902 and Laddie 14110

Born 6/6/59   Black & white   Tim Longton, Quernmore

Awards

English Farmers' Champion 1965
English Aggregate Championship 1965

WHITEHOPE CORRIE 13706, J. M. Wilson	GLEN 12917, H. Porter	JIM 5856, R. Swan FLO 5038, J. T. M. Thomson
	NELL 12916, H. Porter	GARRY 4915, J. Anderson NELL 6086, J. R. Hislop
MEG 12848, J. Bathgate	TAM 8279, T. Watson	MOSS 5176, J. M. Wilson PHIL 7122, T. Watson
	QUEENIE 8655, A. Watson	MIRK 7121, T. Watson MAID 6104, T. Watson

WHITEHOPE CORRIE 13706 *Irish National Champion 1963*
MOSS 5176 *International Aggregate Championship 1949*
Scottish Aggregate Championship 1949 & 1951

Born 14/4/60   Black & white   Tim Longton, Quernmore

Awards

International Supreme Champion 1966
International Farmers' Champion 1964
English National Champion 1966
English Farmers' Champion 1964 & 1966
English Aggregate Championship 1964 & 1966
Captain Whittaker Outwork Cup 1966
J. H. Thorp Memorial Trophy 1966

CHIP 12270, P. Mason	┌ROY 8519, J. Wilson	┌ROY 5406, J. H. Holliday └BUTE 4340, D. Kay
	└JILL 7859, T. Lofthouse	┌DUKE 6017, H. Huddleston └QUEEN 6054, J. Wilson
SPY 13755, T. Longton	┌BEN 5592, D. Dickson	┌TOSS 5009, T. Crozier └BEAT, Robertson
	└SPY 5577, W. Jolly	┌MOSS 4551, J. D. McPherson └SNIP 4341, W. Jolly

MOSS 4551   *English Driving Champion 1947 & 1948*

Born 27/1/63   Black & white   M. W. Cook, Whitby

Awards

English Farmers' Champion 1967

	┌ CAP 4295, M. W. Cook	┌CAP, A. G. Hyslop └QUEEN, H. Taylor
CAP 13274, M. W. Cook		
	└ LASSIE 10680, M. W. Cook	┌GLEN 5965, C. Milburn └NELL 6317, M. W. Cook
	┌ WHITEHOPE NAP 8685, J. M. Wilson	┌GLEN 6123, W. McClure └MEG 5141, W. McClure
GAEL 14463, T. T. McKnight		
	└ DOT 11228, T. T. McKnight	┌JIM 5856, R. Swan └TIB 5881, D. Young

GAEL 14463   *International Supreme Champion 1967*
International Brace Champion 1967
Scottish National Champion 1964
Scottish Farmers' Champion 1964
Scottish Driving Champion 1967
Scottish Brace Champion 1965, 1966 & 1967
International Aggregate Championship 1965 & 1967
Scottish Aggregate Trophy 1965 & 1967
Brace Aggregate Trophy 1967
Captain Whittaker Outwork Cup 1967
WHITEHOPE NAP 8685   *Scottish National Champion 1955*

Born 7/5/63   Black & white   J. H. Holliday, Pately

Awards

J. H. Thorp Memorial Trophy 1968

VIC II 17569, **E. Holliday**	**VIC 10928, W. Sanderson**	**PATCH 6531, T. Roberts** **MONI 8788, E. P. Evans**
	QUEEN II 11541, Holmes Brothers	**HOPE 7029, J. Anderson** **MAID 10892, D. Brotherston**
BETT 16260, **E. Holliday**	**MOSS 11029, J. H. Holliday**	**ROY 5406, J. H. Holliday** **BESS 7936, M. Kay**
	BETH 14446, C. J. Leslie	**MOSS 11241, E. Holliday** **BETH 12661, E. Holliday**

MOSS 11029   *International Supreme Champion 1957*
                  International Aggregate Championship 1957
                  English Aggregate Championship 1957 & 1959
                  J. H. Thorp Memorial Trophy 1958
ROY 5406   *English National Champion 1951*
                  English Driving Champion 1950
HOPE 7029   *International Farmers' Champion 1954*
                  Scottish Aggregate Trophy 1954

1969　　**BOSWORTH COON 34186**　Hungerford

Born 16/4/64　Black, white & mottled　L. Evans, Towcester

Awards

International Supreme Champion 1968
International Farmers' Champion 1969
English Farmers' Champion 1969
International Aggregate Championship 1969
English Aggregate Championship 1968 & 1969
Captain Whittaker Outwork Cup 1968
J. H. Thorp Memorial Trophy 1969

BOSWORTH SCOT 22120, L. Evans	BEN 13864, R. MacKay	WHITEHOPE NAP 8685, J. M. Wilson TIBBY 6582, R. MacKay
	LASS 11713, D. Dickson	BEN 5592, D. Dickson NELL 5426, D. Dickson
FLY 13724, L. Evans	HAIG 9190, T. Jones	SPEED 4382, J. R. Millar FLY 9168, J. Duncan
	FLY 9731, R. Davies	PATCH 6531, T. Roberts JUNO 4869, R. Davies

BOSWORTH SCOT 22120　*International Driving Champion 1962*
HAIG 9190　*Welsh Driving Champion 1960*
WHITEHOPE NAP 8685　*Scottish National Champion 1955*
SPEED 4382　*Scottish Aggregate Trophy 1952*
JUNO 4869　*The Challis Shield 1957*

Bosworth Coon and Descendants

Bosworth Coon 34186 was probably the most successful trial dog in southern England. He represented England on four occasions, winning the Supreme Championship in 1968 at Towyn, making it an emotional victory for Llyr Evans who had been born and brought up in that neighbourhood. He had left his homeland in 1938 and settled in the Midlands, where he became a very successful and popular competitor. He was a team member on many occasions: with Fan 6938 in 1954 and 1955; with Rap, half-brother to Bosworth Coon, in 1973; with Coon's sire, Bosworth Scott 22120 the 1962 International Driving Champion, and Bosworth Moss 16054, both of these last dogs out of David Dickson's Lass 11713. In 1976 his Chip 62102, by Coon out of J. Coggin's Spottie 46442, a daughter of Wiston Cap, was English National Champion, and the following year was seventh in the Supreme Championship, won by J. Thomas and Craig 59425.

Bosworth Coon was third in the 1967 English National, won by M. Cook and Maid 28779, daughter of T. T. McKnight's Gael, and in 1969 he was English National Champion, and reserve to the Supreme Champion, H. Huddleston's Bett 40428. He was eleventh in the 1972 Supreme Championship won by J. Templeton and Cap 50543.

Not only a powerful worker, Coon was also a popular stud dog, many of his offspring proving to be top quality working collies. Bred to Tot Longton's Gyp 38336, a daughter of J. M. Wilson's Bill II 17937, he produced an exceptional litter, containing Gyp 56601, and Hadwin's Quen 56602, dam of R. MacPherson's 1975 and 1979 Supreme Champion, Zac 66166.

Mated to Wiston Cap, Gyp 56601, produced Kerry 84042, the dam of Thomas Longton's Bess 101142. Among her many International Sheep Dog Society Awards were the 1986 Supreme Champion, and 1985 English National Champion titles. Bess's daughter, Gem 147666, by Tony Iley's Goss 91940, a son of J. Hastie's Jace 62098, herself a daughter of Bosworth Coon and Gyp 38336, has continued the success of this breeding line by winning the 1992 English National, and being fourth in the 1992 Supreme Championship won by R. Dalziel's Wisp 161487.

Among Coon's many successful descendants was David Carlton's Tony 66922, winner of the 1976 English Shepherds' Aggregate Championship, and a son of Jace. George Reed's Patch of Thornby 59392, sired by Coon, was the 1974 English Driving Champion. Coon's grandson, E. J. Evans' Brocken Glen 105526, was second in the 1980 Welsh National Championship to H. G. Jones' young Bwlch Taff 113243, and qualified for the Supreme Championship, won by T. Watson and Jen 93965.

Mr Llyr Evans – Supreme Champion – Towyn, 1968, with Bosworth Coon

W. J. Wallace

John Russell's Lad 64612, the 1975 International Farmers' Champion, was a son of Coon out of H. Youngs's Sue 52445, a daughter of Wiston Cap and R. Gwilliam's Wattie 37429, whose lineage can be traced directly back to W. J. Wallace's Hemp 4504, who was a son of his Foch 2344. Foch was second in the 1938 Supreme Championship won by his kennelmate Jed 1492, who had been the 1933 English National Champion. There was sadness behind their success for they were missing their master's little son who had recently died. These two dogs had been fond of their little playmate and always ran happily back to him after their trial runs, and now after their greatest success there was no little boy to welcome them.

Jed was a granddaughter of Meg 306, the 1922 Supreme Champion, owned by W. J. Wallace's father, William Wallace, Otterburn, who had previously won the 1907 Supreme Championship with Moss 22, a son of Herdman's Tommy 16. Moss was exported to New Zealand where he was renamed Border Boss, and became a noted stud dog.

At one time, William Wallace was shepherd at Hindhope and was employed there when Mr Elliott presented the collie, Noble, to Queen Victoria. He was second to Adam Telfer at the 1881 Byrness Trial, and had competed at the first Byrness Trial in 1876, won by Adam Telfer's father, Walter. William Wallace died in 1945 aged ninety.

As a lad, W. J. Wallace had handled Meg 306, in trials, so it was a fairy-tale to win at Southport International with her granddaughter and to be second with Foch, her great-grandson.

W. J. Wallace became famous for his display team of eight dogs, giving demonstrations at agricultural shows and the like. One dog was blind but the spectators never realised, for the dog obeyed every command immediately.

To return to Hemp 4504. Richard Gwilliam mated him to his bitch Susan 4046, a daughter of J. M. Wilson's Cap 3036, and so started a line of sound working collies, with the eventual prefix 'Clun' to denote their breeding.

R. Gwilliam's Wattie 37429 and Spottie 37430, litter sisters from L. Suter's 1964 Supreme Champion, Craig 15445 and out of Fly 33034, were both mated to Wiston Cap, the former producing Sue 52445, dam of J. Russell's Lad 64612, and the latter producing R. Coggan's Spottie 46442, dam of L. Evans' Chip 62102, both bitches having been bred to Bosworth Coon.

Bred to Wiston Cap, Wattie 37429 also produced R. Gwilliam's Susan 42639, who mated to her half-brother, J. Richardson's 1975 Scottish National Champion, Mirk 52844, produced John James' 1975 English National Champion, Mirk 68102, and R. Gwilliam's brood bitch Clun Gael 95727.

An earlier litter from Susan, by Tim Longton's 1966 Supreme Champion Ken 17166, included R. Ollerenshaw's Ken 47974 who was second in the 1972 English National and seventh in the 1971 Supreme Championship, won by J. Murray's Glen 47241, a son of Wiston Cap.

From Cornwall, the 1982 English National Champion, Harry Thomas' Penpel Bess 107127, was a great-granddaughter of Susan, and also of Bosworth Coon.

Susan 42639, dam of J. James' 1975 English National
Champion, Mirk 68102

W. J. Wallace and his team of border collies

1970   **GLEN II 48637**   **Manchester**

IAN CURRIE

Born 5/8/67   Black, white & tan   Tim Longton, Quernmore

Awards

English Farmers' Champion 1970
J. H. Thorp Memorial Trophy 1970

GLEN 29405, J. M. Perrings	NAP 18410, A. Jones	WHITEHOPE NAP 8685, J. M. Wilson DOT 11228, T. T. McKnight
	MEG 17289, J. Roberts	CAIN 8325, H. Darbishire JESS 13516, Mrs. B. Owen
JEN 42152, J. M. Perrings	WISTON CAP 31154, J. Richardson	CAP 15839, J. Richardson FLY 25005, W. S. Hetherington
	JILL 33862, T. Anderton	ROB 21959, T. Longton MEG 24631, W. Miller

GLEN 29405   *English Shepherds' Aggregate Championship 1967*
WISTON CAP 31154   *International Supreme Champion 1965*
                     International Shepherds' Champion 1966
                     Scottish Driving Champion 1969
WHITEHOPE NAP 8685   *Scottish National Champion 1955*
ROB 21959   *International Brace Champion 1969*
                     International Brace Aggregate Championship 1969
                     English Brace Champion 1968 & 1969

Born 5/6/66   Black & white   R. C. MacPherson, Hallbankgate

Awards

English Farmers' Champion 1971
J. H. Thorp Memorial Trophy 1971

BEN 15884, R. C. MacPherson	┌ ROBIN 5499, A. Jones	┌ MAC 5498, J. Evans └ MEG 6782, G. Jones
	└ BET 13783, J. Williams	┌ SPOT 9476, A. Jones └ MEG 12580, G. Williams
JILL 15588, T. Graham	┌ WHITEHOPE NAP 8685, J. M. Wilson	┌ GLEN 6123, W. McClure └ MEG 5141, W. McClure
	└ JED 13266, G. Robertson	┌ VIC 4368, D. Murray └ JEN 11334, G. Robertson

ROBIN 5499   *Welsh Brace Champion 1952 & 1955*
WHITEHOPE NAP 8685   *Scottish National Champion 1955*
SPOT 9476   *Welsh Brace Champion 1961*
VIC 4368   *International Brace Champion 1953, 1954 & 1955*
        International Driving Champion 1951
        International Brace Aggregate 1951, 1953 & 1955
        Scottish National Champion 1952
        Scottish Driving Champion 1950, 1951 & 1952
        Scottish Brace Champion 1947, 1951, 1952, 1953 & 1954

56

Born 26/4/68   Black & white   H. Huddleston, Lancaster

Awards

English Farmers' Champion 1972
J. H. Thorp Memorial Trophy 1972
English Aggregate Championship 1972
Feedmobile Challenge Cup 1972

JOE 33190, T. Harper
┌ BILL 21775, G. Pennefather
│   ┌ JIM 12967, W. Hardisty
│   └ FLY 11362, W. Hardisty
└ NELL 16527, T. Harper
     ┌ SAM 13329, J. Rutherford
     └ TIP 14670, J. Gumbley

UDALE MADDIE 38121, H. Huddleston
┌ SPIKE 17745, W. Huddleston
│   ┌ JOE 9652, W. Routledge
│   └ JANE 14911, G. Holliday
└ PATTIE 23125, H. Huddleston
     ┌ SPUTNICK 18687, W. Huddleston
     └ UDALE BIDDY 18318, J. Rowling

JIM 12967   *English National Champion 1961*
J. H. Thorp Memorial Trophy 1961

The Champions of Lancashire

In Lancashire on the western slopes of the Pennines, resides a family of sheepdogs whose line can be traced back to the early registered dogs and beyond. It may well be that the association of this ancient line with an equally deep-rooted local farming family is unique.

During the 1890s a family of excellent hill dogs was becoming well known in the locality. They were bred by Philip Metcalf, who sold a bitch pup to the Huddleston family, and in 1905 another member of the family acquired a pup named Nell, from this original bitch. Nell became a locally renowned trial winner and hill worker. From Nell came Nip, who sired Fly, the first of this line to be mated to an International Sheep Dog Society registered dog – E. Lucas' Scot 545, a son of G. Caig's Fleet 203, (a grandson of Supreme Champion Kep 13) and T. Ferguson's Maid 209.

From this mating T. Longton acquired a blue bitch, Nell, and her daughter Mossie was mated to the famous North Country sire, T. C. Martindale's Ken 1194. The brothers, Harry and William Huddleston, as young lads, were given two bitch pups, Maddie 2656, and Fan 2401, from this litter. This line has remained unbroken in the Huddleston family to this day.

This bloodline has often produced dogs with slate-blue coloured coats. This colour has become very desirable to those who compete in the show ring with their border collies. The blue dogs have increased in numbers since the importation of two blue collies from New Zealand, which have been bred to many British border collie bitches. These dogs are only registered with the Kennel Club, and are not eligible for I.S.D.S. registration.

Lille, bred to Hemp 153, was dam of T. Gilholm's Jet 352. Jet mated to Adam Telfer's Supreme Champion Haig 252, produced Lassie 518, the paternal great-grandam of Ken 1194.

Ken's dam, T. Ferguson's Maid 209, was a granddaughter of T. P. Brown's Supreme Champion Lad 19. She was born in 1918 and died in 1936, having produced forty-four pups in her long life. Her dam, J. Hunter's Old Trim 39, was of unrecorded breeding. It is interesting to see that Maid 209 was thus paternal grandam and also maternal great-great-grandam to Maddie 2656 and Fan 2401.

Harry Huddleston's Maddie 2656 was mated to a neighbouring unregistered dog, Glen, producing Maddie 4337. When trials commenced after the 1939–45 War, she represented England on three occasions, each time competing in the Supreme Championship, and was third to Ashton Priestley's Pat in the 1951 International.

Mated to J. Gorst's Shep 6107, a blue dog, she produced Maddie III 10992, Bet 6260 and Queen 8810. These two latter bitches belonged to J. Gorst, Harry Huddleston's cousin. Bet was in the English team in 1951, 1953 and 1956, and was English National Champion in 1953.

She was grandam to the 1969 Supreme Champion, Bett 40428, owned by 'the other' Harry Huddlestone of Arkholme. Queen was 1957 English National Champion, and also was second in the 1959 National.

In the 1951 Supreme Championship Bet came fifth behind Ashton Priestley's Pat 4203. She won the 1953 English National Championship by just one point from Harry Huddleston's Duke, and came sixth in the Supreme Championship behind W. J. Evans's Roy 7696.

The good-natured cousinly rivalry continued at the 1957 English National when Queen won the Championship by half a point from Harry Huddleston's Kep 13954, a son of J. Gilchrist's Supreme Champion Spot 3624, with J. Chapman's Lad 11027, in third place just half a point behind Kep! Queen and Lad were by Shep, as was Bet.

Shep 6107, was great-grandsire to Lionel Pennefather's Irish National Champion of 1962 and 1966, Bess 17145, and his brother, H. Huddleston's Duke 6017, also a blue dog, was great-grandsire to Tim Longton's 1966 Supreme Champion, Ken 17166.

J. Gorst's Shep was sired by H. Huddleston's Glen 4339, a son of W. Renwick's Glen 2213, (grandson of G. P. Brown's Supreme Champion Spot 308 and Hunter's Fly 165), and his dam was E. Huddleston's unregistered Queenie, a daughter of T. C. Martindale's Ken 1194, and Mossie. Shep was therefore a great-grandson of Ken and Mossie, who were grandparents of Maddie 4337.

Harry Huddleston's Udale Sim 52690, who won the 1972 English National Championship

*J. M. Renwick's Glen 5107, Brace Champion 1947 and 1950
with Moss*

on better outrun, lift and fetch points, from R. Ollerenshaw's Ken 47974, a son of T. Longton's Ken, was descended directly through seven unbroken generations of bitches, all bred by Harry Huddleston, down from Ken and Mossie, who herself belonged to E. Huddleston. Udale Sim was reserve to J. J. Templeton's Supreme Champion Cap 50543, in the 1972 International, and he represented Great Britain in 1973 at the Expo World Championship in New Zealand, making such a resounding impression, that Harry Huddleston was later persuaded to send him back alone, to be used at stud. Very tragically Sim was found dead on arrival in Singapore.

H. Huddleston with Udale Sim

59

This poem was written by Udale Sim's grieving breeder, to the memory of a loyal partner.

Udale Sim

A border collie was Udale Sim;
Seldom has the likes of him
Graced trial field or hill.
With steady pace and level head,
Be it a half mile cast or single shed,
He proved his canine skill.

Then from the land of the great white cloud
A message came both clear and loud,
'We want that Sim out here.'
And so to Sim we said goodbye
With just the semblance of a sigh,
Although without a tear.

Alas, alas, it was not to be,
For dear old Sim was not to see
Again that great land-in-the-sun.
For when they stopped at Singapore
Our poor old Sim, he was no more.
His life's last trial was run.

Now he was such a loyal friend,
Faithful to the very end.
When I put him on the train
I wonder what was on his mind—
Thinking I was so unkind?
For his eyes showed intense pain.

I've wondered just how much he knew,
What of the future he knew—
That he and I should part?
Sure of the truth of what I said
When I was told that Sim was dead—
'He died of a broken heart.'

H. Huddleston

'The other' Harry Huddleston, of Arkholme, who has competed so successfully in trials, for over fifty years, and has been an English team member on fourteen occasions, won the Supreme Championship in 1969 with Bett 40428, sired by J. Gorst's Roy 14152, a son of his 1953 English National Champion, Bet 6260. In 1989 the English National was won by Harry Huddleston with Jim 150661, a son of J. R. Thomas' English Shepherds' Champion Don 108889.

The Longtons

The Gorst, Huddleston and Longton families are related, though perhaps the Longton name is the best known by the modern trial enthusiasts.

Tim Longton Senior won the 1949 English National with Dot 4844, a daughter of H. Huddleston's unregistered Cap. She was reserve to the 1954 Supreme Champion, J. McDonald's Mirk 5444. The 1950 English National was won by Thomas Longton, Tim's son, known to all as Tot, with Mossie 6235, who repeated her success in 1956. Tot Longton became one of the greatest exponents of brace handling, winning nine English Brace Championships and one International Brace Championship, the latter with Lad 41928, and Rob 21959, one of the North Country's most consistent trials winners.

Tot Longton's elder brother, Will, was also a respected dog handler, winning the 1957 English Shepherds' Championship with Roy 7729. His brother, Jack, has competed regularly in the English team, but it is Tim Longton, another brother, who has rivalled Tot's successes.

Tot Longton's Gyp 38336, a granddaughter of Whitehope Nap 8685, proved to be one of his most successful dogs. She qualified to run in all sections of the 1971 International, gaining third place in the qualifying trial, fourth in the Brace Championship, and finishing up reserve to the Supreme Champion, J. Murray's Glen 47241, having run the Supreme Championship gathering course twice, as the first twenty sheep were found to be mismarked. Her granddaughter Jess 88627, was reserve English National Champion 1983, and later that year she became Supreme Champion on the storm-lashed Aberystwyth course, a fitting culmination to Tot Longton's long and illustrious trials career.

His son Thomas is set fair to emulate his father's trial successes, winning the 1986 Supreme Championship with Bess 101142, who had been English National Champion in 1985, and qualifying for the Supreme Championship in the same year. She was also third in the 1986 English National. Bess was a granddaughter of Wiston Cap 31154, and Tot Longton's Gyp 56601, who was a daughter of Gyp 38336, and by Bosworth Coon. Bess was dam of Thomas Longton's 1992 English National Champion,

Gem 147666, and of Tweed 140476, and of Maggie 140478.

Bess has won four English Brace Championships, two with Lassie 91601 – one with Maggie, and one with Gem, who has also won this award with Tweed, in 1988, 1989 and 1991. These two have been in the English team several times

he was farm manager for Blackburn Corporation, and won the English Shepherds' Championship with Nell 7077. In 1965 he won the first of five English Nationals, and later won four Brace Championships – with Roy 54175 and Cap 67711, in 1973, 1974 and 1975 and in 1978 with Bess 89022 and Tweed 96630, the 1981 English

Tot Longton with Mossie 6235 and Bute 6236 (lying down)

and both have qualified to run in the Supreme Championship.

Tot's brother Tim has also won the Supreme Championship – in 1966, with Ken 17166, a great-grandson of Harry Huddleston's Duke 6017. Ken was English National Champion also in 1966.

Tim Longton's first award in International Sheep Dog Society trials came in 1951 when

National Champion. He has been a member of the English team nearly thirty times and is still competing.

His son Timothy is following the family tradition and has won the English Brace Championships with Gel 124181 and Cap 161769, in 1988 and 1990. Gel was reserve for the English team in 1991, and was fourth in the 1987 English National.

Tim Longton's grandson, Brian Dodd, has also inherited the skill of dog handling. When aged twenty he won the 1988 English National Championship with Laddie 151099, a son of Tim Longton's red Tweed, and captained a team which contained Thomas Longton with Gem, and Jack Longton with Queen.

Successful trial competitors these men and dogs may be, but trial competition is the 'icing on the cake' for such as these, who earn their living with sheep and cattle on the harsh Pennine Fells. It is in such conditions that the Border Collie learns its job, proves its worth, and cannot be other than the best.

At the 1993 Armathwaite International, Tim Longton was presented with the Wilkinson Sword, in appreciation of all he has done for sheepdogs and the Society.

The Wilkinson Sword Trophy presented to Tim Longton by Eric Halsall, 1993, on behalf of the Society

Born 10/5/65   Black & white   T. E. Elliott, Bamford

Awards

English Farmers' Champion 1973

	┌ **TEDDY 13305**, A. Rogerson	┌ **MIRK 10209**, J. Robertson └ **MIST 13304**, H. Rogerson
TWEED 33075, A. D. Cockburn ┤		
	└ **TRIM 7552**, A. D. Cockburn	┌ **NAP 3732**, T. Lothian └ **NELL 6879**, W. J. Evans
	┌ **ROY 14401**, W. Renwick	┌ **ROY 4921**, J. Purdie └ **FLO 9197**, T. Courtney
BESS 22235, A. D. Cockburn ┤		
	└ **BELLE 19061**, A. D. Cockburn	┌ **MIRK 13296**, D. McTeir └ **QUEEN 9726**, A. D. Cockburn

MIRK 13296   *International Aggregate Championship 1964*
                  Scottish Aggregate Championship 1964
                  Scottish Shepherds' Aggregate Championship 1964 & 1965
                  International Shepherds' Champion 1964
                  International Driving Champion 1964
                  Scottish Driving Champion 1964

NELL 6879   *Welsh Aggregate Championship 1951*
                  International Farmers' Champion 1953
                  Brace Aggregate Championship 1956
                  Welsh Brace Champion 1951, 1953 & 1956

Born 27/11/68   Black & white   Tim Longton, Quernmore

Awards

English Farmers' Champion 1974
English Brace Champion with CAP 67711, 1973, 1974 & 1975
J. H. Thorp Memorial Trophy 1974

SWEEP 28626, R. Relph	⌈WHITEHOPE CORRIE 13706, J. McKee	⌈GLEN 12917, H. Porter ⌊NELL 12916, H. Porter
	⌊BESS 17145, G. Pennefather	⌈MOSS 12265, G. Capstick ⌊DOROTHY 14608, E. Metcalfe
JESS 35508, R. Relph	⌈BOY 20380, W. Todd	⌈SWEEP 12276, G. Scott ⌊FLEECE 11049, F. Land
	⌊JEAN 22985, J. Emerson	⌈ROY 12187, J. Roderick ⌊FLY 15210, W. V. Price

WHITEHOPE CORRIE 13706   *Irish National Champion 1963*
BESS 17145   *Irish National Champion 1962 & 1966*
  Irish Brace Champion 1964
  Irish Driving Champion 1963
FLEECE 11049   *English Shepherds' Champion 1958*
  English Shepherds' Aggregate Championship 1958

J. E. James with Fly 34035 and Mirk 68102

Born 14/7/71   Black, white & tan   J. James, Leominster

Awards

English Farmers' Champion 1975
J. H. Thorp Memorial Trophy 1975

MIRK 52844, J. Richardson	WISTON CAP 31154, J. Richardson	CAP 15839, J. Richardson FLY 25005, W. S. Hetherington
	LASSIE 23501, J. McDonald	SWEEP 18393, E. Dixon QUEEN 16968, A. Noble
SUSAN 42639, R. Gwilliam	WISTON CAP 31154, J. Richardson	CAP 15839, J. Richardson FLY 25005, W. S. Hetherington
	WATTIE 37429, R. Gwilliam	CRAIG 15445, L. Suter FLY 33034, H. Price

MIRK 52844 *International Shepherds' Champion 1975*
Scottish Shepherds' Aggregate Championship 1975
Scottish National Champion 1975
Scottish Shepherds' Champion 1973 & 1975
Scottish Driving Champion 1975
The 'Alexander Andrew' Trophy 1975
J. M. Wilson Challenge Shield 1975

WISTON CAP 31154 *International Supreme Champion 1965*
International Shepherds' Champion 1966
Scottish Driving Champion 1969

CRAIG 15445 *Welsh Aggregate Championship 1964*
Captain Whittaker Outwork Cup 1964
International Supreme Champion 1964

Born 6/4/70   Black & white   L. Evans, Towcester

Awards

English Farmers' Champion 1976
J. H. Thorp Memorial Trophy 1976
Ivy Parry Trophy 1976
English Aggregate Championship 1976

BOSWORTH COON 34186,
L. Evans

    BOSWORTH SCOT 22120, L. Evans

        BEN 13864, R. MacKay
        LASS 11713, D. Dickson

    FLY 13724, L. Evans

        HAIG 9190, T. Jones
        FLY 9731, R. Davies

SPOTTIE 46442, J. Coggan

    WISTON CAP 31154, J. Richardson

        CAP 15839, J. Richardson
        FLY 25005, W. S. Hetherington

    SPOTTIE 37430, R. Gwilliam

        CRAIG 15445, L. Suter
        FLY 33034, G. Price

BOSWORTH COON 34186 *International Supreme Champion 1968*
International Farmers' Champion 1969
English National Champion 1969
English Farmers' Champion 1969
International Aggregate Championship 1969
English Aggregate Championship 1968 & 1969
Captain Whittaker Outwork Cup 1968
J. H. Thorp Memorial Trophy 1969

BOSWORTH SCOT 22120 *International Driving Champion 1962*

WISTON CAP 31154 *International Supreme Champion 1965*
International Shepherds' Champion 1966
Scottish Driving Champion 1969

CRAIG 15445 *Welsh Aggregate Championship 1964*
Captain Whittaker Outwork Cup 1964
International Supreme Champion 1964

HAIG 9190 *Welsh Driving Champion 1960*

L. Evans with Chip 62102

E. B. CARPENTER

68

Lady Sheepdog Handlers

Until the late 1970s there were few ladies competing at even local trials, and certainly not at National level, so at a time when a woman's place was considered to be 'in the kitchen,' it was a great achievement when Mrs Annie McCormack won the 1958 Scottish Driving Championship with Swan 8233, and became the first lady to compete at an International. In 1962 Mrs McCormack gained a team place with Ness 14695, a daughter of Swan, and competed at the Beaumaris International.

She had a collection of hand-painted teacups, each portraying one of her collie dogs, and a full set of teacups portraying her famous Swan 8233.

It was to be fifteen years before another lady gained a team place. This was Jean Hardisty, who won the 1977 English National Championship with Flash 79000, emulating her father W. Hardisty who won the 1961 title with Jim 12967, the great-grandsire of Flash. Jean Hardisty, now Mrs Bousefield, was the first lady to captain a National team, and to compete in the Supreme Championship, which she did with Taff 91192, in 1978, having been sixth in the English National that year.

Her father had represented England at the 1960 International with Jim, coming fifth in the Supreme Championship, won by E. L. Daniel and Ken 13306. The following year Jim was fourth in the Supreme Championship, won by Alan Jones and Roy 15393, and his half-sister, Snip, 11496, was twelfth in the Supreme.

Mr Hardisty had previously won the 1957 English Brace Championship with Snip and Fly 11362, her full sister; both these bitches were in the 1962 English team, Fly coming ninth in the Supreme Championship.

Jim, Snip and Fly were sired by W. Goodfellow's Laddie 8049, Scottish National Champion in 1958.

In 1980 Jean Thomson ran her black and tan, ten-year-old Wullie 111993, who had worked in local trials to such effect that he gained merit registration to enable him to compete in the Scottish National, and go forward to compete in the International at Bala.

Another well-known competitor, and author, Viv Billingham, won a place in the 1982 Scottish team with her home-bred Garry 98341. She was second in the 1990 Scottish Brace Championship with Holly 160182 and Tweedhope Glen 169258.

Barbara Sykes gained an English team place with Meg 115981, in 1983, and her daughter Vickie competed in the 1989 International Young Handlers Championship with Moss 137368, a son of Meg. Over the years this award has been won by several lassies – in 1987 Fiona McMillan with Gael 134686; in 1988 Jean Mason with Slade 141825 and in 1990 by Belinda Benn with Glen 124915. A young handler from each country competes for this honour, hotly contested on the singles course.

In 1989 Julie Deptford, who had recently moved from England to live in Scotland, was third with Gwen 160435 in the Scottish National won by S. Davidson and Craig 120006 after a re-run with R. Dalziel and Wisp 161487. Julie and Gwen won the Qualifying Trial and International Shepherds' Championship, and competed in the Supreme Championship on the demanding Margam Park course. Two years later Julie and Gwen won the Scottish National Championship, and she also won the Brace Championship with Bess 161886 and Nell 170326, who were fourth in the International Brace Championship.

Julie guided Bess and Nell to win the 1992 Scottish Brace Championship, and they went on to be second in the International Brace Championship.

Katy Cropper worked Trim 157047 and Max 166230 to represent England in the 1990 International, and another English lady, Rhos Edwards, was fourth with Don 142576, in the 1993 National won by Paul Turnbull and Nap 188631. Rhos also competed in the Armathwaite International, won by Alasdair Macrae and Nan 186565, with Paul Turnbull and Nap in second place. Nap had suffered severe injuries to his hindquarters, and was carefully nursed back to fitness by Paul and his wife.

These are the élite of sheep dog trial lady handlers, but at open trials all over the British Isles there are many very competent ladies competing and regularly being highly placed in the prize lists.

Jean Hardisty with Flash 79000

Mrs A. McCormack and daughter Eileen

Mrs McCormack with Ness 14695, 1962 International

Born 5/2/73   Black & white   Miss J. Hardisty, Sedbergh

Awards

English Farmers' Champion 1977
J. H. Thorp Memorial Trophy 1977
Ivy Parry Trophy 1977

ROY 33183, W. Hardisty
┌ BILL 21775, G. Pennefather
  ┌ JIM 12967, W. Hardisty
  └ FLY 11362, W. Hardisty
└ NELL 16527, T. Harper
  ┌ SAM 13329, J. Rutherford
  └ TIP 14670, J. Gumbley

FAN 56631, W. Hardisty
┌ TINY 46609, H. Jones
  ┌ SPOT 24981, J. Gilchrist
  └ DOT 31602, A. Watson
└ NAN 35374, H. Jones
  ┌ DON 18421, A. Livingstone
  └ MEG 15602, A. Ainslie

JIM 12967   *English National Champion 1961*
            J. H. Thorp Memorial Trophy 1961
FLY 11362   *English Brace Champion 1957*
SPOT 24981 *International Aggregate Championship 1966*
            Scottish Aggregate Championship 1966
            Scottish Shepherds' Aggregate Championship 1966
            Scottish National Champion 1965 & 1966
            Scottish Shepherds' Champion 1965 & 1966

Born 23/8/73　　Black & white　　K. Brehmer, Hexham

Awards

English Shepherds' Aggregate 1977
English Shepherds' Championship 1978
English Driving Champion 1978
J. H. Thorp Memorial Trophy 1978
Ivy Parry Trophy 1978

STANLEY N. R., not known

NOT KNOWN, R. Haggas

Born 24/2/73   Black & white   H. Loates, Retford

Awards

English Farmers' Champion 1979
Ivy Parry Trophy 1979

ROY 45152, **C. Storey**	WISTON CAP 31154, J. Richardson	CAP 15839, J. Richardson FLY 25005, W. S. Hetherington
	JILL 33862, T. Anderton	ROB 21959, T. Longton MEG 24631, W. Miller
MEG 56350, **W. S. Hetherington**	BOSWORTH COON 34186, L. Evans	BOSWORTH SCOT 22120, L. Evans FLY 13724, L. Evans
	LASSIE 47237, S. MacLean	KEN 17166, T. Longton RISCA 41256, Mrs. E. Rogers

WISTON CAP 31154   *International Supreme Champion 1965*
International Shepherds' Champion 1966
Scottish Driving Champion 1969

BOSWORTH COON 34186   *International Supreme Champion 1968*
International Farmers' Champion 1969
English National Champion 1969
English Farmers' Champion 1969
International Aggregate Championship 1969
English Aggregate Championship 1968 & 1969
Captain Whittaker Outwork Cup 1968
J. H. Thorp Memorial Trophy 1969

BOSWORTH SCOT 22120   *International Driving Champion 1962*

ROB 21959   *International Brace Champion 1969*
International Brace Aggregate Championship 1969
English Brace Champion 1968 & 1969

KEN 17166   *International Supreme Champion 1966*
International Farmers' Champion 1964
English National Champion 1966
English Farmers' Champion 1964 & 1966
English Aggregate Championship 1964 & 1966
Captain Whittaker Outwork Cup 1966
J. H. Thorp Memorial Trophy 1966

DART 92163

R. FAWCETT

Born 1/5/75   Black & white   A. Foster, Grange over Sands

Awards

English Shepherds' Champion 1980
English Driving Champion 1979
J. H. Thorp Memorial Trophy 1980
Pedigree Chum Silver Salver 1980
International Shepherds' Champion 1980
International Aggregate Championship 1980
English Aggregate Championship 1980 & 1984
English Shepherds' Aggregate Championship 1979 & 1980
Captain Whittaker Outwork Cup 1984
McDiarmid Trophy 1979 & 1980

KEN 47143, F. Coward	ROB 21959, T. Longton	BOB 12684, J. Gilchrist MINDRUM NELL 11106, R. S. Fraser
	MOSS 38505, J. Hadwin	MAC 28179, T. Wilson MEG 28964, W. Swire
GEM 48614, A. Foster	WISTON GLEN 35175, H. Graveson	TAM II 14387, J. Purdie WISTON ANGELA 16439, W. S. Hetherington
	TESS 41857, H. Graveson	MOSS 10625, H. Graveson LASSIE 21507, E. Wilson

ROB 21959   *International Brace Champion 1969*
English Brace Champion 1968 & 1969
International Brace Aggregate Championship 1969
MINDRUM NELL 11106   *English Shepherds' Champion 1955*

TWEED 96630 Bolton Abbey

Born 17/4/76   Brown & white   Tim Longton, Quernmore

Awards

English Farmers' Champion 1980 & 1981
English Brace Champion with BESS 89022, 1978
J. H. Thorp Memorial Trophy 1981
International Farmers' Champion 1980

JIM 55048, T. Emerson	┌WISTON CAP 31154, J. Richardson	┌CAP 15839, J. Richardson └FLY 25005, W. S. Hetherington
	└NELL 26198, W. Welsh	┌CAP 13733, R. Shennan └LASSIE 22615, R. Shennan
NELL 54547, S. Emerson	┌SPOT 24981, J. Gilchrist	┌BOB 12684, J. Gilchrist └WISTON NAN III 9896, P. McG. Hepburn
	└QUEEN 16549, L. Redpath	┌NICKEY 6368, F. Dickson └LASSIE 10224, L. Redpath

WISTON CAP 31154   *International Supreme Champion 1965*
International Shepherds' Champion 1966
Scottish Driving Champion 1969
SPOT 24981   *International Aggregate Championship 1966*
Scottish Aggregate Championship 1966
Scottish Shepherds' Aggregate Championship 1966
Scottish National Champion 1965 & 1966
Scottish Shepherds' Champion 1965 & 1966

C. H. BARRETT

Born 20/3/78   Black & white   S. H. Thomas, Par

Awards

English Farmers' Champion 1982
English Driving Champion 1982
J. H. Thorp Memorial Trophy 1982
Ivy Parry Trophy 1982

CAP 78525, S. H. Thomas	SHEP II 49061, S. H. Thomas	WISTON CAP 31154, J. Richardson KIM 39897, J. Irving
	LASSIE 71318, S. H. Thomas	BOSWORTH COON 34186, L. Evans SUSAN 42639, R. Gwilliam
GAEL 63582, S. H. Thomas	TWEED 29403, J. Gordon	BILL II 18890, J. Gordon TIB 23211, N. Gordon
	BESS 25554, A. Fyvie	CAP 15839, J. Richardson TRIM 23277, P. Cowie

WISTON CAP 31154 *International Supreme Champion 1965*
International Shepherds' Champion 1966
Scottish Driving Champion 1969
BOSWORTH COON 34186 *International Supreme Champion 1968*
International Farmers' Champion 1969
English National Champion 1969
English Farmers' Champion 1969
International Aggregate Championship 1969
English Aggregate Championship 1968 & 1969
Captain Whittaker Outwork Cup 1968
J. H. Thorp Memorial Trophy 1969

S. H. Thomas

S. H. Thomas from Par, Cornwall, a champion ploughman, accomplished stick dresser, and bell-ringer in his local church, was the first West Country handler to win an English National, which he did in 1982 with his home-bred Penpell Bess 107127. Her sire, Cap 78525, and Gwyn Jones' 1976 Supreme Champion, Shep 73360, were half-brothers, both sired by Harry Thomas'

Shep II 49061, a son of Wiston Cap. Shep 73360, was out of Harry's home-bred Tamsin 66472, and Cap was out of his Lassie 71318, a daughter of Bosworth Coon and R. Gwilliam's good breeding bitch, Susan 42639, herself a daughter of Wiston Cap. Bess's dam, Gael 63582, was a maternal granddaughter of J. Richardson's Cap 15839, the sire of Wiston Cap.

S. H. Thomas with Penpell Bess

Born 19/8/77   Black, white & tan   D. W. Lloyd, Leominster

Awards

English Farmers' Champion 1983

MIRK 52844, G. Lloyd	┌ WISTON CAP 31154, J. Richardson	┌ CAP 15839, J. Richardson └ FLY 25005, W. S. Hetherington
	└ LASSIE 23501, J. McDonald	┌ SWEEP 18393, E. Dixon └ QUEEN 16968, A. Noble
JUNE 86004, T. J. Jones	┌ MOSS 72131, R. E. Nicholls	┌ CRAIG 47577, E. Griffith └ MEG 44766, T. J. Jones
	└ TOSS 57887, J. J. Nicholls	┌ MOSS 41957, R. E. Nicholls └ FLOSS 48108, R. E. Nicholls

MIRK 52844   *International Shepherds' Champion 1975*
Scottish Shepherds' Aggregate Championship 1975
Scottish National Champion 1975
Scottish Shepherds' Champion 1973 & 1975
Scottish Driving Champion 1975
Alexander Andrew Trophy 1975
J. M. Wilson Challenge Shield 1975
WISTON CAP 31154   *International Supreme Champion 1965*
International Shepherds' Champion 1966
Scottish Driving Champion 1969
MOSS 41957   *Welsh National Champion 1972*
Welsh Farmers' Champion 1972

Born 17/9/81   Black & white   A. Elliott, Alston

Awards

English Farmers' Champion 1984
J. H. Thorpe Memorial Trophy 1984

CAP 97169, S. P. Walton	SHEP 67185, K. Shield	DRIFT 51202, T. T. McKnight / GYP 54408, N. Thompson
	JED 79816, K. Shield	NAP 28777, G. Hutton / JEAN 41257, R. Baird
LANGLOCH NELL 84216, A. Elliott	JIM 64812, J. Davidson	SWEEP 39603, J. Richardson / MORAG 29500, W. McKay
	NELL 64328, J. Davidson	ROY 42037, J. Renwick / JED 47579, J. Renwick

DRIFT 51202 *International & Scottish Driving Champion 1970*
SWEEP 39603 *International & Scottish Driving Champion 1968*
Scottish Shepherds' Champion 1968

ANIMAL PHOTOGRAPHY

Tim Longton with (left) Bess 101142 and (right) Maggie 140478

Born 19/12/76   Black, white & tan   T. W. Longton, Quernmore

Awards

International Supreme Champion 1986
English Farmers' Champion 1985
English Brace Champion with LASSIE 91601, 1979 & 1982
English Brace Champion with MAGGIE 140478, 1985
International Aggregate Championship 1986
English Aggregate Championship 1986
Captain Whittaker Outwork Cup 1986
R. Fortune Trophy 1986
Lord Mostyn Plate 1986
I. S. D. S. Blue Riband 1986
Pedigree Chum Supreme Championship Trophy 1986
Rhiwlas Trophy 1986
Langs' Scotch Whisky Quaiche 1986
J. H. Thorp Memorial Trophy 1985
Ivy Parry Trophy 1985

```
                          ┌ MOSS 57707, A. Jones        ┌ MOSS 41957, R. E. Nicholls
   GLEN 80138,            │                             └ NELL 39432, R. G. Evans
   Mrs. M. Arthurs        │
                          └ NELL 61154, A. Jones        ┌ CRAIG 47577, E. Griffith
                                                        └ FLY 49709, J. R. Griffith

                          ┌ WISTON CAP 31154, J. Richardson  ┌ CAP 15839, J. Richardson
   KERRY 84042,           │                                  └ FLY 25005, W. S. Hetherington
   T. Longton             │
                          └ GYP 56601, T. Longton       ┌ BOSWORTH COON 34186, L. Evans
                                                        └ GYP 38336, T. Longton
```

WISTON CAP 31154   *International Supreme Champion 1965*
                    International Shepherds' Champion 1966
                    Scottish Driving Champion 1969
MOSS 41957   *Welsh National Champion 1972*
              Welsh Farmers' Champion 1972
BOSWORTH COON 34186   *International Supreme Champion 1968*
                       International Farmers' Champion 1969
                       English National & Farmers' Champion 1969
                       International Aggregate Championship 1969
                       English Aggregate Championship 1968 & 1969
                       Captain Whittaker Outwork Cup 1968
                       J. H. Thorp Memorial Trophy 1969
GYP 38336   *International & English Driving Champion 1971*
             English Aggregate Championship 1971
             English Brace Champion 1971 & 1972

Tim Longton with Bess 101142

82

Born 4/9/83   Black & white   J. Cropper, Rossendale

Awards

English Farmers' Champion 1986
J. H. Thorp Memorial Trophy 1986

DRYDEN JOE 104626, R. Dalziel	┌ GLEN 75630, R. Fortune	┌ CAP 67230, T. T. McKnight └ SHELL 68768, T. T. McKnight
	└ DRYDEN QUEEN 70345, A. McGregor	┌ SPOT 24981, J. Gilchrist └ CHRIS 60920, A. McGregor
FLOSS 88122, J. Hawkins	┌ FLEET 38813, J. Cropper	┌ ROCK 27425, J. Bathgate └ TRIM 26864, J. Bonella
	└ WYCHNOR HOPE 73538, J. Hawkins	┌ MIRK 28776, J. Hettrick └ GAEL 57306, E. Kelly

DRYDEN JOE 104626   *Scottish National Champion 1986*
J. M. Wilson Challenge Shield 1986
Scottish Shepherds' Champion 1986
Scottish Driving Champion 1986
Alexander Andrew Trophy 1986
Scottish Shepherds' Champion 1979
GLEN 75630   *Scottish Brace Champion 1977*

FLEET 38813 *International Brace Champion 1973*
English Driving Champion 1968 & 1970
Brace Aggregate Championship 1973

SPOT 24981 *International Aggregate Championship 1966*
Scottish Aggregate Championship 1966
Scottish Shepherds' Aggregate Championship 1966
Scottish National Champion 1965 & 1966
Scottish Shepherds' Champion 1965 & 1966

MIRK 28776 *Scottish National Champion 1971*
Scottish Farmers' Champion 1971
Alexander Andrew Trophy 1971

J. Cropper with Cap 142018

AUSTIN BENNETT

Born 19/9/81   Black, white & tan   S. B. Price, Cressage

Awards

International Supreme Champion 1987
English Farmers' Champion 1987
English Aggregate Championship 1987
R. Fortune Trophy 1987
Lord Mostyn Plate 1987
I. S. D. S. Blue Riband 1987
Pedigree Chum Supreme Championship Trophy 1987
Rhiwlas Trophy 1987
Langs' Scotch Whisky Quaiche 1987
Sun Alliance Salver 1987
Ivy Parry Trophy 1987

BOBBY 119815, T. Bowey	MOSS 91079, T. Bowey	DRIFT 68728, J. Bathgate MEG 78015, J. Ironside
	SLIP 102578, T. Bowey	GLEN 75630, R. Fortune NELL 53708, P. Hetherington
SANDIE 122755, J. Wilson	MAC 115688, J. Wilson	SWEEP 86362, W. Johnston MAID 82040, J. McGregor
	VERA 93999, J. Wilson	GARRY 72142, D. Brown FLY 81317, J. Gray

GLEN 75630   *Scottish Brace Champion 1977*
NELL 53708   *Scottish National & Shepherds' Champion 1970*
                   Alexander Andrew Trophy 1970

Born 13/5/83   Black & white   B. Dodd, Quernmore

Awards

English Farmers' Champion 1988
J. H. Thorp Memorial Trophy 1988
Ivy Parry Trophy 1988

TWEED 96630, T. Longton	┌JIM 55048, T. Emmerson	┌WISTON CAP 31154, J. Richardson └NELL 26198, W. Welsh
	└NELL 54547, S. Emmerson	┌SPOT 24981, J. Gilchrist └QUEEN 16549, L. Redpath
BESS 89022, M. Mason	┌ROY 69452, M. Arthurs	┌MIRK 52844, J. Richardson └JEN 57299, Mrs. H. Kirkland
	└NELL 41732, N. Woods	┌TOSS 24644, J. M. Wilson └NIP 16878, T. Longton

TWEED 96630 *English National Champion 1981*
English Farmers' Champion 1980 & 1981
English Brace Champion 1978
J. H. Thorp Memorial Trophy 1981
International Farmers' Champion 1980

WISTON CAP 31154 *International Supreme Champion 1965*
International Shepherds' Champion 1966
Scottish Driving Champion 1969

SPOT 24981 *International Aggregate Championship 1966*
Scottish Aggregate Championship 1966
Scottish Shepherds' Aggregate Championship 1966
Scottish National Champion 1965 & 1966
Scottish Shepherds' Champion 1965 & 1966

MIRK 52844 *International Shepherds' Champion 1975*
Scottish Shepherds' Aggregate Championship 1975
Scottish National Champion 1975
Scottish Shepherds' Champion 1973 & 1975
Scottish Driving Champion 1975
Alexander Andrew Trophy 1975
J. M. Wilson Challenge Shield 1975

NIP 16878 *English Brace Champion 1968*

Born 9/10/84   Black & white   H. Huddleston, Carnforth

Awards

English Farmers' Champion 1989
J. H. Thorp Memorial Trophy 1989
Ivy Parry Trophy 1989

DON 108889, J. R. Thomas	CRAIG 59425, J. R. Thomas	CHIP 29946, L. Suter
		JILL 49652, H. Hawken
	MAID 97071, D. Jones	DON 73710, W. Welsh
		KAY 78706, D. Jones
MIST 106881, J. Townson	TWEED 92756, D. Guild	BEN 86497, D. Nicol
		MAUDE 56368, D. Nicol
	PHIL 73572, R. Taylor	CRAIG 47703, T. Watson
		MIST 45263, R. Taylor

DON 108889   *English Shepherds' Champion 1984*
            English Aggregate Championship 1982
            English Shepherds' Aggregate Championship 1982

CRAIG 59425   *International Supreme Champion 1977*
International Shepherds' Champion 1976 & 1977
International Aggregate Championship 1976 & 1977
Captain Whittaker Outwork Cup 1977
R. Fortune Trophy 1977
Lord Mostyn Plate 1977
I. S. D. S. Blue Riband 1977
Pedigree Chum Supreme Championship Trophy 1977
Welsh Aggregate Championship 1976 & 1977
Welsh Shepherds' Aggregate Championship 1973, 1975, 1976 & 1977
Welsh National Champion 1977
Welsh Shepherds' Champion 1976 & 1977
Challis Shield 1977

TWEED 92756 *Scottish Farmers' Champion 1984*
Scottish Driving Champion 1981
Scottish Aggregate Championship 1984

DON 73710 *International Shepherds' Champion 1979*
Scottish Shepherds' Aggregate Championship 1979
Captain Whittaker Outwork Cup 1975
Scottish Shepherds' Champion 1978

H. Huddleston with Jim 150661

Born 11/7/84   Black & white   J. Harrison, Shap

Awards

English Farmers' Champion 1990

ROY 114678, J. Templeton	┌ **MOSS 103923, J. Templeton**	┌ **HEMP 72301, A. J. Campbell** └ **QUEEN 74047, H. MacKenzie**
	└ **LASS 92191, T. Stevenson**	┌ **GLEN 75630, W. Beattie** └ **WINK 49224, C. Graham**
JAN 128236, H. Fergusson	┌ **BEN 88284, S. L. Davidson**	┌ **BEN 50504, J. A. MacLeod** └ **MIST 75908, D. MacKenzie**
	└ **MEG 115134, B. Cunningham**	┌ **SAN 90558, A. Marr** └ **JILL 100829, B. Cunningham**

ROY 114678   *International Farmers' Champion 1985, 1987 & 1989*
International Aggregate Championship 1985
International Brace Aggregate Championship with **BEN 119873**, *1984*
International Brace Championship with **BEN**, *1984*
International Driving Champion 1983 & 1987
Scottish Aggregate Championship 1981, 1982, 1983 & 1985
Feedmobile Trophy 1985 & 1989
McDiarmid Trophy 1981, 1985 & 1989

Captain Whittaker Outwork Cup 1987 & 1989
Pedigree Chum Silver Salver 1985 & 1987
Scottish National & Farmers' Champion 1982, 1983 & 1985
Scottish Brace Champion with **BEN 119873***, 1982, 1983 & 1984*
Scottish Driving Champion 1983 & 1987
Alexander Andrew Trophy 1982, 1983 & 1985
J. M. Wilson Challenge Shield 1982, 1983 & 1985

MOSS 103923 *Scottish Aggregate Championship 1979*
Feedmobile Trophy 1979

BEN 88284 *Scottish National & Farmers' Champion 1980*
Scottish Brace Champion with **SHEP 80763***, 1981*
Alexander Andrew Trophy 1980
J. M. Wilson Challenge Shield 1980

HEMP 72301 *Scottish Driving Champion 1977*
GLEN 75630 *Scottish Brace Champion with* **JILL 55741***, 1977*

J. Harrison with Craig 148254

Born 27/9/81   Black & white   T. Brownrigg, Kirkby Stephen

Awards

English Farmers' Champion 1991
J. H. Thorpe Memorial Cup 1991
Allison Award 1991

	┌ROBBIE 38315, T. J. Watkins	┌BROCKEN ROBBIE 24636, E. B. Carpenter └FLEECE 22145, T. J. Watkins
ROY 97270, J. Errington	└NELL 65799, M. Page	┌ROY 45152, C. Storey └FLY 34035, J. James
	┌UDALE SIM 52690, H. Huddleston	┌JOE 33190, T. Harper └UDALE MADDIE 38121, H. Huddleston
JESS 96076, A. Dodds	└LASSIE 77725, A. Dodds	┌BRIGG 58613, J. Errington └LASSIE 37287, G. Coatsworth

NELL 65799   *Welsh Shepherds' Aggregate Championship 1974 & 1978*
Welsh National Champion 1973
Welsh Shepherds' Champion 1973, 1974 & 1978
Welsh Brace Champion with **FLY 108143**, *1980*

UDALE SIM 52690   *English Aggregate Championship 1972*
Feedmobile Cup 1972
English National Champion 1972
English Farmers' Champion 1972
J. H. Thorp Memorial Trophy 1972

GEM 147666 **Kirkby Lonsdale**

T. W. LONGTON

Born 22/3/84   Black, white & tan   T. W. Longton, Quernmore

Awards

English Aggregate Championship 1992
English Brace Champion with BESS 101142, 1987
English Brace Champion with TWEED 140476, 1989 & 1991
English Driving Champion 1992

	┌MIRK 37953, A. Penrice	┌BEN 12262, J. R. Millar └MEG 17910, A. Penrice
GOSS 91940, A. Iley	└JACE 62098, J. Hastie	┌BOSWORTH COON 34186, L. Evans └GYP 38336, T. Longton
BESS 101142, T. W. Longton	┌GLEN 80138, Mrs M. Arthurs	┌MOSS 57707, A. Jones └NELL 61154, A. Jones
	└KERRY 84042, T. Longton	┌WISTON CAP 31154, J. Richardson └GYP 56601, T. Longton

BESS 101142   *International Supreme Champion 1986*
International & English Aggregate Championships 1986
I. S. D. S. Blue Riband 1986
Captain Whittaker Outwork Cup 1986
R. Fortune Trophy 1986
Lord Mostyn Plate 1986
Rhiwlas Trophy 1986
Pedigree Chum Supreme Championship Trophy 1986

Langs' Scotch Whisky Quaiche 1986
English National & Farmers' Champion 1985
English Brace Champion with **LASSIE 91601**, *1979 & 1982*
English Brace Champion with **MAGGIE 140478**, *1985*
J. H. Thorp Memorial Trophy 1985
Ivy Parry Trophy 1985
English Brace Champion with **GEM 147666**, *1987*

BEN 12262 *Scottish Aggregate Championship 1960*
International Farmers' Champion 1960
Scottish Driving Champion 1957

BOSWORTH COON 34186 *International Supreme Champion 1968*
International Farmers' Champion 1969
International Aggregate Championship 1969
English Aggregate Championship 1968 & 1969
Captain Whittaker Outwork Cup 1968
English National & Farmers' Champion 1969
J. H. Thorp Memorial Trophy 1969

GYP 38336 *International & English Driving Champion 1971*
English Aggregate Championship 1971
English Brace Champion with **LAD 41928**, *1971 & 1972*

WISTON CAP 31154 *International Supreme Champion 1965*
International Shepherds' Champion 1966
Scottish Driving Champion 1969

J. MOCKFORD

Born 20/5/85   Black & white   P. Turnbull, Morpeth
Awards

English Aggregate Championship 1993
Feedmobile Trophy 1993
McDiarmid Trophy 1993
Eden Valley Mineral Water Co. Crystal Carafe 1993
English Farmers' Champion 1993
J. H. Thorp Memorial Trophy 1993

CRAIG 102464, P. Turnbull	**GLEN 75630, R. Fortune**	**CAP 67230, T. T. McKnight** **SHELL 68768, T. T. McKnight**
	PHIL 92911, T. Hamilton	**MIRK 52844, J. Richardson** **JUNE 59734, W. Cormack**
JESS N. R., M. Graham	**GLEN N. R., J. J. Chapman**	**LAD 16149, Holmes Bros.** **Not known**
	BET 79954, J. J. Chapman	**MIRK 43504, J. Errington** **JILL 34406, J. Errington**

GLEN 75630   *Scottish Brace Champion with* **JILL 55741**, *1977*
MIRK 52844   *International Shepherds' Champion 1975*
                 Scottish Shepherds' Aggregate Championship 1975
                 Scottish National Champion 1975
                 Scottish Shepherds' Champion 1973 & 1975
                 Scottish Driving Champion 1975
                 Alexander Andrew Trophy 1975
                 J. M. Wilson Challenge Shield 1975
JUNE 59734   *Scottish National & Farmers' Champion 1973*
                 Alexander Andrew Trophy 1973

Scottish National Winners

James Gardner, winner of the first Scottish sheepdog trial at Carnwath, ca. 1876

James Scott

98

J. Scott's Kep 13

James Reid and Loos II, 'The Mother of Champions'

Mr James Reid, International Sheep Dog Society secretary for thirty-two years, became involved in the breeding of the border collie and was instrumental, with C. B. MacPherson of Kingussie, in exporting many of the best working dogs of the day, especially to Australia and New Zealand. Few poorly paid shepherds could afford to resist selling a dog for a high price, and they could always train another to replace the old workmate. Mr Reid bred one of the great bitches of the breed – Loos II 435, given as a pup to Mr Wm Wallace, Fingland. She was an excellent worker, and won the 1925 International Farmers' Championship. She became known as the 'Mother of Champions', breeding particularly well to Dickson's Hemp 153, a great-grandson of Tommy 16, who was bred by Adam Telfer. Hemp 153 was second to Spot 303 in the 1925 Supreme Championship and was International Farmers' Champion in 1924. Loos II 435, was dam of eleven International Champions and sixteen National Champions and was herself a great-great-granddaughter of Tommy 16, who was the root of one of the most successful sheepdog bloodlines.

J. M. Wilson's Supreme Champion Fly 824, was by Hemp 153 out of Loos, as was Nell 1627 who won the Scottish National in 1935, 1936 and 1939. Mated to Craig 1048, a son of Hemp 153, Loos produced J. M. Wilson's famous Roy 1665, the only dog to date to win the Supreme Championship three times. Nickey

Mr and Mrs Wallace with Loos

Fingland Loos 435

1823, Scottish National Champion in 1933 and International Farmers' Champion the same year, later exported to Mr Ferrer, Queensland, was also by Craig out of Loos. Nickey was a litter sister to J. M. Wilson's Roy 1665.

Tommy 16 is very important in the development of the modern border collie; one cannot stress too greatly how much he has influenced the whole breed, in Australia and New Zealand as well as in Britain. His son, William Wallace's (Otterburn) Supreme Champion Moss 22, was exported to James Lilico, New Zealand, becoming known there as Border Boss.

The 1913 Supreme Champion, T. P. Brown's Lad 19, also sired by Tommy was exported to James Lilico. Lad grieved for his previous owner, to whom he had been particularly devoted, and refused to show any interest in sheep for months, until one day he suddenly ran out to gather some ewes and from then on he settled to work with all his old skill and enthusiasm. The modern imports from New Zealand show bench kennels, to the show fraternity in England, can be traced through many generations to Lad and his contemporaries exported to Australia and New Zealand. These modern imports into Britain are not eligible for International Sheep Dog Society registration, and with their excessive coats and heavy-boned, short legs differ greatly from the border collies working on the New Zealand sheep stations.

Thomas Armstrong's Supreme Champion Sweep 21 (1910 and 1912), and his Supreme Champion Don 17 (1911 and 1914), both bred from Trim 37, were maternal grandsons of Tommy, and both were exported to New Zealand and later went to Australian kennels.

G. P. Brown's 1923 Supreme Champion Spot 308, who also won the Scottish National that year, was exported to Sam Stoddart in America. Spot was line bred to Tommy, his paternal granddam being by Tommy and his paternal great-great-granddam, Trim 37, also by Tommy. Spot founded the border collie breed in America, and was registered number one in the North America Sheepdog Society's stud book. Spot was taken from his dam, Ruby 207, at six weeks old, and a week later the bitch and her remaining puppies contracted distemper and all died.

Between winning the Supreme Championship and being exported, Spot was bred to twenty-five bitches. One particularly successful litter was from Thomas Hunter's Fly 165, an important key brood bitch of the breed. From this litter by Spot, came Moss 454, who was second to his own son, Mark Hayton's Glen 698 Supreme Champion, 1926. Moss was exported by C. B. MacPherson to James Moore, Australia, who had many of the British bred dogs in his Australian and Tasmanian kennels.

In Australia Moss 454 was bred to Caley (of Thornhill), a daughter of Kep 13, thus founding the famous Boveagh line. Caley had previously been exported in whelp to David Murray's Toss, 3001.

C. B. MacPherson's Moss 454

The Brown Family and Their Dogs

G. P. Brown's Spot II 604, a son of Spot 308, was International and Scottish Shepherds' Champion in 1928, and Nan 490, his dam, was out of T. Hunter's Fly 165. Fly was dam of T. Hunter's famous Sweep 164, International Shepherds' Champion in 1923 and 1924, and sire of many good working dogs before being exported to New Zealand.

G. P. Brown, the first shepherd to win the Supreme Championship, was the youngest of three brothers, all well-known shepherds and dog handlers in the Border country. Thomas P. Brown won the 1913 Supreme Championship with Lad 19, a son of Tommy 16 and Andrew Brown's Old Maid, number one in the society's stud book, and a daughter of A. Renwick's Don.

On one occasion the three brothers were on their way to a trial at Duns. They travelled by pony and trap to Earlston, where they went into a hotel while waiting for the train, to continue the journey. Several dogs were with them, and unnoticed, Old Nell 205 went round to the kitchen door, where an angry mother cat

attacked her. Nell returned to the street but found no sign of her master. When the Browns started for the station they called her to no avail, so reluctantly they boarded the train. Just outside the station Andrew recognised Nell bringing a bunch of sheep down a field. He pulled the communication cord, called the dog, who left the sheep and raced to the train, running perilously alongside until it stopped, and popped into the carriage as the door was opened. Mr Reid the society's secretary was also on the train and he dealt with the railway officials at Duns, who took no further action in the matter. And Nell won first prize at the trial!

T. P. Brown, who, like most shepherds, was a kindly man who thought much of his dogs, sold a promising young bitch, Tess, to a butcher in Perth. Eight weeks later he heard scratching at the door. Opening it he was amazed to see Tess, weary and thin, her paws raw and bleeding, but gently waving her bedraggled tail. She had travelled around two hundred miles over strange country and had either to swim the Firth of Forth or to creep across the railway bridge, which allows little room between the rails and the parapet if a train passes. One can

G. P. Brown's Old Nell

T. P. Brown with (left to right) Maid of Oxton, Lad 19 and Nell

only wonder how she found her way and over-came the many obstacles that must have faced her. Needless to say, the butcher had his money returned, and Tess remained with the gentle man she loved so dearly.

Lad Junior was not so fortunate. After the First World War, when sheep and cattle were still driven to the markets, Mr Brown was taking a flock of lambs to Lanark mart. Various farms close to Lanark had certain fields in which these flocks grazed overnight, prior to market day.

Mr Brown was busy on the morning of the market, sorting out several different flocks and setting his lambs on the road early, for penning in the mart. He had Lad Junior in charge of his flock, and sent him to the head of the lambs to prevent them catching up with the flock in front of them. In flanking to pass them, Lad leapt over a wall but sadly he fell to his death – he had unwittingly leapt the wall of Kirkfieldbank bridge, and fell to the rocks bordering the river below. He was alive when they reached him, but died soon after of his injuries.

These are now legendary men and dogs. Yet they were flesh and blood, a fact brought home to me when privileged to meet and talk with members of their families – history came alive.

J. M. Wilson

To crown numerous awards in International Sheep Dog Society trials J. M. Wilson, reputed to be the greatest of sheepdog handlers, won eleven Nationals and nine International Supreme Championships and his successes have yet to be surpassed. Nell 1627, won the Scottish National in 1935, 1936 and 1939, only being prevented by her half-brother Roy 1665, who beat her by half a point, from winning the 1937 National.

Roy who was disinterested in sheep in his youth, became a legend in sheepdog annals. He had distemper from which he fortunately recovered, only to have a serious fight with his half-brother Jix. The sight in one eye was severely damaged, but as it improved so too did Roy's interest in work, and he proceeded to win the Scottish Brace Championship in 1934, with Fly 824; the International Farmers' Championship in 1935, and among his many other awards he won the 1934, 1936 and 1937 Supreme Championships; the only dog to date, to have thrice won the highest honour a border collie can attain.

102

The last Scottish National before the Second World War was won by J. M. Wilson with Nell and in 1946 when trials resumed, he again won the National with Glen 3940. W. J. Hislop's Sweep 3834, brother to Glen was on equal points, but Glen won on a runoff. Sweep was to become Scottish National Champion two years later. Glen was 1946 Supreme Champion, and Sweep was International Farmers' Champion. Glen again won the Supreme Championship in 1948; his kennel mate, Moss 5176, was second and Sweep was third – these three dogs were all out of J. Kirk's Nell 3514, a daughter of J. M. Wilson's Cap 3036. Because of the cessation of trials through the war, Cap was unable to prove his prowess on the trial field, but he was such an able hill dog that his fame spread and bitches were sent to him from all over Great Britain. His name appears in the majority of extended pedigrees of modern border collies. Cap's most famous daughter was J. Kirk's Nell 3514, dam of J. M. Wilson's Glen and Moss and also W. J. Hislop's Sweep. She was granddam to Whitehope Nap and great-granddam to J. Gilchrist's Spot 24981; and thus in the breeding of many of todays' collies. She was a successful trial dog in her own right, but is best remembered for her quality progeny.

J. M. Wilson's Moss 5176, sire of his 1950 Supreme Champion, Mirk 4438, was destined to be 'bridesmaid', being reserve Supreme Champion to Mirk, and in 1949 to D. W. Daniel's Supreme Champion, Chip 4924. Moss was a much sought-after stud dog, many successful and famous dogs being bred from him.

J. M. Wilson retired from trial competition after winning his ninth Supreme Championship in 1955 at Edinburgh, with Bill 9040, who was later exported to America where he won the North American Championship in 1958. Whitehope Nap 8685, was reserve Champion to Bill at Edinburgh. He had previously won the Scottish National earlier in the year, with Bill in second place. Nap was a smooth-coated, powerful, black and white dog who passed his powerful method of work on to his offspring. Many later Champions were from his breeding line, inheriting his power and speed, and his 'sheep wisdom'.

Her Majesty the Queen honoured J. M. Wilson in 1957 with the M.B.E., for his services to agriculture. One of his most precious possessions was a gold pocket watch presented to him by King George V, after he and Alex Millar gave the Royal Family a command performance of their collies' skills at Balmoral. Sadly, J.M. died in 1975 as the result of a car accident.

David Murray

David Murray O.B.E., a quiet, unassuming gentleman, won the Scottish National Championship in 1952 with his famous dog Vic 4368. He was, however, better known for his Brace class successes with Vic and his son, Number 6152. With these dogs he won four successive Scottish Brace Championships in 1951 to 1954, and three successive International Brace Championships 1953 to 1955. Vic was Scottish Driving Champion in 1950, 1951 and 1952 and International Driving Champion in 1951. David Murray had previously won the 1938 Scottish National with Sweep 1962, who was also Scottish and International Driving Champion, and in 1947, Sweep's son, Toss 3001, was Scottish Driving Champion. In 1960 Murray's Glen 12063, won the Scottish and International Driving Championships.

In 1945, at my first visit to a sheepdog trial, David Murray's dog Vic so impressed me with his gleaming coat and rippling muscles, as he paced purposefully behind his sheep, that I became 'hooked' on sheepdog work, and the history of the breed.

At one trial, before I plucked up courage to compete, I was persuaded against my better judgement to return the sheep to the letting-out pen, but made the mistake of using inexperienced Lassie 9868, instead of Ben 9474, who could have done the job without my feeble interference! Lassie allowed the flock to spread and we were about to find ourselves rather out of our depth, when I noticed the sheep drawing together, and proceeding towards the pen in an orderly manner. Looking round I saw that Vic had been sent to restore order, and once the sheep were gathered together he was quietly recalled, and Lassie and her grateful (and relieved) handler, finished the job. A kindly helping hand from a true gentleman.

'Film-star' Dogs

David Murray and his daughter Jean appeared in the film *My Dog, Number*, in which Number was the chief character, showing a collie's work through a hill farming year. Sadly, Jean died a few years later, which was a great blow to David Murray. He also appeared in a film about sheep farming and his dog Turk played the role of Flash in the film, *Flash the Sheepdog*. This film was shown in the local cinema at Peebles and David and Turk were invited to appear in the theatre, but David died suddenly just before the show, so his son, David, took Turk to the theatre, but Turk was very unhappy. A few months later David lent Turk to a shepherd friend. The dog disappeared and despite every effort to find him, he was never seen again.

Other versatile border collies have become 'film-stars'. In the film *Owd Bob* W. B. Bagshaw's Glyn played the part of Owd Bob, but Black Wull was played by a German Shepherd dog, although, in the book, he was also a sheep-dog. W. B. Bagshaw donated the International Driving Championship Trophy in memory of his father J. B. Bagshaw, at the inception of the Driving class, in 1937. The three National Driving classes began in 1938.

Father and son were successful competitors, and were very much involved with the organisation of the famous Longshaw trials.

Mark Hayton's Pal Glen, and Arthur Hayton's Pattie 1515, 1934 and 1938 International Shepherds' Champion, took part in the film, *Song of the Plough*. Arthur Hayton won the English Shepherds' Championship in three consecutive years, 1936, 1937 and 1938, with Jock, and won the 1935 English Brace Championship with Pattie. Mark Hayton's Pat 2219, who was 1937 English National Champion, was later stolen and sadly never heard of again. It was Mark Hayton who wrote these words, as true today as in the 1930s – 'It is not by the boot, the stick, the kennel and chain that a dog can be trained, or made man's loyal friend, but only by love. For those who understand, no explanation is needed, and for those who do not, no explanation will prevail.' His Glen 698, won the 1926 Supreme Championship, with his sire, C. B. MacPherson's Moss 454, in second place.

Joe Relph and Jeff took part in the film *Border Collie*, and his Moss 2032, was in the films *Shepherd of the Hills* and *Flemish Farm*. He won the 1937 English Brace Championship with Moss and Bess 6338 and his Fleet 4555, who won the 1946 English Aggregate Championship, and the 1948 English Brace Championship in partnership with Spy 4553, played the 'hero' in *Loyal Heart*. Fleet, Cap 6360, and Spy accompanied Joe Relph in the Lord Mayor's Procession in London, many in the crowds recognising Fleet as the film-star dog. Fleet was sire of Ashton Priestley's 1951 Supreme Champion Pat 4203, and had himself been reserve to J. M. Wilson's Glen in the 1946 Supreme Championship. I have a personal interest in Pat as he sired Lassie 9868, the foundation bitch of the Brocken family of border collies.

In 1973 W. J. Evans' Queen played Flossie in *Fish*, a children's T.V. serial filmed in South Wales; the story of a lonely little boy whose life changed when Flossie, a stray sheepdog, appeared in the village.

Bagshaw's Glyn 1855

1922	SPOT 303	Lanark
1925		Stirling
1926		Stirling
1927		Stranraer

Born –/3/21   Black & white   A. Millar, Newmilns

Awards

International Supreme Champion 1925
Scottish National Champion 1922, 1925, 1926 & 1927

CAP 237, W. Telfer
- GLEN 34, W. Wallace
  - Not known
  - Not known
- MADDIE I, 38, J. A. Reid
  - DON I 17, T. Armstrong
  - MADDIE 8, W. B. Telfer

FAN 230, R. Douglas
- SWEEP, W. Hedley
  - Not known
  - Not known
- JED, J. Thompson
  - Not known
  - Not known

Born 1920   Black & white   G. P. Brown, Oxton

Awards

International Supreme Champion 1923
International Shepherds' Champion 1922

BEN 249, G. P. Brown	DON 217, C. Hardisty	DON 17, T. Armstrong MEG 27, J. Renwick
	FAN 208, G. P. Brown	TOMMY 16, I. Herdman NELL 205, T. P. Brown
RUBY 207, G. P. Brown	SKIP, J. McKnight	Not known Not known
	MOSS, A. Harrison	Not known Not known

Exported to Sam Stoddart in United States

DON 17   *International Supreme Champion 1911 & 1914*
Exported to New Zealand and thence to Australia

106

Born –/1/17   Black & white   A. Millar, Newmilns

RISP II 238, A. Millar	JIM, J. Johnstone	Not known Not known
	FLOSS, J. Weir	Not known Not known
NANCY 242, A. Millar	DON 17, T. Armstrong	DON, W. Burns TRIM 37, T. Armstrong
	JED, R. Oliver	Not known Not known

DON 17   *International Supreme Champion 1911 & 1914*
Exported to New Zealand and thence to Australia
NANCY 242   *Exported to New Zealand*

A. Millar's Mux 20 and Risp 15

The Millars and Their Dogs

1922 saw the commencement of the National trials in England, Scotland and Wales. Throughout the twenties the Scottish trials were dominated by Alex Millar, who won eight Nationals, seven of them consecutively. His Spot 303, Supreme Champion 1925, won four Scottish Nationals, including that of 1922.

Nancy 242, daughter of T. Armstrong's Supreme Champion Don 17 (1911 and 1914), was exported to James Lilico, New Zealand, but her daughter Tot 155 remained with Alex Millar to win the 1924 National. Mated to Vim 685, who was lost at sea when returning from Ireland, Tot produced Ben 891, International Farmers' Champion in 1928 and 1930, and Scottish National Champion in 1930. Ben sired the 1934 Scottish National Champion Ken 1477, who gained full points to win the title, before being exported to New Zealand.

Alex Millar's Mirk 836, Scottish National Champion in 1928 and 1929 was by Dickson's Hemp 153, out of Mist 332, whose sire was Walter Telfer's Cap 237, sire of Spot 303.

Alex Millar with Frisk, a dog bred from a line of locally well-respected working collies, was first competitor at the post at the first International trial in 1906 at Gullane: he had been granted permission by the committee to have an early run, as it was his wedding day!

His son, J. R. Millar, was almost as successful a handler as his father, winning four Scottish National Championships and many other awards in National and International trials. Drift 4380, a son of J. Purdie's Tam, the sire of J. Gilchrist's Supreme Champion Spot 3624 (1947), was his first National Champion (1947), followed two years later with Ben 4931, sired by J. M. Wilson's Supreme Champion of 1946 and 1948, Glen 3940. He next won the Scottish National in 1953 with Tam 7032, a son of Ben; and in 1969 with Ken II 18754, who was a grandson of Tam. Ken II's sire, J. R. Millar's Ben 12262, as well as gaining other awards, was International Farmers' Champion in 1960. Speed 4382, another of J. R. Millar's team dogs, won the Scottish Aggregate Trophy in 1952.

Alex Millar with (left to right) Mirk 836, Ben 891, Spot 303 and Tot 155

MIRK 836

Born 20/5/26   Black & white   A. Millar, Newmilns

Awards

International Brace Champion with BEN 891, 1929, 1931 & 1932
Scottish Brace Champion with BEN 891, 1932

HEMP 153, T. Dickson	YARROW 23, A. Telfer	TYNE 145, I. Herdman NELL (MEG), J. Renwick
	FENWICK JED 33, A. Telfer	MOSS, A. Telfer WYLIE, G. Snaith
MIST 332, A. Craig	CAP 237, W. Telfer	GLEN, W. Wallace MADDIE I 38, J. A. Reid
	FLY 221, J. F. Wilson	GLEN 34, W. Wallace JED 220, J. F. Wilson

HEMP 153   *International Farmers' Champion 1924*
MIRK 836 *was full brother to J. M. Wilson's Supreme Champion* **CRAIG 1048**, *1930*

T. M. Dickson's Hemp 153

Born 1926   Black & white   A. Millar, Newmilns

Awards

International Farmers' Champion 1928 & 1930
International Brace Champion with MIRK 836, 1929, 1931 & 1932
International Aggregate Championship 1930
Scottish Brace Champion with MIRK 836, 1932

VIM 685, A. Millar	TOSS, K. Jamieson	Not known Not known
	JESS 52, J. Weir	JIM, J. Russell JENNY, A. Hamilton
TOT 155, A. Millar	RISP II, 238, A. Millar	JIM, J. Johnstone FLOSS, J. Weir
	NANCY 242, A. Millar	DON 17, T. Armstrong JED, R. Oliver

TOT 155   *Scottish National Champion 1924*
DON 17   *International Supreme Champion 1911 & 1914*
VIM 685 *was lost at sea, while returning from Ireland*
JENNY, *Alex Hamilton, was a daughter of* **TOMMY 16** *& Old Maid 2, A. Hamilton,*
     who was out of A. Brown's Old Maid I and A. Renwick's **DON 146.**

CRAIG 1048

*J. M. Wilson with Nell 1627 (left) and
Craig 1048 (right)*

Born 8/6/27   Black & white   J. M. Wilson, Moffat

Awards

International Supreme Champion 1930
International Farmers' Champion 1929
Scottish Brace Champion with FLY 824, 1931
International Aggregate Championship 1932

	┌YARROW 23, A. Telfer	┌TYNE 145, I. Herdman └NELL (MEG), J. Renwick
HEMP 153, T. Dickson		
	└FENWICK JED 33, A. Telfer	┌MOSS, A. Telfer └WYLIE, G. Snaith
	┌CAP 237, W. Telfer	┌GLEN 34, W. Wallace └MADDIE I 38, J. A. Reid
MIST 332, A. Craig		
	└FLY 221, J. F. Wilson	┌GLEN 34, W. Wallace └JED 220, J. F. Wilson

HEMP 153   *International Farmers' Champion 1924*

111

Born 7/4/31   Black & white   J. M. Wilson, Moffat

Awards
International Farmers' Champion 1933
Scottish Aggregate Championship 1933

```
                                    ┌ HEMP 153, T. Dickson      ┌ YARROW 23, A. Telfer
                                    │                           └ FENWICK JED 33, A. Telfer
CRAIG 1048, J. M. Wilson ──────────┤
                                    │                           ┌ CAP 237, W. Telfer
                                    └ MIST 332, A. Craig        └ FLY 221, J. F. Wilson

                                    ┌ LADDIE 317, J. A. Reid    ┌ ROY, Hindmarsh
                                    │                           └ JED, Hindmarsh
LOOS II 435, W. Wallace ───────────┤
                                    │                           ┌ TOM, T. Gilholm
                                    └ LOOS I 45, J. A. Reid     └ LILLE 26, T. Gilholm
```

NICKEY 1823 *exported to Australia*

CRAIG 1048   *International Supreme Champion 1930*
                  International Farmers' Champion 1929
                  Scottish Brace Champion 1931
                  International Aggregate Championship 1932
LOOS II 435   *International Farmers' Champion 1925*
HEMP 153   *International Farmers' Champion 1924*

Born 29/3/29   Black & white   A. Millar, Newmilns

Awards

International Farmers' Champion 1934
International Aggregate Championship 1934
Scottish Aggregate Championship 1934

BEN 891, A. Millar	⌐VIM 685, A. Millar	⌐TOSS, K. Jamieson └JESS, J. Weir
	└TOT 155, A. Millar	⌐RISP II, 238, A. Millar └NANCY 242, A. Millar
FLY 76, T. Howie	⌐TAM, T. Galloway	⌐Not known └Not known
	└JEN, A. K. Galloway	⌐Not known └Not known

BEN 891   *International Farmers' Champion 1928 & 1930*
               International Brace Champion 1929, 1931 & 1932
               International Aggregate Championship 1930
               Scottish Brace Championship 1932
TOT 155   *Scottish National Champion 1924*

1935	**NELL 1627**	Helenburgh
1936		Helenburgh
1939		Peebles

Born 18/5/30   Black & white   J. M. Wilson, Moffat

Awards

International Brace Champion with ROY 1665, 1937 & 1938
International Aggregate Championship 1935
Scottish Aggregate Championship 1935
Scottish Brace Champion with FLY 824, 1933
Scottish Brace Champion with ROY 1665, 1936, 1937 & 1938

HEMP 153, T. Dickson	┌ YARROW 23, A. Telfer	┌ TYNE 145, I. Herdman └ NELL (MEG), J. Renwick
	└ FENWICK JED 33, A. Telfer	┌ MOSS, A. Telfer └ WYLIE, G. Snaith
LOOS II 435, W. Wallace	┌ LADDIE 317, J. A. Reid	┌ ROY, Hindmarsh └ JED, Hindmarsh
	└ LOOS I 45, J. A. Reid	┌ TOM, T. Gilholm └ LILLE 26, T. Gilholm

HEMP 153   *International Farmers' Champion 1924*
LOOS II 435   *International Farmers' Champion 1925*
FENWICK JED 33 *was exported to New Zealand*

Born 7/4/31   Black & white   J. M. Wilson, Moffat

Awards

International Supreme Champion 1934, 1936 & 1937
International Farmers' Champion 1935
International Brace Champion with NELL 1627, 1937 & 1938
International Aggregate Championship 1936 & 1937
Scottish Aggregate Championship 1936 & 1937
Scottish Brace Champion with FLY 824, 1934
Scottish Brace Champion with NELL 1627, 1936, 1937 & 1938

CRAIG 1048, J. M. Wilson
- HEMP 153, T. Dickson
  - YARROW 23, A. Telfer
  - FENWICK JED 33, A. Telfer
- MIST 332, A. Craig
  - CAP 237, W. Telfer
  - FLY 221, J. F. Wilson

LOOS II 435, W. Wallace
- LADDIE 317, J. A. Reid
  - ROY, Hindmarsh
  - JED, Hindmarsh
- LOOS I 45, J. A. Reid
  - TOM, T. Gilholm
  - LILLE 26, T. Gilholm

CRAIG 1048   *International Supreme Champion 1930*
     International Farmers' Champion 1929
     International Aggregate Championship 1932
     Scottish National Champion 1931 & 1932
     Scottish Brace Champion 1931
LOOS II 435   *International Farmers' Champion 1925*
HEMP 153   *International Farmers' Champion 1924*

Born 18/8/32   Black   D. Murray, Peebles

Awards

Scottish Driving Champion 1938

CRAIG 1048, J. M. Wilson	HEMP 153, T. Dickson	YARROW 23, A. Telfer FENWICK JED 33, A. Telfer
	MIST 332, A. Craig	CAP 237, W. Telfer FLY 221, J. F. Wilson
NAN 1438, D. Murray	DON, A. McNicol	Not known Not known
	MEG II 79, A. McNicol	CHANCE, A. McNicol MEG, A. McNicol

CRAIG 1048   *International Supreme Champion 1930*
              International Farmers' Champion 1929
              International Aggregate Champion 1932
              Scottish National Champion 1931 & 1932
              Scottish Brace Champion 1931
HEMP 153   *International Farmers' Champion 1924*
MEG   *A. McNicol was by T. P. Brown's* **LAD 19**
CHANCE   *A. McNicol was by A. Millar's* **RISP II 238**

No trials were held during the war years, 1940–45

1946 **GLEN 3940** Stirling

Born 15/9/43   Black & white   J. M. Wilson, Innerleithen

Awards
International Supreme Champion 1946 & 1948
International Farmers' Champion 1948
International Aggregate Championship 1946 & 1948
Scottish Aggregate Championship 1946 & 1948

	┌BEN 1572, A. Riddell	┌GLEN 603, T. Hunter └SLY I 1087, P. Dignan
GLEN 3510, W. Hislop	└BEAT I, J. Guthrie	┌Not known └Not known
	┌CAP 3036, J. M. Wilson	┌SAM 2336, H. Cullens └PEN 2572, H. Cullens
NELL 3514, J. Kirk	└MOSS 1827, J. McCaskie	┌MOSS 1677, A. Storie └NICKEY 1823, T. Dickson

NICKEY 1823   *Scottish National Champion 1933*
International Farmers' Champion 1933
Scottish Aggregate Championship 1933

Born 23/1/44   Black & white   J. R. Millar, Dalry

Awards
Scottish Driving Champion 1946

	┌JIGGS 2378, W. Elliott	┌BEN 1572, A. Riddell └TIB I, J. Anderson
TAM 3465, J. Purdie	│	
	└MEG 2787, J. Hislop	┌ROY 2772, D. Rogerson └BETTY 1852, D. Rogerson
	┌Not known	
NORA, A. Carmichael	│	
	└Not known	

Handlers at the 1948 International Trial. Kneeling, left to right: Harry Huddleston, with Maddie; Griff Pugh with Sweep; David Stone with Jake. Standing: R. O. Williams with Lad; J. M. Wilson; W. J. Hislop; Tom Bonella with Spot; David Murray with Vic; R. J. Hughes with Jaff; J. H. Roberts with Roy. W. J. Hislop's Sweep stands in the foreground.

W. J. Hislop's Tam 4214 (left) and
Sweep 3834 (right)

Born 11/6/42   Black & white   W. J. Hislop, Gordon

Awards
International Farmers' Champion 1946
International & Scottish Driving Champion 1948

GLEN 3510, W. J. Hislop	┌ **BEN 1572, A. Riddell**	┌ **GLEN 603, T. Hunter** └ **SLY I 1087, P. Dignan**
	└ **BEAT I, J. Guthrie**	┌ Not known └ Not known
NELL 3514, W. J. Hislop	┌ **CAP 3036, J. M. Wilson**	┌ **SAM 2336, H. Cullens** └ **PEN 2572, H. Cullens**
	└ **MOSS 1827, J. McCaskie**	┌ **MOSS 1677, A. Storie** └ **NICKEY 1823, T. Dickson**

NICKEY 1823   *Scottish National Champion 1933*
International Farmers' Champion 1933
Scottish Aggregate Championship 1933
SWEEP 3834 and **GLEN 3940** *were full brothers*

119

Born 16/6/45   Black, white & mottled   J. R. Millar, Dalry

GLEN 3940, J. M. Wilson	GLEN 3510, W. Hislop	BEN 1572, A. Riddell BEAT I. J. Guthrie
	NELL 3514, J. Kirk	CAP 3036, J. M. Wilson MOSS 1827, J. McCaskie
JESS 5471, R. Brown	SWEEP, Wallace	Not known Not known
	MINNIE 1758, W. Wallace	CRAIG 1048, J. M. Wilson LOOS II 435, W. Wallace

GLEN 3940   *International Supreme Champion 1946 & 1948*
               International Farmers' Champion 1948
               International Aggregate Championship 1946 & 1948
               Scottish Aggregate Championship 1946 & 1948
               Scottish Farmers' Champion 1946
CRAIG 1048   *International Supreme Champion 1930*
               International Farmers' Champion 1929
               International Aggregate Championship 1932
               Scottish Brace Champion 1931
               Scottish National Champion 1931 & 1932
LOOS II 435   *International Farmers' Champion 1925*
W. Wallace's **MINNIE 1758**, *was a full sister to J. M. Wilson's* **ROY 1665**

J. M. Wilson with Tib 6903, Glen 3940, Mirk 4438 and Moss 5176

Born 19/4/44   Black & white   J. M. Wilson, Innerleithen

Awards
International Supreme Champion 1950
International Aggregate Championship 1950
Scottish Aggregate Championship 1950

SPOT 3369, J. McDonald	⌐MOSS, W. Amos	⌐Not known └Not known
	└MEG, J. McDonald	⌐Not known └Not known
CHRIS 4065, J. Cole	⌐CAP 3036, J. M. Wilson	⌐SAM 2336, H. Cullens └PEN 2572, H. Cullens
	└QUEEN 3113, J. Gilchrist	⌐WATT, J. Gilchrist └QUEEN, J. Gilchrist

Born 24/3/46   Black, white & tan   J. M. Wilson, Innerleithen

MIRK 4438, J. M. Wilson	SPOT 3369, J. McDonald	MOSS, W. Amos
		MEG, J. McDonald
	CHRIS 4065, J. Cole	CAP 3036, J. M. Wilson
		QUEEN 3113, J. Gilchrist
QUEEN 4205, J. M. Wilson	SPOT 3032, A. Storie	JIX 1707, F. Sutcliffe
		TIB, R. Anderson
	PHIL 2662, J. M. Wilson	KEN 1477, A. Millar
		FAN II, G. Gilholm

MIRK 4438   *International Supreme Champion 1950*
           International Aggregate Championship 1950
           Scottish Aggregate Championship 1950
           Scottish National Champion 1950

KEN 1477   *International Farmers' Champion 1934*
           International Aggregate Championship 1934
           Scottish Aggregate Championship 1934
           Scottish National Champion 1934

E. B. CARPENTER

Born 1/4/45   Black & white   D. Murray, Peebles

Awards

International Brace Champion with NUMBER 6152, 1953, 1954 & 1955
International Driving Champion 1951
Brace Aggregate Championship with NUMBER 6152, 1951, 1953 & 1955
Scottish Brace Champion with TOSS 3001, 1947
Scottish Driving Champion 1950, 1951 & 1952
Scottish Brace Champion with NUMBER 6152, 1951, 1952, 1953 & 1954

BEN 4475, R. Phillips	⌐GLEN 2479, R. Anderson	⌐ROB 2203, R. Anderson ⌐MIST 1717, G. Anderson
	⌐QUEEN 3596, J. M. Wilson	⌐BOY, J. M. Wilson ⌐PHIL 2662, J. M. Wilson
FLY 5506, D. Murray	⌐SWEEP 1962, D. Murray	⌐CRAIG 1048, J. M. Wilson ⌐NAN 1438, D. Murray
	⌐FLY, A. Henderson	⌐Not known ⌐Not known

SWEEP 1962   *Scottish National Champion 1938*
                 Scottish Driving Champion 1938
CRAIG 1048   *International Supreme Champion 1930*
                 International Farmers' Champion 1929
                 International Aggregate Championship 1932
                 Scottish Brace Champion 1931
                 Scottish National Champion 1931 & 1932

Born 9/2/49   Black, white & mottled   J. R. Millar, Dalry

Awards

Scottish Brace Champion with JIM 10503, 1955

BEN 4931, J. R. Millar	┌GLEN 3940, J. M. Wilson	┌GLEN 3510, W. Hislop └NELL 3514, J. Kirk
	└JESS 5471, R. Brown	┌SWEEP, Wallace └MINNIE 1758, W. Wallace
MEG II 4348, A. Burns	┌TAM II 3742, A. Burns	┌TAM I 1313, A. Burns └FLY, J. Lambie
	└BET, H. Patterson	┌Not known └Not known

BEN 4931   *Scottish National Champion 1949*
MEG II 4348   *Scottish Shepherds' Champion 1949*
GLEN 3940   *International Supreme Champion 1946 & 1948*
                   International Farmers' Champion 1948
                   International Aggregate Championship 1946 & 1948
                   Scottish Aggregate Championship 1946 & 1948
                   Scottish Farmers' Champion 1946

1954 **SPOT II 6775** Aberdeen

Born 19/2/47   Black, white & mottled   W. R. Little, Walkerburn

GLEN 3957, S. Banks	GLEN 3510, W. Hislop	BEN 1572, A. Riddell BEAT I, J. Guthrie
	NELL 3514, W. Hislop	CAP 3036, J. M. Wilson MOSS, 1827, J. McCaskie
TIB 4458, S. Banks	SPOT 3369, J. McDonald	MOSS, W. Amos MEG, J. McDonald
	LINT, C. Scott	Not known Not known

GLEN 3957 *was full brother to J. M. Wilson's* **GLEN 3940**, *International Supreme Champion*

Competitors at the Southdean Trial in the 1950s. Left to right: W. Work, unknown, J. Gilchrist,
H. Greenslade, W. R. Little, unknown, W. Goodfellow

125

Born 2/1/51   Black & white   J. M. Wilson, Innerleithen

GLEN 6123, W. McClure	┌MARK 4991, J. Jones	┌SWEEP 3483, McHarrie └MEG, Lambie
	└FLOSS 5058, J. Jones	┌JAFF I 2598, R. Williams └BET 4353, R. Williams
MEG 5141, W. McClure	┌JIM, N. R. Scott	
	└NELL 3514, J. Kirk	┌CAP 3036, J. M. Wilson └MOSS 1827, J. McCaskie

Scott's **JIM** *was full brother to W. J. Hislop's* **GLEN 3510.**
JAFF I 2598   *Welsh National Champion 1937*

126

TILLYOCHIE MOSS 7878 **Golspie**

SCOTTISH FARMER

Born 28/5/49   Black & white   T. Bonella, Kinross

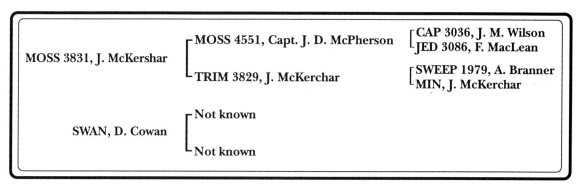

MOSS 3831, J. McKershar
— MOSS 4551, Capt. J. D. McPherson
— CAP 3036, J. M. Wilson
— JED 3086, F. MacLean
— TRIM 3829, J. McKerchar
— SWEEP 1979, A. Branner
— MIN, J. McKerchar

SWAN, D. Cowan
— Not known
— Not known

MOSS 4551   *English Driving Champion 1947 & 1948*

SCOTTISH FARMER

Born 14/4/51   Black & white   J. J. Templeton, Mauchline

Awards

International Aggregate Championship 1957
Scottish Aggregate Championship 1957 & 1959
Scottish Brace Champion with HOPE 9943, 1958

	┌TAM 3465, J. Purdie	┌JIGGS 2378, W. Elliott └MEG 2787, J. Hislop
ROY 4921, J. Purdie	│	
	└TRIM, J. Purdie	┌Not known └Not known
	┌YORK 4734, J. Graham	┌SPOT 3690, T. Bonella └JEAN 3934, J. Graham
MOSS 5018, J. J. Templeton	│	
	└JESS 4019, J. Templeton	┌CAP 3036, J. M. Wilson └MIDGE 3370, P. Dignan

SCOTTISH FARMER

Born 12/4/50 Black, white & tan W. Goodfellow, Newcastleton

BEN 5592, D. Dickson	┌ TOSS 5009, T. Crozier	┌ TOSS, Scott └ WINNIE, Scott
	└ BEAT, Robertson	┌ Not known └ Not known
PHIL 6252, D. Dickson	┌ GLEN 3940, J. M. Wilson	┌ GLEN 3510, W. Hislop └ NELL 3514, J. Kirk
	└ MEG 4228, D. Dickson	┌ TOSS 5009, T. Crozier └ TRIM 2665, D. Dickson

GLEN 3940 *International Supreme Champion 1946 & 1948*
International Farmers' Champion 1948
International Aggregate Championship 1946 & 1948
Scottish Aggregate Championship 1946 & 1948
Scottish National Champion 1946

W. J. Hislop with Jim 12572 (left) and
Sweep 13146 (right)

Born 29/1/56   Black & white   W. J. Hislop, Gordon

Awards

Scottish Driving Champion 1959

TAM 10502, B. Cunningham	TOSS 4059, J. Pollock	CAP 3036, J. M. Wilson NICKEY 3368, W. Wardrop
	MEG 7246, B. Cunningham	SPEED 4382, J. R. Millar FLY 5383, B. Cunningham
MEG 11706, A. B. Bathgate	MIRK 10209, J. Robertson	MIRK 4438, J. M. Wilson MEG 4966, R. Balderstone
	JED 9925, J. Robertson	MOSS 5176, J. M. Wilson JED 7375, R. Blackie

SPEED 4382   *Scottish Aggregate Championship 1952*
MIRK 4438   *International Supreme Champion 1950*
            International Aggregate Championship 1950
            Scottish Aggregate Championship 1950
            Scottish National Champion 1950
MOSS 5176   *International Aggregate Championship 1949*
            Scottish Aggregate Championship 1949 & 1951

SCOTTISH FARMER

Born 5/8/55   Black & white   R. Short, Duns

Awards

International Shepherds' Champion 1960
Scottish Shepherds' Champion 1958 & 1960
Scottish Shepherds' Aggregate Championship 1960

ROB 9913, R. S. Fraser	┌SCOTT 7072, R. S. Fraser	┌NICKEY 4698, R. S. Fraser └NELL 4696, F. Dickson
	└BET 9898, R. Garside	┌MOSS, J. Thomson └JED 4597, J. Thomson
JED 6882, R. Short	┌WATT 5326, W. Anderson	┌SWEEP 5084, W. Anderson └TWIG 5368, G. Lowes
	└NELL 5147, R. S. Fraser	┌SPOT 3032, A. Storie └BETTY 3583, R. S. Fraser

NICKEY 4698   *International Shepherds' Champion 1948*
　　　　　　　English Shepherds' Aggregate Championship 1948 & 1949
　　　　　　　English Shepherds' Champion 1948

Born 26/9/54   Black & white   W. J. Hislop, Gordon

ROY 5048, J. Hogarth	SWEEP 3834, W. Hislop	GLEN 3510, W. Hislop NELL 3514, W. Hislop
	BET, W. Forrester	Not known Not known
BESS 8642, J. Hogarth	GLEN 3868, J. Hogarth	SPOT 3369, J. McDonald CHRIS 4065, J. Cole
	JED 7496, D. Lothian	NAP 3732, T. Lothian TOT 3397, D. Brotherston

SWEEP 3834   *Scottish National Champion 1948*
International Farmers' Champion 1946
International & Scottish Driving Champion 1948

Born 12/3/59   Black & white   T. Bonella, Kinross

Awards

Scottish Aggregate Championship 1963
Scottish Farmers' Champion 1962

	┌ TWEED 9601, J. M. Wilson	┌ MOSS 5176, J. M. Wilson └ TRIM 8859, R. Anderson
GLEN 13902, R. Osborne	└ MEG 7587, R. Osborne	┌ CHIEF 5560, J. Douglas └ JILL 6480, J. Douglas
	┌ KING 11251, T. Steele	┌ WHITEHOPE NAP 8685, J. M. Wilson └ RAY 9610, P. McG. Hepburn
NELL II 15075, R. Osborne	└ FAY 8448, R. Osborne	┌ MOSS 5176, J. M. Wilson └ JOY 5290, K. Wood

TWEED 9601   *International Supreme Champion 1958*
                International Aggregate Championship 1958
                English Aggregate Championship 1958
                English National Champion 1959
                English Driving Champion 1961
                English Brace Champion 1958 & 1960
MOSS 5176   *International Aggregate Championship 1949*
                Scottish Aggregate Championship 1949 & 1951
WHITEHOPE NAP 8685   *Scottish National Champion 1955*

Born 24/3/55   Black & white   J. Hogarth, Selkirk

Awards

Scottish Farmers' Champion 1963
Scottish Brace Champion with GLEN 14250, 1960 & 1961

	┌ TOSS 5009, Crozier	┌ TOSS, Scott └ WINNIE, Scott
BEN 5592, D. Dickson		
	└ BEAT, Robertson	┌ Not known └ Not known
	┌ HEMP 8822, T. Johnston	┌ MOSS 5176, J. M. Wilson └ JUNE 6901, T. Johnston
MEG 10935, D. Armstong		
	└ MEG II 9321, A. Chapman	┌ CRAIG 7874, A. Anderson └ NELL 7875, A. Anderson

MOSS 5176   *International Aggregate Championship 1949*
Scottish Aggregate Championship 1949 & 1951

SCOTTISH FARMER

Born 6/4/57   Black & white   T. T. McKnight, Canonbie

Awards

International Supreme Champion 1967
International Brace Champion with DOT III 18925, 1967
International Aggregate Championship 1965 & 1967
Scottish Aggregate Championship 1965 & 1967
Brace Aggregate Championship with DOT III 18925, 1967
Captain Whittaker Outwork Cup 1967
Scottish National Champion 1964
Scottish Farmers' Champion 1964
Scottish Driving Champion 1967
Scottish Brace Champion with DOT III 18925, 1965, 1966 & 1967

WHITEHOPE NAP 8685, J. M. Wilson	**GLEN 6123, W. McClure**	**MARK 4991, J. Jones** **FLOSS 5058, J. Jones**
	MEG 5141, W. McClure	**JIM, N. R. Scott** **NELL 3514, J. Kirk**
DOT 11228, T. T. McKnight	**JIM 5856, R. Swan**	**DRIFT 4380, J. R. Millar** **MEG 5623, D. Young**
	TIB 5881, D. Young	**MOSS 4551, Capt. J. McPherson** **JED 4770, D. Young**

WHITEHOPE NAP 8685 *Scottish National Champion 1955*
DRIFT 4380 *Scottish Driving Champion 1946*
MOSS 4551 *English Driving Champion 1947 & 1948*

Gael 14463 and Her Progeny

One of the most outstanding bitches in border collie history – probably the most outstanding bitch of all time – was Thompson McKnight's Gael 14463, a daughter of power dog Whitehope Nap 8685. She had been destined for New Zealand sheep runs, but fate decreed otherwise. Her dam, Dot 11228, died, so Gael remained to carry on the normal farm chores, and she became a worthy great-granddaughter of J. Kirk's famous brood bitch, Nell 3514. Her potential to pass on to her descendants the finest qualities of a working border collie, was as great as Nell's had been.

Gael's trial career is the finest of any bitch in the sheepdog world. For seven consecutive years she competed in the International trials, coming fourth in the 1964 Supreme Championship, won by L. Suter's Craig 15445. She was reserve in the 1965 Supreme Championship, won by Wiston Cap. Gael and her daughter Dot III 18925, sired by J. Brown's Sam 16555, won the 1965, 1966 and 1967 Scottish Brace Championships, and the 1967 International Brace Championship.

Gael won the 1964 Scottish National, and aged ten, she crowned her long and successful career with the supreme accolade – the 1967 Supreme Championship, at Stirling, where in 1961 she had made her International debut.

In the same year her daughter Dot III was reserve to her, and won the Qualifying trials, gaining the International Farmers' Championship, with Gael in third place, and together they won the International Brace Championship.

Dot's litter brother D. Young's Dusk 18923, was the 1965 Scottish and International Driving Champion, and the 1966 Scottish Farmers' Champion.

Gael, a quality brood bitch, mated to Miles Cook's Cap 13274, produced Maid 28779, who after winning the 1967 English National for her owner Miles Cook, competed at the International won by her illustrious dam.

Maid's litter brother Mirk 28776, handled by Thomson McKnight, won the 1971 National.

While John Hettrick, Mirk's owner, was in the process of moving home into England, he left his dogs in the care of his friend, Thomson McKnight, who had bred Mirk and who wanted to run Mirk in the National. So to comply with International Sheep Dog Society rules, Mr Hettrick, then an English resident, had to make the decision to transfer Mirk to Mr McKnight.

Mirk justified this decision by winning the 1971 Scottish National, and after competing in the International, his registration was transferred back to a proud Mr Hettrick.

George Hutton's Nap 28777, a renowned North Country hill collie, was also a litter brother of Mirk and Maid, and his son Nip 68389, after being second in the 1974 English National won by Tim Longton and Roy 54175, became runner-up in the 1974 Supreme Championship won by Gwyn Jones and Bill 51654, and won the McDiarmid Trophy in the 1974 International. In partnership with Shona 62645 he won the 1974 and 1975 International Brace Championships and was English Driving Champion in 1977.

Gael

We farmers and shepherds
Who drove o'er the dale
Mourn sadly thy passing
Dear friendly old Gael.

Of all the great dogs
Whose tails ever curled
You proved yourself top
Of the whole canine world.

No words can be said
No words can be penned
That would e'er do thee justice,
Old servant and friend.

Twelve times you have heard
The cuckoo's sweet call,
Twelve times have you witnessed
The russet leaves fall.

You worked on the farm
And at the trials so game,
But never yet knew
How great was your fame.

Today far and wide
Many pedigree claims
Your blood and your style
Flow strong in their veins.

Your trials are run
So peacefully sleep
Till the great final gather
When men are as sheep.

Though the curtain of time
Puts our minds in a fog,
We'll love and remember thee
Wee collie dog.

Joe Johnstone

Peter Hetherington's Nell 53708, a grand-daughter of Gael, represented Scotland on seven occasions, winning the 1970 Scottish National and the International Shepherds' Championship at the 1973 International Centenary trial. With her son Hemp 59856, she was 1976 and 1978 Scottish Brace Champion.

Bred to T. T. McKnight's Jaff 38313, who in partnership with Dot III, won the 1969 Scottish Brace Championship, Gael produced Mike Perrings' Kyle 47050, the 1970 English and International Shepherds' Champion, and a popular stud dog who, like his sire, produced many successful progeny.

David Shennan's Meg 63230, a grand-daughter of Jaff and Dot III, was the 1976 Scottish National Champion, having been third in the 1974 National, and in 1975 Meg was third in the Supreme Championship, won by R. MacPherson's Zac 66166.

These are just a few of the many successful descendants of a very special bitch, who has made a lasting contribution to the modern border collie family.

Gael, a legend in her own lifetime, died of a heart attack in 1968, mourned by the sheepdog world, who recognised her unique qualities.

Jaff's promising career was cut short when he was found killing a neighbour's poultry and shot. Tragedy struck again when Jaff's son, Drift, out of Dot III, died after eating from the carcase of a calf that had been put down by the vet. The lethal injection present in the flesh, poisoned Drift, who at three years old, had already won the Scottish and International Driving Championships.

And so Thompson McKnight lost not only his promising trial dogs but also two valuable stud dogs, whose breeding potential had already been proven.

The Scottish National Team, 1966

1965   **SPOT 24981**   **Inverness**

1966   **Kilmartin**

Born 7/5/62   Black & white   J. Gilchrist, Roslin

Awards

International Aggregate Championship 1966
Scottish Aggregate Championship 1966
Scottish Shepherds' Aggregate Championship 1966
Scottish Shepherds' Champion 1965 & 1966

BOB 12684, J. Gilchrist	**SPOT 7320, J. Gilchrist**	ROY 5323, W. Renwick JED 4941, J. Gilchrist
	NELL 10141, G. Hunter	MOSS 5176, J.M. Wilson PHIL 7122, T. Watson
WISTON NAN III, 9896, P. Mc. G. Hepburn	**MOSS 5176, J. M. Wilson**	MIRK 4438, J. M. Wilson NELL 3514, J. Kirk
	ANNE 4545, W. S. Hetherington	TAM 3465, J. Purdie TRIM, J. Purdie

MOSS 5176   *International Aggregate Championship 1949*
                    Scottish Aggregate Championship 1949 & 1951
MIRK 4438   *International Supreme Champion 1950*
                    International Aggregate Championship 1950
                    Scottish National Champion 1950
                    Scottish Aggregate Championship 1950
ANNE 4545 *was full sister to J. Gilchrist's* **SPOT 3624**, *International Supreme Champion 1947*

The Gilchrists and Their Dogs

John Gilchrist's Spot 3624, a son of J. Purdie's Tam 3465 and his unregistered Trim, was Supreme Champion at Cardiff in 1947. Partnered by his son Ben 5714, he was 1948 Scottish and International Brace Champion, winning these Championships again in 1949, with another son, Glen 6425. Even today Spot's descendants can often be recognised by a white streak over the hips.

Spot 24981, a great-great-grandson of Spot 3624, was narrowly beaten into second place by Tim Longton's Ken 17166, in the 1966 Supreme Championship. He was Scottish National Champion in 1965 and 1966, and though a contemporary of Wiston Cap, he also became a popular stud dog. Later generations have combined the lines of these two great dogs.

In 1976 John Gilchrist won the Scottish Shepherds' Aggregate and Scottish Driving Championships with Bob 79686, a son of Spot 24981.

Another extensively used stud dog by Spot 24981, was Elwyn Griffith's Craig 47577. Before Wiston Cap's prepotency was recognised, a daughter of his was mated to Craig, producing six puppies, all becoming outstanding workers of great quality. Among them was Captain Grant Jones' Tos 61152, the 1974 Welsh National Champion, and Alan Jones' Nell 61154, dam of 1976 Welsh National Champion Craig 72737,

and Taff 80135. This bitch had been punished in puppy days for going to sheep on her own, so great was her working instinct, but when old enough for training, she was too frightened to look at sheep. When her litter was weaned she was put down as useless, her great breeding potential lost and unrecognised, and her working ability ruined.

James Gilchrist was not as successful in the International Sheep Dog Society Trials as his brother, and was better known for breeding good class dogs. His Roy 5323, later owned by W. Renwick, was a son of John Gilchrist's Spot 3624 and Queen 3113. From the unplanned mating of Roy and James' bitch Jed 4941, came Spot 7320, with whom James represented Scotland at the 1956 International, coming fifth in the Supreme Championship, won by G. Redpath and Moss 6805, despite Spot's failure to pen a particularly wild and rebellious ewe.

Spot's son, Bob 12684, owned by John Gilchrist, became a very popular stud dog, and mated to P. G. McGregor Hepburns' Wiston Nan III 9896, he produced Scottish National Champion Spot 24981. W. S. Hetherington's great brood bitch Ann 4545, a white-coated dog, was great-great-grandam of Wiston Cap.

James Gilchrist won the 1971 Scottish Driving Championship with Tam 25605, a son of Bob 12684, and the same award in 1973 with Mirk 47857, sired by Tam.

Descendants of these 'Gilchrist' dogs can be found in the pedigrees of very many of the modern working dogs, in all parts of the world.

Born 8/5/61   Black, white, tan & mottled   A. McMillan, Dalrymple

Awards

Scottish Farmers' Champion 1967

	┌─ ROY 8803, D. Houston	┌DAVE 4381, J. R. Millar └WENDY 4131, D. Houston
ROB 9802, A. Lambie		
	└─ BESS 6547, A. Lambie	┌GLEN 4403, J. Denniff └SHEILA 5074, T. Rogerson
	┌─ GLEN 14081, A. Lambie	┌TWEED 9601, J. M. Wilson └MAID 9093, H. Paton
TOT 17056, J. Blain		
	└─ MOSSIE 15499, J. McGarva	┌ROY 8993, J. Templeton └TIB 14209, J. McGarva

TWEED 9601   *International Supreme Champion 1958*
International Aggregate Championship 1958
English Aggregate Championship 1958
English National Champion 1959
English Driving Champion 1961
English Brace Champion 1958 & 1960

ROY 8993   *International Aggregate Championship 1957 (shared with H. J. Holliday's* **MOSS 11029**)
Scottish Aggregate Championship 1957 & 1959
Scottish Brace Champion 1958
Scottish National Champion 1957

SCOTTISH FARMER

Born 18/11/61   Brown & white   J. Kerr, Maybole

Awards

Scottish Farmers' Champion 1968
Alexander Andrew Trophy 1968

NAP 16043, W. McMillan	NAP 11691, D. Moodie	WULL 9459, W. McClure FLY 8899, W. McClure
	DOT 11228, T. T. McKnight	JIM 5856, R. Swan TIB 5881, D. Young
MEG 17826, W. Kerr	SWEEP 12662, W. McMillan	TWEED 9601, J. M. Wilson NELL 5520, D. Moodie
	FLY 8899, W. McMillan	GLEN 6123, W. McClure MEG 5141, W. McClure

NAP 16043   *International & Scottish Driving Champion 1963*
MEG 17826   *Scottish Driving Champion 1966*
NAP 11691   *International & Scottish Driving Champion 1961*
TWEED 9601   *International Supreme Champion 1958*
            International Aggregate Championship 1958
            English Aggregate Championship 1958
            English National Champion 1959
            English Driving Champion 1961
            English Brace Champion 1958 & 1960

FLY 8899 *was litter sister to* **WHITEHOPE NAP 8685**

John Kerr

John Kerr sold Queen 24078 as a puppy, because, like most shepherds, he disliked her colour – brown and white, instead of the ubiquitous black and white. However, he later liked her style of work and bought her back at fifteen months. He had won the 1966 Scottish Driving Championship with her dam, Meg 17826, and two years later Queen was Scottish National Champion.

I believe the only other brown-coated collies to win a National were J. Brady's Buff 23069, twice Irish National Champion, and son of Whitehope Corrie 13706; Tim Longton's English Champion, Tweed 96630; Selwyn Jones' Vickey 15968, the 1963 Welsh Champion; J. Brady's Gyp 33128, Irish National Champion 1970; and J. McSwiggan's Rock 36024, Irish National Champion 1971.

Members of the Scottish National Team, 1969

Born 8/6/60　　Black & white　　J. R. Millar, Dalry

Awards

Scottish Farmers' Champion 1969
Alexander Andrew Trophy 1969

BEN 12262, J. R. Millar	┌ **BEN 6304, M. Lindsay**	┌ **CAP 3036, J. M. Wilson** └ **NELL II 3037, J. M. Wilson**
	└ **JEN 11334, G. Robertson**	┌ **BEN 5592, D. Dickson** └ **NELL 11322, J. R. Millar**
BET 15066, W. Paul	┌ **TAM 7032, J. R. Millar**	┌ **BEN 4931, J. R. Millar** └ **MEG II 4348, A. Burns**
	└ **FLY 5239, W. Paul**	┌ **SPEED 4382, J. R. Millar** └ **TOT 5237, W. Paul**

BEN 12262　*International Farmers' Champion 1960*
　　　　　　　Scottish Aggregate Championship 1960
　　　　　　　Scottish Driving Champion 1957
TAM 7032　*Scottish National Champion 1953*
　　　　　　　Scottish Brace Champion 1955
BEN 4931　*Scottish National Champion 1949*
SPEED 4382　*Scottish Aggregate Championship 1952*
MEG II 4348　*Scottish Shepherds' Champion 1949*

The Wiston 'Line'

W. S. Hetherington was a shrewd and well-known collie breeder whose prefix 'Wiston' is famous worldwide. Among the numerous famous dogs bearing this prefix are Supreme Champions Wiston Cap and Wiston Bill 36391, both from W. S. Hetherington's Fly 25005, bred from J. M. Wilson's Bill II 17937, and J. Hogarth's Lassie 19421. Three of Wiston Cap's sons have become Supreme Champions – J. Murray's Glen 47241 (1971), J. Templeton's Cap 50543 (1972) and G. Jones' Bill 51654 (1974). Four of his grandchildren have also won the Supreme Championship – G. Jones' Shep 73360 (1976); R. Shennan's Mirk 67512 (1978); E. W. Edwards' Bill 78263 (1981 and 1982) and T. W. Longton's Bess 101142 (1986).

FRANK MOYES

W. S. Hetherington, the breeder of Wiston Cap, in his 85th year, still with dog at foot

144

Wiston Cap 31154, Supreme Champion in 1965. A great hill dog, he had a tremendous influence on the modern border collie, having served more bitches than any other dog within the breed

John Richardson won the 1968 Scottish Shepherds' Championship with Sweep 39603, and the 1973 and 1975 Scottish Shepherds' Championships with Mirk 52844. In 1975 Mirk also went on to win the Scottish National Championship. Both dogs were by Wiston Cap out of J. McDonald's Lassie 23501.

The Scottish National has been won by Wiston Cap's son, D. McTeir's Ben 56646 in 1972; by his granddaughter, D. Shennan's Meg 63230, in 1976 and by his grandson, R. Shennan's Mirk 67512, in 1979; by his great-granddaughter, W. Rae's Connie 84203 in 1977; by his great-grandsons, H. Logan's Star 109497 in 1981, and by A. Macrae's Mirk 96612, in 1984.

The English National has been won by his daughter, H. Loates' Wiston Jill 79096, in 1979; his grandsons, J. James' Mirk 68102 in 1975, Tim Longton's red Tweed 96630 in 1981, and D. Lloyd's Jim 103518 in 1983; by his great-granddaughter, S. H. Thomas' Bess 107127 in 1982; by his great-grandson, B. Dodd's Laddie 151099 in 1988.

The Welsh National has been won by his granddaughter, M. Page's Nell 65799 in 1973; his grandsons, A. G. Jones' Tos 61152 in 1974, H. G. Jones' Bwlch Taff 113243 in 1980 and 1981; by his great-grandsons, A. Jones' Craig 72737 in 1976, M. Page's Cap 108145 in 1982, J. Burke's Glen 113361 in 1984, A. Owen's Ben 129820 in 1985; and his great-granddaughter, H. Owen's Spotan 134842, in 1986.

The Irish National has been won by his daughter, M. Graham's Gay 69947 in 1976, who also won the Manx Championship; by his grandson, H. Logan's Sweep 87666, in 1980; and by his great-grandson, J. Irvine's Shep 109351 in 1983

These successes alone prove the phenomenal influence that Wiston Cap has had on the modern border collie, and the clever blending of the old bloodlines by W. S. Hetherington, to produce such an outstanding dog, whose name appears in the majority of modern pedigrees.

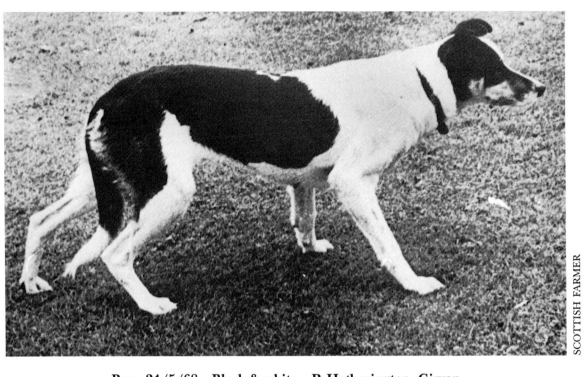

SCOTTISH FARMER

Born 24/5/68   Black & white   P. Hetherington, Girvan

Awards

International Shepherds' Champion 1973
Scottish Aggregate & Scottish Shepherds' Aggregate Championship 1973 & 1977
Scottish Shepherds' Champion 1970
Alexander Andrew Trophy 1970
Scottish Brace Champion with HEMP 59856, 1976 & 1978

LAD 37094, P. Hetherington	LAD 14294, Holmes Bros.	VIC 10928, W. Sanderson QUEEN II 11541, A. Owen
	GAEL 14463, T. T. McKnight	WHITEHOPE NAP 8685, J. M. Wilson DOT 11228, T. T. McKnight
SLIP 43837, P. Hetherington	JAFF 38313, T. T. McKnight	BROCKEN ROBBIE 24636, Mrs E. B. Carpenter FLEECE 22145, T. J. WATKINS
	GEN 39142, T. T. McKnight	WISTON CAP 31154, J. Richardson BEAT 32666, R. Blackie

LAD 37094 *Scottish Brace Champion 1968*
GAEL 14463 *International Supreme Champion 1967*
International Brace Champion 1967
International & Scottish Aggregate Championship 1965 & 1967
Brace Aggregate Championship 1967
Captain Whittaker Outwork Cup 1967
Scottish National & Scottish Farmers' Champion 1964
Scottish Driving Champion 1967
Scottish Brace Champion 1965, 1966 & 1967
JAFF 38313 *Scottish Brace Champion 1969*
WHITEHOPE NAP 8685 *Scottish National Champion 1955*
WISTON CAP 31154 *International Supreme Champion 1965*
International Shepherds' Champion 1966
Scottish Driving Champion 1969

P. Hetherington with Nell 53708

Born 27/1/63   Black & white   T. T. McKnight, Canonbie

Awards

Scottish Farmers' Champion 1971
Alexander Andrew Trophy 1971

CAP 13274, M. Cook	CAP 4295, M. Collin	CAP, A. G. Hyslop QUEEN, H. Taylor
	LASSIE 10680, M. Cook	GLEN 5965, C. Milburn NELL 6317, M. Cook
GAEL 14463, T. T. McKnight	WHITEHOPE NAP 8685, J. M. Wilson	GLEN 6123, W. McClure MEG 5141, W. McClure
	DOT 11228, T. T. McKnight	JIM 5856, R. Swan TIB 5881, D. Young

GAEL 14463   *International Supreme Champion 1967*
International Brace Champion 1967
International & Scottish Aggregate Championship 1965 & 1967
Brace Aggregate Championship 1967
Captain Whittaker Outwork Cup 1967
Scottish National & Scottish Farmers' Champion 1964
Scottish Driving Champion 1967
Scottish Brace Champion 1965, 1966 & 1967
WHITEHOPE NAP 8685   *Scottish National Champion 1955*
MIRK 28776 *was litter brother to M. Cook's* **MAID 28779**, *English National Champion 1967*

Born 8/1/69   Black & white   D. McTeir, Sanquhar

Awards

International Shepherds' Champion 1972
Scottish Shepherds' Aggregate Championship 1972
Scottish Shepherds' Champion 1972
Alexander Andrew Trophy 1972

WISTON CAP 31154, J. Richardson	CAP 15839, J. Richardson	COON 10011, J. Richardson LYN 13707, R. Frame
	FLY 25005, W. S. Hetherington	BILL II 17937, J. M. Wilson LASSIE 19421, J. Hogarth
BESS 39525, D. Russell R.O.M.	JIM, N. R. J. Simpson	
	TESS, N. R. D. Russell	

WISTON CAP 31154   *International Supreme Champion 1965*
International Shepherds' Champion 1966
Scottish Driving Champion 1969

SCOTTISH FARMER

Born 4/8/69   Black & white   W. Cormack, Thurso

Awards

Scottish Farmers' Champion 1973
Alexander Andrew Trophy 1973

MOSS 48201, J. Coghill	SPOT 24981, J. Gilchrist	BOB 12684, J. Gilchrist WISTON NAN III 9896, P. McG. Hepburn
	QUEEN 23040, A. McLay	ROY 8993, J. Templeton QUEEN 13141, D. W. Taylor
JUNE 53107, J. Coghill	SPOT 24981, J. Gilchrist	BOB 12684, J. Gilchrist WISTON NAN III 9896, P. McG. Hepburn
	BESS 20879, A. McLay	TAM II 14387, J. Purdie LASSIE 12694, T. Wilson

SPOT 24981 *International Aggregate Championship 1966*
  Scottish Aggregate Championship 1966
  Scottish Shepherds' Aggregate Championship 1966
  Scottish National & Scottish Shepherds' Champion 1965 & 1966

ROY 8993 *International Aggregate Championship 1957 (shared with H. J. Holliday's* **MOSS 11029***)*
  Scottish Aggregate Championship 1957 & 1959
  Scottish National Champion 1957
  Scottish Brace Champion 1958

LASSIE 12694 *Scottish Shepherds' Champion 1957*

Born 11/2/67   Black & white   D. MacDonald, Perth

Awards

Scottish Shepherds' Champion 1974
Alexander Andrew Trophy 1974

GLEN 15845, J. Lothian	TIDE 11318, J. C. McCaskie	GARRY 4915, J. Anderson TIDE 4126, T. Kerr
	LINDA 12959, J. McCaskie	GARRY 8253, J. Fleming FLY 9258, J. C. McCaskie
FLOSS 58139, D. MacDonald	BEN 16172, C. MacKechnie	MIRK 8012, R. Macrae NAN 7699, G. MacKechnie
	MEG 13452, D. MacDonald Snr.	WHITEHOPE NAP 8685, J. M. Wilson GYP 8747, W. S. Hetherington

WHITEHOPE NAP 8685   *Scottish National Champion 1955*

151

1975   **MIRK 52844**   **Troon**

Born 13/4/68   Black, white & mottled   J. Richardson, Duns

Awards

International Shepherds' Champion 1975
Scottish Shepherds' Aggregate Championship 1975
Scottish Shepherds' Champion 1973 & 1975
Scottish Driving Champion 1975
Alexander Andrew Trophy 1975
J. M. Wilson Challenge Shield 1975—first

WISTON CAP 31154,
J. Richardson
┌ CAP 15839, J. Richardson ┌ COON 10011, J. Richardson
└ LYN 13707, R. Frame
└ FLY 25005, W. S. Hetherington ┌ BILL II 17937, J. M. Wilson
└ LASSIE 19421, J. Hogarth

LASSIE 23501, J. McDonald
┌ SWEEP 18393, E. Dixon ┌ BEN 13163, D. Dickson
└ PHIL 7122, W. Watson
└ QUEEN 16968, A. Noble ┌ JEFF 14422, T. Watson
└ QUEEN 12652, P. Jaffray

WISTON CAP 31154   *International Supreme Champion 1965*
International Shepherds' Champion 1966
Scottish Driving Champion 1969
JEFF 14422   *Scottish Aggregate Championship 1961*
Scottish Driving Champion 1962

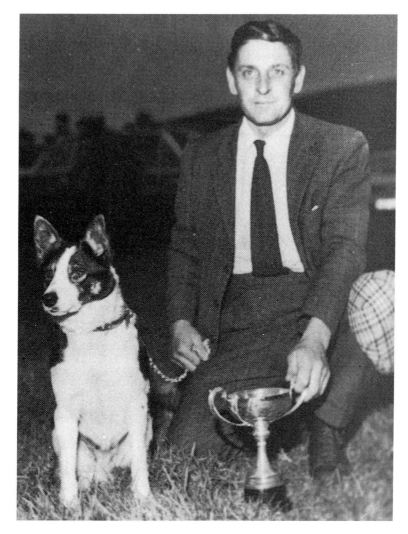

Born 22/4/70   Black, white & tan   D. Shennan, Girvan

Awards

International Aggregate Championship 1975
Scottish Aggregate Championship 1975
Scottish Farmers' Champion 1974 & 1976
Alexander Andrew Trophy 1976
J. M. Wilson Challenge Shield 1976

```
                                    ┌ BROCKEN ROBBIE 24636, Mrs E. B. Carpenter
                ┌ JAFF 38313, T. T. McKnight   └ FLEECE 22145, T. J. Watkins
DRIFT 51202, T. T.
   McKnight
                └ DOT III 18925, T. T. McKnight ┌ SAM 16555, J. Brown
                                                └ GAEL 14463, T. T. McKnight

                ┌ WISTON CAP 31154, J. Richardson ┌ CAP 15839, J. Richardson
GAEL 54350, W.                                    └ FLY 25005, W. S. Hetherington
   Murray
                └ LASSIE 45019, J. Rae ┌ SPOT 24981, J. Gilchrist
                                       └ BESS 35015, W. Murray
```

DRIFT 51202 *International & Scottish Driving Champion 1970*

JAFF 38313 *Scottish Brace Champion 1969*

DOT III 18925 *International Farmers' Champion 1967*
International Brace Champion 1967
International Brace Aggregate Championship 1967
Scottish Brace Champion 1965, 1966, 1967 & 1969

WISTON CAP 31154 *International Supreme Champion 1965*
International Shepherds' Champion 1966
Scottish Driving Champion 1969

GAEL 14463 *International Supreme Champion 1967*
International Brace Champion 1967
International & Scottish Aggregate Championship 1965 & 1967
Brace Aggregate Championship 1967
Captain Whittaker Outwork Cup 1967
Scottish National & Scottish Farmers' Champion 1964
Scottish Driving Champion 1967
Scottish Brace Champion 1965, 1966 & 1967

SPOT 24981 *International Aggregate Championship 1966*
Scottish Aggregate Championship 1966
Scottish Shepherds' Aggregate Championship 1966
Scottish National & Shepherds' Champion 1965 & 1966

Born 5/1/74   Black, tan & white   W. Rae, Castle Douglas

Awards

Scottish Shepherds Champion 1977
Alexander Andrew Trophy 1977
J. M. Wilson Challenge Shield 1977

SWEEP 51651, R. Shennan	⌐**SWEEP 39603, J. Richardson**	⌐WISTON CAP 31154, J. Richardson └LASSIE 23501, J. McDonald
	└**NELL 33597, I. Kerr**	⌐BOB 12684, J. Gilchrist └NELL III 19128, P. McG. Hepburn
MIST 60399, A. Davidson	⌐**MOSS 47113, A. Beattie**	⌐BILL II 17937, J. M. Wilson └CHRIS 14589, A. Beattie
	└**GAEL 51597, J. Gray**	⌐WISTON CAP 31154, J. Richardson └DOT 43897, J. Gray

SWEEP 39603   *International Driving Champion 1968*
Scottish Shepherds' Champion 1968
Scottish Driving Champion 1968

WISTON CAP 31154   *International Supreme Champion 1965*
International Shepherds' Champion 1966
Scottish Driving Champion 1969

1978   **NAN 85606**   **Earlston**

Born 1/4/74   Black, white & tan   D. Shennan, Girvan

Awards

Scottish Farmers Champion 1978
Scottish Driving Champion 1978
Alexander Andrew Trophy 1978
J. M. Wilson Challenge Shield 1978

MOSS 77473, J. G. Brownlie	┌MOSS 60437, W. McConnell	┌TWEED 34916, J. McE. Jack └DOT 45558, W. McConnell
	└MEG 63230, W. Rae	┌DRIFT 51202, T. T. McKnight └GAEL 54350, W. Murray
FLY 74537, J. G. Brownlie	┌GLEN 64001, J. McE. Jack	┌SWEEP 51651, R. Shennan └NELL 22932, J. McE. Jack
	└FLY 23160, D. Shennan	┌ROY 14746, D. Shennan └NELL 12945, A. Burns

MEG 63230   *International Aggregate Championship 1975*
Scottish Aggregate Championship 1975
Scottish National Champion 1976
Scottish Farmers' Champion 1974 & 1976
Alexander Andrew Trophy 1976
J. M. Wilson Challenge Shield 1976
DRIFT 51202   *International & Scottish Driving Champion 1970*
ROY 14746   *International Farmers' Champion 1963*

The Shennan Brothers

Two brothers who have regularly been members of the Scottish team, from the early 1960s to the present time, are David and Robert Shennan. Both have won their country's National Championship.

Robert Shennan competed in 1962 with Cap 13733; in 1965 with Bill II 18890; in 1966 with Tweed 29403; in 1970 with Sweep 51651; and in 1971 with Garry 49864; and then came Mirk 67512, a grandson of Wiston Cap. Mirk was second in the 1978 National, and later in the year he became Supreme Champion. He was the 1979 National Champion, and also Scottish and International Driving Champion. He was fourth in the 1976 Scottish National and third in the 1980 National. Nell 112637, upheld these successes, coming fourth and fifth respectively in the 1981 and 1985 Nationals.

David Shennan competed in 1964, 1966, 1967, 1968 and 1969 with Fly 23160, who was seventh in the 1967 Supreme Championship. Her kennelmate, Maid 51269, was second in the 1969 National, won by J. R. Millar with Ken II 18754, and seventh in the Supreme Championship, and continued her successes by being reserve to the 1970 Supreme Champion,

D. McTeir's Wiston Bill 36391, and in 1971 she was International Farmers' Champion and ninth in the Supreme Championship. She was third in the 1972 Supreme Championship, won by J. Templeton and Cap 50543.

To retrace a few years – David's, Roy 14746, was International Farmers' Champion in 1963 and eighth in the Supreme Championship.

In 1976 David's Meg 63230, a daughter of T. T. McKnight's Drift 51202, won the National, after a runoff with T. Watson's Mirk II 80772, both dogs having equal points. Mirk II was the Shepherds' Champion. This was the first runoff in a Scottish National since 1946, when J. M. Wilson's Glen 3940 took the title from W. Hislop's Sweep 3834, who later won the 1948 National. Meg was reserve to the 1976 Supreme Champion, G. Jones' Shep 73360, was third in the 1974 National and represented Scotland in 1975 and 1979.

David Shennan was eighth in the 1977 Supreme Championship with Fly 73340, a daughter of Wiston Cap, and in 1978, Nan 85606, a granddaughter of Fly 23160, was Scottish National Champion and was eighth in the Supreme Championship. In 1993 David was once more in the team – with Bill 177773, who was fourth in the National.

Born 23/1/71   Black, white & mottled   R. Shennan, Turnberry

Awards

International Supreme Champion 1978
International Aggregate Championship 1978
Scottish Aggregate Championship 1978
International Driving & Scottish Driving Champion 1979
Scottish National & Scottish Farmers' Champion 1979
Alexander Andrew Trophy 1979
Captain Whittaker Outwork Cup 1978
R. Fortune Trophy 1978
Lord Mostyn Plate 1978
I.S.D.S. Blue Riband 1978
Pedigree Chum Supreme Championship Trophy 1978
Warnock Trophy 1978
J. M. Wilson Challenge Shield 1979

```
                          ┌─WISTON CAP 31154, J. Richardson    ┌CAP 15839, J. Richardson
       MIRK 52844, J.     │                                    └FLY 25005, W. S. Hetherington
         Richardson       │
                          └─LASSIE 23501, J. McDonald          ┌BILL II 17937, J. M. Wilson
                                                               └LASSIE 19421, J. Hogarth

                          ┌─BEN 18073, J. Fleming              ┌TEDDY 13305, A. Rogerson
                          │                                    └JED 9925, J. Robertson
    JAN 39653, J. Nelson  │
                          └─NELL 13934, A. Mackie              ┌GARRY 8253, J. Fleming
                                                               └MEG 13209, A. Mackie
```

MIRK 52844   *International Shepherds' Champion 1975*
              Scottish Shepherds' Aggregate Championship 1975
              Scottish National Champion 1975
              Scottish Driving Champion 1975
              Scottish Shepherds' Champion 1973 & 1975
              Alexander Andrew Trophy 1975
              J. M. Wilson Challenge Shield 1975

WISTON CAP 31154   *International Supreme Champion 1965*
                    International Shepherds' Champion 1966
                    Scottish Driving Champion 1969

R. Shennan with Mirk 67512

159

1980   **BEN 88284**   **Thornhill**

Born 29/11/74   Black & white   S. Davidson, Sandbank

Awards

Scottish Farmers' Champion 1980
Scottish Brace Champion with SHEP 80763, 1981
Alexander Andrew Trophy 1980
J. M. Wilson Challenge Shield 1980

BEN 50504, J. A. MacLeod	JAFF 38313, T. T. McKnight	BROCKEN ROBBIE 24636, Mrs E. B. Carpenter FLEECE 22145, T. J. Watkins
	FAY 42928, W. Cuthbert	RAY 16206, W. Cuthbert TESS 23793, W. Cuthbert
MIST 75908, D. MacKenzie	SPOT 24981, J. Gilchrist	BOB 12684, J. Gilchrist WISTON NAN III 9896, P. McG. Hepburn
	GAEL 44425, P. McG. Hepburn	GARRY 28375, D. Murray MEG 33723, W. Weir

SPOT 24981   *International Aggregate Championship 1966*
                   Scottish Aggregate Championship 1966
                   Scottish Shepherds' Aggregate Championship 1966
                   Scottish National & Scottish Shepherds' Champion 1965 & 1966
JAFF 38313   *Scottish Brace Champion 1969*

E. B. CARPENTER

Born 21/6/78   Black, white & tan   J. H. Logan, Appin

Awards

Scottish Farmers' Champion 1981
Alexander Andrew Trophy 1981
Warnock Trophy 1981
J. M. Wilson Challenge Shield 1981

MOSS 103923, J. Templeton	**HEMP 72301, A. J. Campbell**	**MIRK 52844, J. Richardson** **MEG 49547, A. J. Campbell**
	QUEEN 74047, H. MacKenzie	**SWEEP 58327, W. Merchant** **BET 63604, A. MacIntosh**
BESS 77614, J. McGregor	**BEN 56646, D. McTeir**	**WISTON CAP 31154, J. Richardson** **BESS 39525, D. Russell**
	BELLE 45916, J. McGregor	**DON 18755, R. Osborne** **NELL 15388, J. Walker**

MOSS 103923   *Scottish Aggregate Championship 1979*
Feedmobile Challenge Cup 1979
HEMP 72301   *Scottish Driving Champion 1977*
BEN 56646   *International Shepherds' Champion 1972*
Scottish Shepherds' Aggregate Championship 1972
Scottish National & Scottish Shepherds' Champion 1972
Alexander Andrew Trophy 1972

MIRK 52844   *International Shepherds' Champion 1975*
Scottish Shepherds' Aggregate Championship 1975
Scottish National Champion 1975
Scottish Driving Champion 1975
Scottish Shepherds' Champion 1973 & 1975
Alexander Andrew Trophy 1975
J. M. Wilson Challenge Shield 1975

WISTON CAP 31154   *International Supreme Champion 1965*
International Shepherds' Champion 1966
Scottish Driving Champion 1969

The 1981 Scottish Team

FRANK MOYES

1982	**ROY 114678**	Strathaven
1983		Bonchester Bridge
1985		Monymusk

FRANK MOYES

Born 15/3/79   Black, white & tan   J. J. Templeton, Fenwick

Awards

International Farmers' Champion 1985, 1987 & 1989

International Aggregate Championship 1985

Brace Aggregate Championship with BEN 119873, 1984

International Brace Champion with BEN 119873, 1984

International Driving Champion 1983 & 1987

Scottish Aggregate Championship 1981, 1982, 1983 & 1985

Feedmobile Trophy 1985 & 1989

McDiarmid Trophy 1981, 1985 & 1989

Captain Whittaker Outwork Cup 1987 & 1989

Pedigree Chum Silver Salver 1985 & 1987

Scottish Farmers' Champion 1982, 1983 & 1985

Scottish Brace Champion with BEN 119873, 1982, 1983 & 1984

Scottish Driving Champion 1983 & 1987

Alexander Andrew Trophy 1982, 1983 & 1985

J. M. Wilson Challenge Shield 1982, 1983 & 1985

ROY 114678 *& S. L. Davidsons's* **MOSS** *were on equal points (198) at the 1988 Scottish National. After a runoff,* **ROY** *was placed second.*

```
                         ┌─HEMP 72301, A. J. Campbell    ┌MIRK 52844, J. Richardson
   MOSS 103923, J. J.    │                               └MEG 49547, A. J. Campbell
      Templeton          │
                         └─QUEEN 74047, H. MacKenzie     ┌SWEEP 58327, W. Merchant
                                                         └BET 63604, A. MacIntosh

                         ┌─GLEN 75630, W. Beattie        ┌CAP 67230, T. T. McKnight
   LASS 92191, T. Stevenson                              └SHELL 68768, T. T. McKnight
                         │
                         └─WINK 49224, C. Graham         ┌SCOT 28069, G. Young
                                                         └TIB 42313, J. Patterson
```

GLEN 75630 *was better known as* **FORTUNE'S GLEN**, *after the man to whom he later belonged.*

MOSS 103923 *Scottish Aggregate Championship 1979*
Feedmobile Challenge Cup 1979
HEMP 72301 *Scottish Driving Champion 1977*
GLEN 75630 *Scottish Brace Champion 1977*
MIRK 52844 *International Shepherds' Champion 1975*
Scottish Shepherds' Aggregate Championship 1975
Scottish National Champion 1975
Scottish Driving Champion 1975
Scottish Shepherds' Champion 1973 & 1975
Alexander Andrew Trophy 1975
J. M. Wilson Challenge Shield 1975
SCOT 28069 *International Shepherds' Champion 1969*
Scottish Shepherds' Aggregate Championship 1969
Scottish Shepherds' Champion 1969

John Templeton

The illustrious trial career of John Templeton MBE took off with Roy 8993 winning the 1957 Scottish National Championship, and in the same year, being reserve to Supreme Champion, J. Holliday's Moss 11029. Roy's dam, Moss 5018, a granddaughter of J. M. Wilson's Cap 3036, had been given to John Templeton by his uncle, and he had won trials with her before Roy gained his 'cap'. For five consecutive years Roy represented Scotland; in 1957 both he and his full brother, Hope 9943, were in the Scottish National team and together they won the 1958 Scottish Brace Championship. Partnered by Meg 12625, also out of Moss 5018, Roy was second in the 1959 Scottish Brace Championship. He was reserve to the 1960 Scottish National Champion, R. Short's Nell 127436, and third in the 1961 National. Roy's daughter, Maid 14173, partnered by Roy II 16894, and by Nap 17605 respectively, won the 1962 and 1963 Scottish Brace Championships.

Roy was third in the 1959 National and reserve in the Supreme Championship, won by M. Jones and Ben 13879, and Maid 14173, was third in the 1962 Supreme Championship, won by A. T. Lloyd's Garry 17690. Maid's son, Nap 17605, was reserve to the 1965 Scottish Champion, J. Gilchrist's Spot 24981, and fifth in the Supreme Championship, won by Wiston Cap 31154.

In 1966 John Templeton, with Shawsholm Fly 20080, was reserve to the National Champion, Spot 24981, and Fly and Nap were second in the Scottish Brace Championship.

John Templeton, a quiet unassuming gentleman, respected by all, has remained one of Scotland's most successful handlers, being a team member on many occasions since 1957. In 1972 he won the ultimate accolade – the Supreme Championship – with Cap 50543, a son of Wiston Cap, and partnered by Fleet 37588, Cap also won the Scottish and International Brace Championships.

The following year Fleet was second and Cap fifth in the World Championship Trial in America. Both dogs had been sold to an American, but tragically Fleet, with some other dogs, died in a motel fire which occurred after the trial.

In 1980 John Templeton's Max 110507, a son of Tim Flood's Irish National Champion Scot 57965, was third in the Supreme Championship, won by T. Watson and Jen 93965.

In 1981 a new legend appeared in border collie history. Roy 114678 a son of John Templeton's Moss 103923, who had been reserve to Supreme Champion, R. MacPherson's Zac 66166 in 1979, was second in the Scottish National to Harford Logan's Star 109497, who was also by Moss. Roy went on to be third in the Supreme Championship, won by Wyn Edwards' Bill 78263, and the following year Roy was third again to Bill, the Supreme Champion, for the second time.

Roy's team record possibly surpasses all others – he was a team member for nearly a decade in the eighties, and was only out of the singles class in 1984, the year in which he and Ben 119873 represented Scotland in the Brace Class and won the International Brace Championship. Roy was Scottish National Champion in 1982, 1983 and 1985; Scottish Brace Champion with Ben in 1982, 1983 and 1984, and was reserve to Supreme Champion, J. McKenzie's Don 122367 in 1985. He was fifth in the storm-lashed 1983 Supreme Championship at Aberystwyth, won by Tot Longton and Jess 88627. Roy was second in the 1987 Scottish National, won by J. R. Welsh and Jen 134760, and fifth again in the Supreme Championship, won by Sidney Price and Davy 131049. The following year he was second to the Scottish National Champion, S. Davidson's Moss 138632.

Having competed in International Sheep Dog Society Trials regularly from 1981 to 1989, winning numerous awards, Roy, at ten years old, was once more in the Scottish team for the 1989 International at Margam. An old, but extremely fit and determined dog, he ran his heart out on this testing course, many willing him to win this, his final International.

It was not to be. Youth had its day – Wisp became Supreme Champion, and once more Roy, with sheer courage and experience, was reserve to a very worthy champion. He could retire in the knowledge that he had given of his best – always. Seven times he had been placed in the Supreme Championship: second twice, third twice, fifth twice and also tenth. A great record enhanced by nine team placings, including second place in four Nationals, three Scottish Brace Championship titles, and two second places; a win at one International Brace Championship, and second place in two others. He won two Scottish and one International Driving Championship, and gained the respect of the whole sheepdog world.

1992 saw John Templeton again 'knocking on the door', with young Spot 182249, a son of his Ben 119873, gaining third in the Supreme Championship won by Bobby Dalziel and Wisp 161487 – Wisp's second Supreme Championship.

Although John Templeton did not compete at the 1993 International he had the pleasure of seeing his son, J. G. Templeton, gain sixth place in the Scottish team with Nell 173962, a daughter of Roy. She qualified for the final day at the International, and came tenth in the Supreme Championship, won by Alasdair Macrae with Nan 186565, at Armathwaite, where in 1981 Roy had won his first award in the Supreme Championship.

'Young' John Templeton had been a team member with Nell 129513, in 1985, when his father had been Scottish National Champion with Roy. He won the 1984 International Young Handlers Award with Nell, a daughter of his father's Ben 119873.

J. J. Templeton's Ben 119873

FRANK MOYES

Born 16/5/76   Black & white   A. S. Macrae, Lochaline

Awards

Scottish Shepherds' Champion 1984
Alexander Andrew Trophy 1984
Warnock Trophy 1984
J. M. Wilson Challenge Shield 1984

SPOT 82060, G. Redpath	DON 72528, I. Kerr	BEN 56646, D. McTeir NELL 52393, G. Redpath
	CHRIS 60920, W. McKenzie	SCOT 28069, G. Young PHIL 24983, P. McG. Hepburn
NELL 52793, G. Redpath	SWEEP 39603, J. Richardson	WISTON CAP 31154, J. Richardson LASSIE 23501, J. McDonald
	NELL 40698, J. Wilson	CAP 35276, J. Wilson FAN 15237, A. Porteous

SWEEP 39603 *International & Scottish Driving Champion 1968*
Scottish Shepherds' Champion 1968
BEN 56646 *International Shepherds' Champion 1972*
Scottish Shepherds' Aggregate Championship 1972
Scottish National & Scottish Shepherds' Champion 1972
Alexander Andrew Trophy 1972

SCOT 28069 *International Shepherds' Champion 1969*
Scottish Shepherds' Aggregate Championship 1969
Scottish Shepherds' Champion 1969
WISTON CAP 31154 *International Supreme Champion 1965*
International Shepherds' Champion 1966
Scottish Driving Champion 1969

Alasdair S. Macrae

Alasdair S. Macrae, who won the 1984 Scottish National with Mirk 96612, had been reserve to the team the previous year. He had experienced difficulties in travelling to the International, held that year on the gale-lashed Aberystwyth course, and with typical determination, he and his dog had hitch-hiked to the trial, but as the full team had been present, they remained spectators.

Alasdair's Bute 178106 was third in the 1990 National won by J. F. McRobert and Glen 143941, sired by A. S. Macrae's Mirk III 120673, and was reserve in the Supreme Championship, won by G. Jones and Queen 152483. The following year, Bute, then owned by K. Brehmer, was Scottish Driving Champion.

In 1992 A. S. Macrae had Nap 148436, and Corrie 182846, in the team, the latter being reserve to the Supreme Champion, Bobby Dalziel's Wisp 161487. Again in 1993 he had two team dogs: Elwyn Glen 190830, a son of G. Jones' Taff 167290, who came third, and Nan 186565, who, at Armathwaite, won the Supreme Championship, with Elwyn Glen in fourth place.

1986 **DRYDEN JOE 104626** Eddleston

Born 21/9/77   Black & white   R. Dalziel, Ettrick Valley

Awards

Scottish Shepherds' Champion 1979 & 1986
Alexander Andrew Trophy 1986
J. M. Wilson Challenge Shield 1986
Scottish Driving Champion 1986

	┌ CAP 67230, T. T. McKnight	┌ CAP 52841, A. Rogerson └ LASSIE 60521, T. T. McKnight
GLEN 75630, R. Fortune		
	└ SHELL 68768, T. T. McKnight	┌ DRIFT 51202, T.T. McKnight └ SHELL 56986, J. Robinson
	┌ SPOT 24981, J. Gilchrist	┌ BOB 12684, J. Gilchrist └ WISTON NAN III 9896, P. McG. Hepburn
DRYDEN QUEEN 70345, A. McGregor		
	└ CHRIS 60920, A. McGregor	┌ SCOT 28069, G. Young └ PHIL 24983, P. McG. Hepburn

GLEN 75630 *Scottish Brace Champion 1977*
SPOT 24981 *International Aggregate Championship 1966*
Scottish Aggregate Championship 1966
Scottish Shepherds' Aggregate Championship 1966
Scottish National & Scottish Shepherds' Champion 1965 & 1966
DRIFT 51202 *International & Scottish Driving Champion 1970*
SCOT 28069 *International Shepherds' Champion 1969*
Scottish Shepherds' Aggregate Championship 1969
Scottish Shepherds' Champion 1969

A young Scottish shepherd whose hero was the great handler J. M. Wilson once worked a dog for a stranger's appraisal, only later to discover that the stranger was his hero. Bobby Dalziel was the shepherd, and he himself has since developed the same mystical, telepathic partnership with his dogs.

With Dryden Joe 104626, he won the 1979 Scottish Shepherds' Championship, coming third in the team, and that was the beginning of a very successful International Sheep Dog Trials career. Three years later, Joe was seventh in the Supreme Championship, and in 1986 he won the Scottish National and Driving Championships; his kennelmate Nell 118049, was also in the team and she qualified to compete in the Supreme Championship. She was the 1985 International Shepherds' Champion, and was sixth in the Supreme Championship, and was also in the 1983 team.

Wisp 161487 was second in the 1989 National, won by S. L. Davidson and Chief. Bobby Dalziel and Wisp won the Supreme Championship on the difficult Margam Park course. Wisp was second again in the 1991 National, won by Julie Deptford and Gwen 160435, and came fifth in the Supreme Championship. He was the 1992 Scottish National Champion and before a hushed, enthralled audience who all recognised that they were watching the ultimate in understanding between man and dog, Wisp and Bobby Dalziel won their second Supreme Championship, on the long flat Aberystwyth course.

Born 7/4/82   Black & white   J. R. Welsh for T. Hutchinson, Newton Stewart

Awards

Scottish Farmers' Champion 1987
Alexander Andrew Trophy 1987
J. M. Wilson Challenge Shield 1987

BILL 115436, W. Welsh	┌DON 73710, W. Welsh	┌CAP 52841, A. Rogerson
		└MIST OF THORNBY 60944, W. Jardine
	└TAMMY 103528, J. Fleming	┌GARRY 69147, J. Fleming
		└SHELLEY 66940, J. Fleming
MAUD 80584, T. Hutchinson	┌NAP 37421, D. Walker	┌BILL II 18890, R. Shennan
		└NELL 12961, R.Robertson
	└MAUD 33297, D. Walker	┌BILL II 17937, J. M. Wilson
		└QUEEN 24078, J. Kerr

DON 73710   *International Shepherds' Champion 1979*
           Scottish Shepherds' Aggregate Championship 1979
           Scottish Shepherds' Champion 1978
           Captain Whittaker Outrun Cup 1975
QUEEN 24078   *Scottish National & Scottish Farmers' Champion 1968*
           Alexander Andrew Trophy 1968

DONALD McCAIG

Born 1/10/82   Black & white   S. L. Davidson, Dunoon

Awards

International Brace Champion with CHIEF 120006, 1988
Scottish Aggregate Championship 1988
Scottish Farmers' Champion 1988
McDiarmid Trophy 1988
Alexander Andrew Trophy 1988
J. M. Wilson Challenge Shield 1988

BEN 88284, S. L. Davidson	┌ **BEN 50504, J. A. MacLeod**	┌ JAFF 38313, T. T. McKnight └ FAY 42928, W. Cuthbert
	└ **MIST 75908, D. MacKenzie**	┌ SPOT 24981, J. Gilchrist └ GAEL 44425, P. McG. Hepburn
JEN 106192, J. Paterson	┌ **DRIFT 91394, R. Shennan**	┌ MIRK 52844, J. Richardson └ JAN 39653, J. Nelson
	└ **JEN 57299, J. Kirkland**	┌ SPOT 24981, J. Gilchrist └ JEN 47346, J. C. Templeton

BEN 88284   *Scottish National & Scottish Farmers' Champion 1980*
        Scottish Brace Champion 1981
        Alexander Andrew Trophy 1980
        J. M. Wilson Challenge Shield 1980
JAFF 38313   *Scottish Brace Champion 1969*

SPOT 24981	*International Aggregate Championship 1966*
	Scottish Aggregate Championship 1966
	Scottish Shepherds' Aggregate Championship 1966
	Scottish National & Scottish Shepherds' Champion 1965 & 1966
MIRK 52844	*International Shepherds' Champion 1975*
	Scottish Shepherds' Aggregate Championship 1975
	Scottish National & Scottish Driving Champion 1975
	Scottish Shepherds' Champion 1973 & 1975
	Alexander Andrew Trophy 1975
	J. M. Wilson Challenge Shield 1975

S. L. Davidson

S. L. Davidson is a contemporary competitor of Bobby Dalziel and has won three Nationals – with Ben 88284, a grandson of J. Gilchrist's Spot 24981, and of T. T. McKnight's Jaff 38313, in 1980; with Moss 138632, a son of Ben, in 1988; and with Chief 120006, an older, full brother of Moss, in 1989.

His International debut was with Ben in 1978, and he was in the 1979 team with Shep 80763, these two dogs winning the 1981 Scottish Brace Championship. Chief, whose working name was Craig, was in the team in 1984 and in 1985, when he qualified to compete in the Supreme Championship, coming eighth, and in 1987 he was sixth in the Supreme Championship.

Moss was a team member in 1986, and in 1988 he was Scottish National Champion, after a runoff with John Templeton's Roy, both dogs having equal points. Moss was fourth that year in the Supreme Championship, won by M. Jones and Spot 152290, and Moss and Chief won the International Brace Championship. In 1990 Moss and Hope 158875, a son of Chief, were team members, Hope winning the Scottish and International Driving Championships, while Moss and Chief were Scottish Brace Champions. Hope was in the team again in 1992 and came fourth in the National.

FRANK MOYES, COURTESY WSN

*S. Davidson with Moss 138632 (left)
and Chief 120006 (right)*

SCOTTISH FARMER

Born 5/2/80   Black & white   S. L. Davidson, Dunoon

Awards

International Brace Champion with MOSS 138632, 1988
Scottish Farmers' Champion 1989
Alexander Andrew Trophy 1989
J. M. Wilson Challenge Shield 1989
Warnock Trophy 1987 & 1989

	┌ BEN 50504, J. A. MacLeod	┌ JAFF 38313 T. T. McKnight └ FAY 42928, W. Cuthbert
BEN 88284, S. L. Davidson		
	└ MIST 75908, D. MacKenzie	┌ SPOT 24981, J. Gilchrist └ GAEL 44425, P. McG. Hepburn
	┌ DRIFT 91394, R. Shennan	┌ MIRK 52844, J. Richardson └ JAN 39653, J. Nelson
JEN 106192, J. Paterson		
	└ JEN 57299, J. Kirkland	┌ SPOT 24981, J. Gilchrist └ JEN 47346 J. C. Templeton

BEN 88284   *Scottish National & Scottish Farmers' Champion 1980*
                Scottish Brace Champion 1981
                Alexander Andrew Trophy 1980
                J. M. Wilson Challenge Shield 1980

JAFF 38313 *Scottish Brace Champion 1969*

SPOT 24981 *International Aggregate Championship 1966*
                Scottish Aggregate Championship 1966
                Scottish Shepherds' Aggregate Championship 1966
                Scottish National & Scottish Shepherds' Champion 1965 & 1966

MIRK 52844 *International Shepherds' Champion 1975*
                Scottish Shepherds' Aggregate Championship 1975
                Scottish National & Scottish Driving Champion 1975
                Scottish Shepherds' Champion 1973 & 1975
                Alexander Andrew Trophy 1975
                J. M. Wilson Challenge Shield 1975

FRANK MOYES, COURTESY WSN

Born 1/9/83   Black, tan & white   J. McRobert, Tweedsmuir

Awards

Scottish Shepherds' Aggregate Championship 1990
Scottish Shepherds' Champion 1990
Alexander Andrew Trophy 1990
J. M. Wilson Challenge Shield 1990

MIRK III 120673, A. S. Macrae	MIRK 52844, G. Lloyd	WISTON CAP 31154, J. Richardson LASSIE 23501, J. McDonald
	PAT 93851, D. Roberts	ROY 79357, A. Roberts PATSY 54457, G. Williams
NELL 131110, W. Wilson	BEN 88284, S. L. Davidson	BEN 50504, J. A. MacLeod MIST 75908, D. MacKenzie
	MEG 96533, J. Wilson	HEMP 72301, A. J. Campbell BET 63604, A. MacIntosh

MIRK 52844   *International Shepherds' Champion 1975*
Scottish Aggregate Championship 1975
Scottish National Champion 1975
Scottish Shepherds' Champion 1973 & 1975
Scottish Driving Champion 1975
Alexander Andrew Trophy 1975
J. M. Wilson Challenge Shield 1975

BEN 88284   *Scottish National & Farmers' Champion 1980*
Scottish Brace Champion 1981
Alexander Andrew Trophy 1980
J. M. Wilson Challenge Shield 1980

WISTON CAP 31154   *International Supreme Champion 1965*
International Shepherds' Champion 1966
Scottish Driving Champion 1969

HEMP 72301   *Scottish Driving Champion 1977*

The Scottish Team, 1991

LES PARKER, COURTESY WSN

Born 12/11/85   Black, white & tan   Mrs. J. Deptford, Elgin

Awards

International Shepherds' Champion 1989
Scottish Shepherds' Aggregate Championship 1989
Pedigree Pet Food Silver Salver 1989
Scottish Farmers' Champion 1991
J. M. Wilson Challenge Shield 1991
Warnock Trophy 1991
Allison Award 1991

SWEEP 125020, P. Edwards	CAP 91526, J. Thomas	CRAIG 59425, J. Thomas MAID 67640, J. Thomas
	JESS 97492, J. Reed	JASPER 79280, W. Reed EAST OF ENGLAND JAN 83769, J. Reed
FLY 140115, P. Edwards	MAC 116944, W. Jones	TWEED 92886, W. Japp FLY 103521, W. Owen
	PEARL 119614, A. Bunt	GLEN 38768, A. Bunt FLY 80269, A. Bunt

CAP 91526   *International Driving Champion 1981*
Feedmobile Challenge Cup, 1983
CRAIG 59425   *International Supreme Champion 1977*
International Shepherds' Champion 1976 & 1977
International Aggregate Championship 1976 & 1977
Welsh Shepherds' Aggregate Championship 1973, 1975, 1976 & 1977
Welsh Aggregate Championship 1976 & 1977
Captain Whittaker Outwork Cup 1977
R. Fortune Trophy 1977
Lord Mostyn Plate 1977
I.S.D.S. Blue Riband 1977
Pedigree Chum Supreme Championship Trophy 1977
Welsh National Champion 1977
Welsh Shepherds' Champion 1976 & 1977
Challis Shield 1977
JASPER 79280   *International Driving Champion 1978*

Julie Deptford with (left to right) Bess 161886, Nell 170326 and Gwen 160435

AUSTIN BENNETT

Born 24/2/86   Black & white   R. Dalziel, Ettrick Valley

Awards

International Supreme Champion 1989 & 1992
I.S.D.S. Blue Riband 1989 & 1992
International Shepherds' Champion 1992
International Aggregate Championship 1989 & 1992
Scottish Aggregate Championship 1989
Lord Mostyn Plate 1989 & 1992
R. Fortune Trophy 1989 & 1992
Scottish Shepherds' Aggregate Championship 1992
Captain Whittaker Outwork Cup 1992
Pedigree Chum Supreme Champion Challenge Trophy 1989 & 1992
Lang's Supreme Silver Quaiche 1989 & 1992
Sun Alliance Insurance Group Crystal 1989
Caithness Glass 1992
Rhiwlas Trophy 1989 & 1992
Scottish Shepherds' Champion 1989, 1991 & 1992
Alexander Andrew Trophy 1991 & 1992
J. M. Wilson Challenge Shield 1992

GUNNER KEELE 148409, N. Rutter	┌ **DON 108889, J. Thomas**	┌ CRAIG 59425, J. Thomas └ MAID 97071, D. Jones
	└ **FLY 114092, N. Rutter**	┌ ED 94619, R. Bailey └ FLY 73214, R. Bailey
NELL 143510, J. Barr	┌ **BEN 119873, J. Templeton**	┌ GLEN 104763, J. Templeton └ JEN 106069, J. Barr
	└ **NELL 114326, J. Barr**	┌ MOSS 103923, J. Templeton └ NELL 69129, J. Templeton

DON 108889 *English Aggregate Championship 1982*
English Shepherds' Aggregate Championship 1982
English Shepherds' Champion 1984

BEN 119873 *Scottish Brace Champion with Roy 114678, 1982, 1983 & 1984*
International Brace Champion with Roy, 1984
Brace Aggregate Championship 1984

CRAIG 59425 *International Supreme Champion 1977*
International Shepherds' Champion, 1976 & 1977
International Aggregate Championship 1976 & 1977
Welsh Aggregate Championship 1976 & 1977
Welsh Shepherds' Aggregate Championship 1973, 1975, 1976 & 1977
Captain Whittaker Outwork Cup 1977
R. Fortune Trophy 1977
Lord Mostyn Plate 1977
I.S.D.S. Blue Riband 1977
Pedigree Chum Supreme Championship Trophy 1977
Welsh National Champion 1977
Welsh Shepherds' Champion 1976 & 1977
Challis Shield 1977

MOSS 103923 *Scottish Aggregate Championship 1979*
Feedmobile Trophy 1979

AUSTIN BENNETT

Bobby Dalziel and Wisp 161487

FRANK MOYES, COURTESY WSN

Born 15/3/89   Black, white & tan   J. Wilson, Duns

Awards

Scottish Shepherds' Champion 1993
Alexander Andrew Trophy 1993
J. M. Wilson Challenge Shield 1993
Warnock Trophy 1993

JIM 155787, J. H. Logan	⌈ CHIP 77779, J. McSwiggan	⌈ DALE 55615, S. O'Leary ⌊ LYNN 28622, J. McSwiggan
	⌊ LASSIE 139121, Mrs. B. Doyle	⌈ ROY 96930, Mrs. D. Moore ⌊ MIST 112263, M. McNally
NELL 170919, R. Alexander	⌈ VIC 150071, R. Alexander	⌈ DON 108889, J. Thomas ⌊ GEM 110452, J. Wheaton
	⌊ TIB 109671, R. Alexander	⌈ NAP 85273, S. MacFarlane ⌊ QUEEN 98527, W. Stevenson

CHIP 77779   *International Brace Championship with* **JESS 77782**, *1977*
           Irish Brace Championship with **JESS 77782**, *1980*
LYNN 28622   *Irish Brace Champion with* **Rock 36024**, *1969*
DON 108889   *English Aggregate Championship 1982*
           English Shepherds' Aggregate Championship 1982
           English Shepherds' Champion 1984

Welsh National Winners

Born 1921   Black & tan   J. Pritchard, Pwllheli

SWEEP 164, T. Hunter	LADDIE 42, W. Rutherford	MOSS, P. Elliott QUEEN, J. K. Burns
	FLY 165, T. Hunter	DON, A. Hamilton MAID 945, A. Hamilton
FAN 298, G. Gilholm	MOSS III 28, W. Wallace	MOSS, Turnbull LASSIE, W. Scott
	BENTY, T. Gilholm	

SWEEP 164 *International Shepherds' Champion 1923 & 1924, exported to New Zealand in 1926*

MOSS III 28 *was exported to Australia*

T. Hunter's **FLY 165** *was dam of C. B. McPherson's* **MOSS 454** *and T. Hunter's* **MAID 489** *(both by* **SPOT I 308,** *G. P. Brown)*

MAID 489 *was dam of G. Whiting's 1933 Supreme International Champion,* **CHIP 672**

G. Gilholm's **FAN 298** *was full sister to T. Gilholm's famous* **LILLE 26,** *a key brood bitch in the breed*

Born –/6/21   Black & white   T. Roberts, Corwen

Awards
International Supreme Champion 1924

```
                        ┌ KEP 13, J. Scott          ┌ SPOT, R. Snowdon, Longwitton
  LEADER 666, T. Gilholm │                           └ CLEG, Turnbull
                        │
                        └ LASSIE 518, T. Gilholm    ┌ HAIG 252, A. Telfer
                                                     └ JET 352, T. Gilholm

                        ┌ MOSS III 28, W. Wallace   ┌ MOSS, Turnbull
  LILLE 26, T. Gilholm  │                           └ LASSIE, W. Scott
                        │
                        └ BENTY, T. Gilholm
```

KEP 13   *International Supreme Champion 1908 & 1909*
HAIG 252 *International Supreme Champion 1921*
          English National Champion 1924

Tom Roberts – Family Success

Two years after Wales had become a part of the International Society in 1922, Tom Roberts and Jaff 379 won the Supreme Championship, having won the 1923 and 1924 Welsh Nationals. Jaff, a grandson of Scott's Kep 13, Supreme Champion in 1908 and 1909, was himself grandsire to the 1937 Welsh National Champion, R. H. Williams' Jaff 2598, and great-grandsire of Jaff II 2199, John Jones' 1935 Supreme Champion. John Jones (Corwen) and Tom Roberts were cousins, and the family tradition of sheepdog handling has been upheld by John Jones' son, Meirion, who was Welsh National Champion with Craig 67343, in 1979, and won the 1959 Supreme Championship with Ben 13879, joining that élite band of handlers by again winning the Supreme Championship in 1988, with Spot 152290. Among his many International Sheep Dog Society awards Meirion with Tibbie 11113, was reserve Supreme Champion in 1958 to W. J. Evans' Tweed 9601, and Tibbie had also been third in the 1956 Supreme Championship.

John Jones, Trawsfynydd, competed for many years in top class trials, winning the Welsh National in 1932 with Blackie 1635, a son of Scot 564, who was sired by G. Brown's Spot 308 and out of T. Hunter's Fly 165. His 1935 Welsh Champion, Fly 1574, was also by Scot 564, and George Whiting's 1933 Supreme Champion, Chip 672, was also a grandson of Spot 308, and of T. Hunter's Fly 165.

186

J. Pritchard and Juno 618

Born –/8/22 Black & tan E. Pritchard, Pwllheli

Awards

International Shepherds' Champion 1926
Welsh Shepherds' Champion 1927

LADDIE 406, J. Pritchard	┌ SWEEP 164, T. Hunter	┌ LADDIE 42, W. Rutherford └ FLY 165, T. Hunter
	└ FAN 298, G. Gilholm	┌ MOSS III 28, W. Wallace └ BENTY, T. Gilholm
NELL, J. Pritchard		

LADDIE 406 *Welsh National Champion 1922*
SWEEP 164 *International Shepherds' Champion 1923 & 1924*

Hard-fought Trials

In 1926 and 1927 the Welsh National was won by a son of Spot 308 (Supreme Champion 1923) – Edward Morris' Spot 615. His first National Championship was gained after a runoff with John Jones' (Corwen) Cap, both dogs having equal points on 108½. They were presented with an extra test of penning five marked sheep, which had to be shed from fifteen. Cap failed to shed his five in the given time, and Spot, having shed, but failed to pen, was proclaimed the winner. Tom Roberts' Jaff 379 was third that year, and the following year he and J. B. Bagshaw's Lad 305 were on equal points in the Supreme Championship, and the winner, Lad, was decided after a similar test had been worked. Lad was one of the biggest dogs to grace the trials field and in 1925, having won the English National, he was fourth in the Supreme Championship, and in 1926 he was second to Walter Telfer's Queen in the English National.

John Pritchard – Sad Losses

Just prior to the 1925 International the whole world of sheepdog enthusiasts was stunned and sickened when John Pritchard of Criccieth tragically lost two of his dogs; his team dog Laddie being one of them. Laddie 406, was sired by T. Hunter's Sweep 164, and had won the first Welsh National of 1922. The two dogs were found hanged by persons unknown, who had also endeavoured to set fire to the farmhouse and barns.

In the following year John's team entrant, Spotan, a daughter of the ill-fated Laddie, was mysteriously poisoned. The sympathy of sheepdog men everywhere was extended to Mr Pritchard, and James Moore, who had exported so many British sheepdogs, offered to give him one of his best dogs to ease his loss. Through this kind and generous offer he and Mr Pritchard became firm friends, and later Mr Pritchard sent a beautiful bitch, Roos, to Mr Moore.

Roos was mated in Australia to Moss 454, producing Kyneton Moss, while Kyneton Young Moss came from the mating of Moss 454 and Caley (of Thornhill). Several generations later these lines became interwoven in the Boveagh kennels and many of the legendary dogs of Australia and New Zealand trace directly back to these specific lines, founded on Herdman's Tommy 16, the grandson of Old Hemp.

SPOT 615

Born 5/6/23   Black & white   E. Morris, Bethesda

SPOT 308, G. P. Brown	┌ BEN 249, G. P. Brown	┌ DON 217, C. Hardisty └ FAN 208, G. P. Brown
	└ RUBY 207, G. P. Brown	┌ SKIP, J. McKnight └ MOSS, A. Harrison
BEAT 429, R. Forest	┌ LAD, D. Murray	
	└ BEAT 4, J. Waldie	┌ PATE, J. Young └ MAID, J. Skeldon

SPOT 308   *International Supreme Champion 1923*
International Shepherds' Champion 1922
Scottish National Champion 1923
Exported to Sam Stoddart in the United States

Born 12/3/26   Blue, white & tan   R. J. Hughes, Llanerchymedd

BOSS 570, F. Booth	┌SPOT 308, G. P. Brown	┌BEN 249, G. P. Brown └RUBY 207, G. P. Brown
	└FAN 230, R. Douglas	┌SWEEP 188, W. Hedley └JED, J. Thompson
DOT 573, T. Jones	┌HAIG 252, A. Telfer	┌GLEN 34, W. Wallace └MADDIE I 38, J. A. Reid
	└FLY 51, A. P. Swanston	┌LEADER 666, T. Gilholm └MADDIE, Saltoun

SPOT 308   *International Supreme Champion 1923*
International Shepherds' Champion 1922
Scottish National Champion 1923
HAIG 252   *International Supreme Champion 1921*
English National Champion 1924

TOSS 464

Born –/7/22   Black & white   L. J. Humphreys, Towyn

Awards

Welsh Brace Champion with LAD 476, 1931 & 1932

SWEEP 164, T. Hunter	LADDIE 42, W. Rutherford	MOSS, P. Elliott QUEEN, J. K. Burns
	FLY 165, T. Hunter	DON, A. Hamilton MAID 945, A. Hamilton
FLY 337, T. Dickson	HEMP 153, T. Dickson	YARROW 23, A. Telfer FENWICK JED 33, A. Telfer
	MADDIE I 38, J. A. Reid	DON I 17, T. Armstrong MADDIE 8, W. Telfer

SWEEP 164   *International Shepherds' Champion 1923 & 1924*
HEMP 153   *International Farmers' Champion 1924*
DON I 17   *International Supreme Champion 1911 & 1914*

DON I 17 and SWEEP 164   *were exported to New Zealand*

L. J. Humphreys was the most successful Welsh handler prior to the 1939 War, winning six Welsh Nationals; two with Toss 464; two with Lad 990 and two with Moss 2206. In 1931 and 1932 Toss and Lad won the Welsh Brace Championships. Toss represented Wales for ten years, and in 1928 was reserve Supreme Champion, beaten by one point by J. M. Wilson's first Supreme Champion, Fly 824, a daughter of Hemp 153. Toss was a grandson of T. Dickson's Hemp 153, and Lad was a great-great-grandson of Hemp, and Moss was also of the Hemp line.

*L. J. Humphreys, with some of his champion dogs, giving a
demonstration at Hackney Wick Stadium*

LAD 990

Born 15/4/27   Black & white   L. J. Humphreys, Towyn

Awards

International Brace Champion with MEG 1498, 1935
Welsh Brace Champion with TOSS 464, 1931 & 1932

LAD 742, D. Jones	GLEN 571, R. Parry	LAD 305, J. B. Bagshaw SPEEDY 370, J. B. Bagshaw
	JESS 582, J. T. Evans	SWEEP 164, T. Hunter FLY 337, T. Dickson
LASS 572, D. Jones	SPOT I 308, G. P. Brown	BEN 249, G. P. Brown RUBY 207, G. P. Brown
	JED 514, J. R. Hislop	SWEEP 164, T. Hunter BEAT 4, J. Waldie

SPOT I 308   *International Supreme Champion 1923*
              International Shepherds' Champion 1922
              Scottish National Champion 1923
LAD 305   *International Supreme Champion 1927*
              International Farmers' Champion 1926
              English National Champion 1925
SWEEP 164   *International Shepherds' Champion 1923 & 1924*

L. J. Humphrey's Champion dogs, 1930s

Born 19/10/30   Black, white & tan   J. Jones, Trawsfynydd

Awards

International & Welsh Driving Champion 1938
Welsh Aggregate Championship 1937

SCOT 564, J. Matthews	┌ **SPOT I 308, G. P. Brown**	┌ BEN 249, G. P. Brown └ RUBY 207, G. P. Brown
	└ **FLY 165, T. Hunter**	┌ DON, A. Hamilton └ MAID 945, A. Hamilton
FAN 105, J. H. Williams	┌ **MOSS, R. Williams**	┌ CAP 333, Lord Mostyn └ FAIRY, Lord Mostyn
	└ **LASSIE II, W. Peake**	

SPOT I 308   *International Supreme Champion 1923*
                International Shepherds' Champion 1922
                Scottish National Champion 1923
                Exported to Sam Stoddart in the United States

| 1933 | **MOSS 2206** | Margam |
| 1939 | | Llanfairfechan |

Born 7/7/32   Black & white   L. J. Humphreys, Towyn

MOSS 1677, A. Storie
┌ JAFF, R. Johnstone
└ MADDIE, T. Thomson

NICKEY, T. M. Dickson
┌ HEMP 153, T. M. Dickson
│   ┌ YARROW 23, A. Telfer
│   └ FENWICK JED 33, A. Telfer
└ LOOS II 435, W. Wallace
    ┌ LADDIE 317, J. A. Reid
    └ LOOS I 45, J. A. Reid

HEMP 153   *International Farmers' Champion 1924*
LOOS II 435   *International Farmers' Champion 1925*

| 1935 | **FLY 1574** | Beaumaris |

Born 6/4/29   Black & white   J. Jones, Trawsfynydd

SCOT 564, J. R. Matthews
┌ SPOT I 308, G. P. Brown
│   ┌ BEN 249, G. P. Brown
│   └ RUBY 207, G. P. Brown
└ FLY 165, T. Hunter
    ┌ DON, A. Hamilton
    └ MAID 945, A. Hamilton

FLOSS 1245, E. Pryce Jones
┌ JAFF 379, T. Roberts
│   ┌ LEADER 666, T. Gilholm
│   └ LILLE 26, T. Gilholm
└ DOLL, E. V. Jones

SPOT I 308   *International Supreme Champion 1923*
International Shepherds' Champion 1922
Scottish National Champion 1923

JAFF 379   *International Supreme Champion 1924*
Welsh National Champion 1923 & 1924

194

D. W. Davies with Nett (left) and Chip (right)

Born 25/4/26   Black & white   D. W. Davies, Pontypridd

Awards

Welsh Brace Champion with TOGO 1999, 1934

DICK 756, T. Jones	┌ **DICK 342, A. P. Swanston**	┌ **HEMP 153, T. M. Dickson** └ **FAN 230, R. Douglas**
	└ **DOT 573, A. P. Swanston**	┌ **HAIG 252, A. Telfer** └ **FLY 51, A. P. Swanston**
FAN 566, T. Jones	┌ **DICK 550, F. R. Griffiths**	┌ **SWEEP 164, T. Hunter** └ **FAN 479, M. Hayton**
	└ **FLY 551, T. Griffiths**	┌ **SWEEP 164, T. Hunter** └ **FLY 165, T. Hunter**

HEMP 153   *International Farmers' Champion 1924*
HAIG 252   *International Supreme Champion 1921*
                  English National Champion 1924
SWEEP 164   *International Shepherds' Champion 1923 & 1924,*
                  exported to New Zealand in 1926

Born 3/12/34 Black & white R. H. Williams, St Asaph

JAFF II 2011, T. Roberts	JAFF I 379, T. Roberts	LEADER 666, T. Gilholm LILLE 26, T. Gilholm
	LOE 1848, T. Roberts	SANDY, A. Craig HAZEL 681, A. Craig
RUBY 2505, W.Ll.Parry	SPOT 615, E. Morris	SPOT 308, G. P. Brown BEAT 429, R. Forest
	LADY, J. Williams	

JAFF II 2011 *International Farmers' Champion 1938*
          Welsh Aggregate Championship 1938
JAFF I 379 *International Supreme Champion 1924*
          Welsh National Champion 1923 & 1924
SPOT 615 *Welsh National Champion 1926 & 1927*
SPOT 308 *International Supreme Champion 1923*
          International Shepherds' Champion 1922
          Scottish National Champion 1923
          Exported to Sam Stoddart in the United States

A. Craig's **SANDY** *was a son of Dickson's* **HEMP** *153*
A. Craig's **HAZEL 681**, *by W. B. Telfer's* **CAP 237**, *was exported to New Zealand*

Bill Miles

W. F. Miles, who first competed in trials at the age of fifteen in 1921, was awarded the Oldest Competitor Trophy at the Woburn International, 1987, and presented with the Wilkinson Sword at the 1990 International at Alnwick.

He was a Welsh team member in 1933 with Rock 1285, a son of J. M. Wilson's Craig, and has regularly represented Wales during the past sixty years, winning the 1947 Welsh Aggregate Championship with Ken 5015, and the 1949 International Farmers' Championship with Wally. He won the Welsh National in 1938 with Kate 2601, a great-granddaughter of C. B. MacPherson's Moss 454 and Lauder's Meg 57, both of which were later exported – Moss to J. L. Moore's Australian kennels, and Meg to New Zealand.

Bill Miles considers Kate to be the most sagacious dog he has ever known. He purchased her from G. Lauder, and when he collected her at the local station, he found her loose, lying beside the travelling crate, out of which she had chewed her way. The station staff could get nowhere near her, and told him he would never catch her. He walked straight to her, saying, 'What are you doing there Kate?' She jumped up at him as if she had known him all her life, and followed him to the vehicle, while he carried the empty crate. At home he took her straight to the sheep and she worked for him. He was very upset when she later fell to her death down a quarry face, while working on the mountain.

With Wally 4361, he won the 1952 Welsh National and Welsh Driving Championship. Wally's trials' career was marred in later years as he suffered with severe rheumatism, and though he travelled to the 1952 International at Inverness, he was not well enough to compete.

Bill Miles won the Welsh and International Driving Championships with Kay 12084, a daughter of Whitehope Nap, in 1958, when she was also Welsh Driving Champion. She and Sweep 16216 won the 1963 Welsh Brace Championship.

Wally was a grandson of Captain J. D. McPherson's Moss 4551, English Driving Champion in 1947 and 1948. For quite a few years after the 1939–45 War, a contingent of Scottish and North country handlers visited South Wales for the 'August Week' holiday trials, and Captain McPherson with Moss was always among them.

At one Chepstow trial his single did not meet with the judge's approval, and he was asked to single again. In shocked disbelief he did as requested and, with Moss in full control of the ewe, turned to the judge and asked in an indignant voice, 'Do you want her in the b— tent?'

Bill Miles with the Wilkinson Sword

J. DAVIES

197

Born 1/5/36   Black & white   W. F. Miles, Treharris

NIPPIE, G. Lauder

MEG II 1315, G. Lauder
┌ SPOT 1630, C. B. McPherson ┌ BATTY 18, W. Amos
│   └ FLY 165, T. Hunter
│
└ TRIM 73, G. Lauder ┌ MOSS 454, C. B. McPherson
                                              └ MEG 57, G. Lauder

MOSS 454 was exported to J. L. Moore, Australia
MEG 57 was exported to J. Lillico, New Zealand

198

No trials were held during the war years, 1940–45

1946   **JAFF 4313**   **Llanfairfechan**
1948   **Machynlleth**

R. J. Hughes with Jaff 4313 (far right)

Born –/7/38   Black, white & tan   R. J. Hughes, Llanerchymedd

Awards

International & Welsh Driving Champion 1946, 1947 & 1949
Welsh Brace Champion with BEN 4333, 1946

COON 1608, Lord Mostyn	⌐ **MOSS 1318, G. Lauder**	⌐ **MOSS 1677, A. Storie** ⌐ **FAN, A. Storie**
	∟ **TRIM 73, P. Marshall**	⌐ **MOSS 454, C. B. McPherson** ∟ **MEG 57, G. Lauder**
NELL, T. O. Jones		

MOSS 454 *was exported to Australia*
MEG 57 *was exported to J. Lillico, New Zealand*

Jaff 4313 and his Descendants

Many dogs are discarded before they are mentally mature and only later do they develop into efficient, trustworthy shepherding dogs. Such a dog was R. J. Hughes' Jaff 4313 – so it is not just a modern occurrence – and may more often be caused by anxious, impatient owners!

At four years old Jaff was purchased by J. R. Hughes after disappointing several previous owners. Two years later he had become an extremely useful dog, winning the 1946 Welsh National Championship, the Welsh and International Driving Championships, and partnered by his son, Ben 4333, the Welsh Brace Championship. He was Welsh National Champion again in 1948, and his fame as a powerful driving dog grew when he won the 1947 and 1949 Welsh and International Driving Championships.

A popular stud dog, Jaff sired many famous working dogs, breeding particularly well to J. C. Williams' Minn 3387, the highest-pointed Welsh bred dog in the 1952 Welsh National, and a paternal and maternal granddaughter of J. M. Wilson's Cap 3036. They were grandparents to W. J. Evans' 1953 Supreme Champion Roy 7696 from whom came a line of quality dogs, including Alan Jones' great dog Roy 15393 and Herbert Worthington's Hemp 13132.

Among the great-grandsons and granddaughters of Jaff and Minn were the 1954 Welsh National Champion, Gwilliam Owen's Nell 8739, and Wyn Edwards' 1965 Welsh Champion, Nip 17278. W. Jones' 1958 Welsh National Champion Ben 11401, was also a grandson of Jaff.

G. Redpath's Coon 9077, a grandson of Jaff, became 1956 International Shepherds' Champion, the same year that George Redpath won the Supreme Championship with Moss 6805. Moss had previously been the 1952 Scottish and International Shepherds' Champion, and was sired by W. Hislop's Sweep 3834, the 1948 Scottish National Champion. Sweep was also sire of Griff Pugh's Don 6644, Welsh National Champion 1951, and of Joe Deniff's 1954 English National Champion, Sweep 5594.

The 1952 English National Champion, Cecil Holmes' Lad 4453, was out of Bet 4353, a litter sister to Jaff.

Wiston Cap has Jaff in his pedigree four times within seven generations. Jaff's sire, G. Lauder's Coon 1608 (later sold to Lord Mostyn) was a grandson of C. B. McPherson's Moss 454, who was reserve to the 1926 Supreme Champion – his own son – M. Hayton's Glen 698. Moss was a son of G. P. Brown's 1923 Supreme Champion, Spot 308, later sold for £165 to Sam Stoddart in America, where he founded the registered American Border Collie family.

Tragically Jaff was gored by an irate cow and died from his injuries.

Mr John Smith, whose wife is a niece of Mr Hughes, has the following stories to tell. Talking to Mr Robert Williams, who had worked at Ty Croes for some years, he was told of the time when R. J. Hughes' sheep was loaned for Benllech trials. Arriving at the trial Mr Hughes was angry to find a certain cantankerous black sheep had been included in the flock. He commented that 'somebody will have black luck today' – unfortunately he drew the black sheep and the 'black luck'.

Mr Williams recalled Mr Hughes' concern about the difficulty his dog Ben suddenly seemed to be having when working sheep. Ben was examined by the vet who found him to be almost blind. A few years later, Ben now completely blind, was attacked and killed by the same wicked old cow that later killed Jaff.

Mr O. J. Owen, who worked for Mr Hughes in the late 1940s, remembered Jaff well and recalled the many bitches sent to him, being collected from Llanerchymedd station. On arrival at the farm they were thoroughly cleaned and washed, prior to mating.

Although crippled in later life with arthritis, Mr Hughes still trained his dogs and toured his farm by pony and trap.

He attended the 'August Week' trials in South Wales during the late 1940s and early 50s, and I recall him returning to his car to find that his dogs had ripped up the upholstery – real leather in those days. He was not amused!

Born –/12/37   Black & white   R. O. Williams, Trescawan

WHITE 2182, J. Pritchard	┌HEMP 1844, J. Pritchard	┌TOSS, H. Griffiths └BET, H. Griffiths
	└FAN 1336, J. Pritchard	
JESH 2534, R. O. Williams	┌JAFF II 2199, J. Jones	┌JAFF 1267, J. Jones └QUEEN 149, J. Morris
	└JESS 2566, J. Evans	┌SCOT 564, J. R. Matthews └FAN 105, J. H. Williams

WHITE 2182   *International Farmers' Champion 1937*
Welsh Brace Champion 1939

JAFF II 2199   *International Supreme Champion 1935*
Welsh Aggregate Championship 1935
Exported to New Zealand

BLACKIE 1635 *and* **FLY 1574** *were also sired by*
SCOT 564, **BLACKIE** *being full brother to* **JESS 2566**
BLACKIE *and* **FLY** *were respectively 1932 and 1935 Welsh*
Champions

Born 24/9/44   Black & white   W. J. Evans, Magor

	⌐GLEN 3510, W. Hislop	⌐BEN 1572, A. Riddell
GLEN 3940, J. M. Wilson		⌊BEAT I, J. Guthrie
	⌊NELL 3514, J. Kirk	⌐CAP 3036, J. M. Wilson
		⌊MOSS 1827, J. McCaskie
JED, J. Purdie		

GLEN 3940   *International Supreme Champion 1946 & 1948*
International Farmers' Champion 1948
International Aggregate Championship 1946 & 1948
Scottish Aggregate Championship 1946 & 1948
Scottish National Champion 1946

W. J. Evans

While living in Wales, W. J. Evans won the 1949 Welsh National with Sweep 4204, having previously been International Farmers' Champion in 1947 with Jaff 2885, which title he won again in 1953 with Nell 6879, the year that Roy 7696, was Supreme Champion. Jaff, at nine years old, had been third in the 1946 Supreme Championship to J. M. Wilson's Glen 3940, and J. Relph's Fleet 4555.

Nell 6879 won the Welsh Brace Championship in 1951, 1953 and 1956 partnered by Coon 5701, Roy, and Moss respectively. Roy and Moss won the 1957 International Brace Championship.

Residing for a time in England, W. J. Evans promptly won the 1958 English National with Moss 7971, who with Tweed 9601, also won the

English Brace Championship, and a few weeks later Tweed won the Supreme Championship. Tweed, purchased from J. M. Wilson when he retired from trials competition, won the 1959 English National, and he and Moss were English Brace Champions again in 1960.

W. J. Evans won the 1962 English National with Don 13392, a son of Roy, and in 1963 Ben 12953, a son of Whitehope Nap 8685, was English National Champion.

Renowned for his expert sheepdog exhibitions at agricultural shows, with his team of trial winning collies, and his Hungarian horse, Condor, W. J. Evans was summoned by Her Majesty the Queen to give a command performance at Windsor before the Royal Family and their guest, Haile Selassie, Emperor of Ethiopia.

Welsh team 1949 standing (left to right): Ivor Jones, judge, J. H. Halsall (secretary of ISDS), L. J. Humphreys, unknown lady, R. O. Williams, D. Daniel, J. Pritchard, O. G. Thomas. Front row: Hugh Griffith, W. F. Miles, A. Jones, H. Worthington, John Jones, W. J. Evans, R. J. Hughes.

1950   SWEEP 5096   Llandrindod Wells

Born 11/1/45   Tan & white   W. Harris, Ynysybwl

	┌ CAP 3036, J. M. Wilson	┌ SAM 2336, H. Cullens └ PEN 2572, H. Cullens
JIG 6937, D. Stone		
	└ MEG 3640, D. Lothian	┌ ROBBIE 2743, J. Skeldon └ JED, D. Lothian
	┌ ROSS 3289, J. Telford	┌ CAP 3036, J. M. Wilson └ JILL 2735, R. Bonella
MAID 3677, D. Stone		
	└ FLOSS 3572, T. Brotherstone	┌ ROBBIE 2743, J. Skeldon └ BEAT 3095, T. Brotherstone

JILL 2735   *Scottish Shepherds' Champion 1939*

Born 8/3/48   Black & white   G. Pugh, Sealand

Awards

Welsh Driving Champion 1951

	┌ GLEN 3510, W. Hislop	┌ BEN 1572, A. Riddell └ BEAT I, J. Guthrie
SWEEP 3834, W. Hislop		
	└ NELL 3514, W. Hislop	┌ CAP 3036, J. M. Wilson └ MOSS 1827, J. McCaskie
	┌ ROY 1665, J. M. Wilson	┌ CRAIG 1048, J. M. Wilson └ LOOS II 435, W. Wallace
NELL 2768, A. McKelvie		
	└ SIS 1990, A. Craig	┌ ROY 102, R. Stewart └ FLOSS 103, D. Cook

SWEEP 3834   *Scottish National Champion 1948*
                International Farmers' Champion 1946
                International & Scottish Driving Champion 1948
ROY 1665   *International Supreme Champion 1934, 1936 & 1937*
                International Farmers' Champion 1935
                International Brace Champion 1937 & 1938
                International Aggregate Championship 1936 & 1937
                Scottish Aggregate Championship 1936 & 1937
                Scottish National Champion 1937
                Scottish Brace Champion 1934, 1936, 1937 & 1938

CRAIG 1048   *International Supreme Champion 1930*
                              International Aggregate Championship 1932
                              International Farmers' Champion 1929
                              Scottish National Champion 1931 & 1932
                              Scottish Brace Champion 1931
LOOS II 435   *International Farmers' Champion 1925*

Unknown man, Don 6644 and G. Pugh

Born 12/3/42   Black & white   W. F. Miles, Treharris

Awards
International Farmers' Champion 1949
Welsh Driving Champion 1952

DON 2698, **Capt. J. D. McPherson**	┌ MOSS 131, W. Amos └ TRIM, A. Lawrie	┌ GLEN 603, T. Hunter └ LASSIE 68, T. Courtney
CONNIE 2807, **Capt. J. D. McPherson**	┌ ROCK 1321, Capt. J. D. McPherson └ VIM 1984, Capt. J. D. McPherson	┌ TYNE, G. Lauder └ BESS 1028, R. Armstrong ┌ SPOT 763, F. Milne └ MORAG, F. Milne

ROCK 1321 and VIM 1984 *Scottish Brace Champions 1935*
VIM 1984 *was a Beardie*

W. F. Miles with Wally 4361

Born –/–/44　Black , white & mottled　G. Pugh, Bagillt

Awards
Welsh Driving Champion 1953

	┌JIX 1707, F. Sutcliffe	┌CRAIG 1048, J. M. Wilson
SPOT 3032, A. Storie		└LASS, F. Sutcliffe
	└TIB, R. Anderson	
NELL II, A. Storie		

CRAIG 1048　*International Supreme Champion 1930*
International Aggregate Championship 1932
International Farmers' Champion 1929
Scottish National Champion 1931 & 1932
Scottish Brace Champion 1931

Born 1/3/51   Black & white   G. Owen, Sennybridge

Awards
The Challis Shield 1954

SPOT 7061, G. Owen	┌ **GLEN 3940, J. M. Wilson**	┌ **GLEN 3510, W. Hislop** └ **NELL 3514, J. Kirk**
	└ **NELL 6457, Mrs. C. Stephens**	┌ **SPOT 3624, J. Gilchrist** └ **MEG 3893, J. Jeffrey**
TOT 6606, G. Owen	┌ **JAFF 4558, W. J. Thomas**	┌ **JAFF 4313, R. J. Hughes** └ **MINN 3387, J. C. Williams**
	└ **NELL 5699, F. Price**	┌ **DRIFT 4380, J. R. Millar** └ **NAN 4177, D. Livingstone**

GLEN 3940   *International Supreme Champion 1946 & 1948*
International Farmers' Champion 1948
International Aggregate Championship 1946 & 1948
Scottish Aggregate Championship 1946 & 1948
Scottish National Champion 1946

SPOT 3624   *International Supreme Champion 1947*
International Aggregate Championship 1947
International Brace Champion 1948 & 1949
Scottish Aggregate Championship 1947
Scottish Shepherds' Aggregate Championship 1946 & 1947
Scottish Shepherds' Champion 1947
Scottish Brace Champion 1948 & 1949
Scottish Driving Champion 1953

JAFF 4313 *Welsh National Champion 1946 & 1948*
International & Welsh Driving Champion 1946, 1947 & 1949
Welsh Brace Champion 1946
MINN 3387 *The Challis Shield 1952*
DRIFT 4380 *Scottish National Champion 1947*
Scottish Driving Champion 1946

Gwilliam Owen with Nell 8739

GLEN 7690

Born 3/5/50   Black & white   H. Greenslade, Cwmcarn

Awards

International Farmers' Champion 1956
Welsh Driving Champion 1956

SWEEP 4204, W. J. Evans	⌈ **GLEN 3940, J. M. Wilson**	⌈**GLEN 3510, W. Hislop** ⌊**NELL 3514, J. Kirk**
	⌊ **JED, J. Purdie**	
JED 4047, W. James	⌈ **CAP 3036, J. M. Wilson**	⌈**SAM 2336, H. Cullens** ⌊**PEN 2572, H. Cullens**
	⌊ **JED 3565, T. Lothian**	⌈**SWEEP, D. Lothian** ⌊**JED, D. Lothian**

SWEEP 4204   *Welsh National Champion 1949*
GLEN 3940   *International Supreme Champion 1946 & 1948*
               International Farmers' Champion 1948
               International Aggregate Championship 1946 & 1948
               Scottish Aggregate Championship 1946 & 1948
               Scottish National Champion 1946
JED 4047   *Challis Shield 1955 & 1956*

Harry Greenslade

Harry Greenslade, a contemporary of W. J. Evans was a coal miner of Cwmcarn, which nestles in a Welsh valley beneath Mynyddislwyn Mountain, on which one of the oldest and most testing of South Wales trials is held annually. Many are the great names in the world of sheepdog trials who have graced that course, both men and dogs.

Harry Greenslade had no sheep of his own, but his many farming pals allowed him to train his dogs on their mountain pastures. As he didn't have his own transport he used to be driven in a friend's motorcycle and sidecar, seated in the sidecar along with two or three dogs! Not as eye-catching as the ancient, ornate glass motor hearse in which Jack Mathias carried his four dogs!

In 1955 Harry Greenslade and Glen 7690, won the Welsh National Championship, repeating this win in 1956, when Glen was also Welsh Driving Champion, going on to become the International Farmers' Champion at Llandudno.

Glen was a paternal grandson of J. M. Wilson's dual Supreme Champion, Glen 3940, and a maternal grandson of J. M. Wilson's Cap 3036. Via his son Garry 11742, the highest-pointed Welsh bred dog in the 1963 Welsh National (Challis Cup), Glen became grandsire to A. T. Lloyd's 1962 Supreme Champion, Garry 17690, whose dam, Nell 16024, was by D. W. Daniel's dual 1949 and 1952 Supreme Champion, Chip 4924.

Harry Greenslade and Glen 7690

DAILY HERALD

The Daniel Family

With Floss 11400, D. W. Daniel won the Welsh Aggregate Championships in 1955 and 1957, and with Allan 12085, a son of Chip, he won the International Farmers' Championship in 1958.

Eurwyn, his son, has been a regular member of the Welsh team, and won the 1960 Supreme Championship with Ken 13306, a son of Chip and Floss, who was a daughter of T. Bonella's 1956 Scottish National Champion, Moss 7878.

In 1968 Eurwyn's Chip 22797, Ken's son, was reserve Supreme Champion to Llyr Evans' Bosworth Coon 34186, having given a wonderful display of controlled shedding. Chip won the International Aggregate Championship, and Welsh Driving Championship that same year.

In 1982 Meg 96043, and in 1984, Ken 101980, full brother and sister, were Welsh Farmers' Champions, both Nationals being won by shepherds: M. R. Page and Cap 108145 and J. P. Burke and Glen 113361.

In 1992 Eurwyn won his first Welsh National Championship, with Fly 163488, a daughter of Bobby Dalziel's 1986 Scottish National Champion, Dryden Joe 104626. His son, David, competes regularly and has also been a member of the Welsh team.

Fly was a member of the 1993 team, and was ninth in the Supreme Championship.

Glen 7690

(Left to right) T. Bonella with Tillochie Moss 7878; H. Greenslade with Glen 7690 and I. Jones with Rovi 6112

GLEN 7395

Born 24/11/49   Black, white & mottled   W. J. Thomas, Brynmawr

Awards

Welsh Farmers' Champion 1960

	┌GLEN 3510, W. Hislop	┌BEN 1572, A. Riddell └BEAT I, J. Guthrie
GLEN 3940, J. M. Wilson	└NELL 3514, J. Kirk	┌CAP 3036, J. M. Wilson └MOSS 1827, J. McCaskie
	┌SPOT 3624, J. Gilchrist	┌TAM 3465, J. Purdie └TRIM, J. Purdie
MEG II 4088, J. Jeffrey	└MEG 3893, A. Anderson	┌CAP 3036, J. M. Wilson └MIST, J. Jeffrey

GLEN 3940   *International Supreme Champion 1946 & 1948*
International Farmers' Champion 1948
International Aggregate Championship 1946 & 1948
Scottish Aggregate Championship 1946 & 1948
Scottish National Champion 1946
SPOT 3624   *International Supreme Champion 1947*
International & Scottish Aggregate Championships 1947
International & Scottish Brace Champion 1948 & 1949
Scottish Shepherds' Aggregate Championship 1946 & 1947
Scottish Shepherds' Champion 1947
Scottish Driving Champion 1953

Born 15/10/51　Black & white　W. Jones, Llanferres

GLEN N. R., J. W. Jones

FLASH 9618, J. Holmes
- SWEEP 4702, G. Pugh
  - BOY 3890, W. Little
  - FLY 3794, G. Redpath
- JESS 5177, T. S. Roberts
  - JAFF 4313, R. J. Hughes
  - MEG 4386, G. Pugh

SWEEP 4702　*Welsh Aggregate Championship 1948*
JAFF 4313　*International & Welsh Driving Champion 1946, 1947 & 1949*
　　　　　Welsh National Champion 1946 & 1948
　　　　　Welsh Brace Champion 1946

ROY 15393

Born 4/4/57   Black, white & tan   A. Jones, Llithfaen

Awards

International Supreme Champion 1961
International Farmers' & Welsh Farmers' Champion 1961
International Brace Champion with GLEN 17251, 1964
International & Welsh Aggregate Championships 1961
Brace Aggregate Championship with GLEN 17251, 1964
Welsh Driving Champion 1961
Welsh Brace Champion with SPOT 9476, 1961
Welsh Brace Champion with GLEN 17251, 1962 & 1964
Challis Shield 1959 & 1961

ROY 7696, W. J. Evans	⌐ MAC 5498, J. Evans	⌐JAFF 4313, R. J. Hughes └MINN 3387, J. C. Williams
	└ MEG 6782, G. W. Jones	⌐GLEN 2584, J. Jones └MON 3417, T. Jones
JILL 7742, W. J. Evans	⌐ MOSS 5176, J. M. Wilson	⌐MIRK 4438, J. M. Wilson └NELL 3514, J. Kirk
	└ NELL 6879, W. J. Evans	⌐MOSS 6811, A. Jones └FLY N. R., R. Wood

ROY 7696   *International Supreme Champion 1953*
International Brace Champion 1957
International & Welsh Aggregate Championships 1953
Brace Aggregate Championship 1957
Welsh Brace Champion 1953

MOSS 5176   *International Aggregate Championship 1949*
Scottish Aggregate Championship 1949 & 1951

NELL 6879   *International Farmers' Champion 1953*
Brace Aggregate Championship 1956
Welsh Aggregate Championship 1951
Welsh Brace Champion 1951, 1953 & 1956

JAFF 4313   *International & Welsh Driving Champion 1946, 1947 & 1949*
Welsh National Champion 1946 & 1948
Welsh Brace Champion 1946

MINN 3387   *Challis Shield 1952*

MIRK 4438   *International Supreme Champion 1950*
International & Scottish Aggregate Championships 1950
Scottish National Champion 1950

MOSS 6811   *International Aggregate Championship 1952*
Welsh Aggregate Championship 1950 & 1952
Welsh Brace Champion 1952

Alan Jones – a Remarkable Record

One of the most famous Welsh dogs was Alan Jones' Roy 15393, a son of W. J. Evans' Supreme champion, Roy 7696, and grandson of Nell 6879, who was a daughter of Alan's Moss 6811. When only two years old, Roy won the 1959 Welsh National, and two years later he won the Welsh National Championship, Farmers' Championship, Driving Championship, and the Brace Championship, partnered by Spot 9476. He then went on to win the Supreme Championship at Ayr, plus the International and Welsh Aggregate Championships. In 1962, having won the Welsh Brace Championship with Glen 17251, Roy was reserve to Supreme Champion A. T. Lloyds' Garry 17690.

Two years later he and Glen won the Welsh and International Brace Championships, but Roy unfortunately developed a tumour in his back, which was successfully operated on, but left the dog's strength so impaired that he was unable to

run in further trials, although he was able to do ordinary farm work, and lived to a good age.

Alan won the Welsh National in 1962 with Glen; with Lad 44675, in 1971; and with Craig 72737 in 1976, who had been reserve to the Welsh National Champion, Herbert Worthington's Lad 54209, the previous year. In 1977 Craig was reserve to the Supreme Champion, John Thomas' Craig 59425, and made his final team appearance in 1979.

Alan Jones is one of the most consistently successful Welsh contestants, competing from the early 1950s and continuing into the 90s. His first International appearance was in 1951 with Robin 5499, followed in 1952 with Moss 6811, who was reserve to the Supreme Champion D. Daniel's Chip 4924.

Moss and Taff 9248 were both in the 1953 team, and Taff made the team again in 1956, when Spot 9476, a son of J. Gilchrist's Supreme Champion, Spot 3624, was a team member for the first of three consecutive years.

Then came the great Roy 15393, competing in the Welsh team in 1959, 1961 and 1962, followed in 1964 by Glen 17251; Taff 20938 in 1967 and Lad 44675 in 1969. Moss 57707 was in the 1971 team when Lad won the Welsh National Championship, and Moss was reserve to his sire, R. E. Nicholl's Moss 41957, the 1972 Welsh National Champion. Lad was in the 1973 Centenary International, at Bala, where he won the International Farmers' Championship, and his final team place was in 1974.

Spot 97015 was reserve to the 1978 Welsh National Champion, E. N. Davies' Cymro 82447, going on to be third in the Supreme Championship, won by R. Shennan's Mirk 67512.

Alan represented Wales in 1980 with Craig and Spot in the Brace class, and won the International Brace Championship.

He won five Welsh Brace Championships – in 1952 with Robin and Moss; in 1955 with Robin and Jaff 9048; in 1961 with Roy and Spot; in 1962 and 1964 with Roy and Glen; and many other International Sheep Dog Trial awards over the years.

Alan was very seriously ill during 1982, but made a wonderful recovery to resume his winning ways; 1983 saw him once again in the Welsh team with Lad 130299; and in 1985 Vic 117838 was in the team and won the Driving Championship, with Lad also a team mate.

Returning to trials after recovering from a serious operation, Alan had two dogs in the 1986 team – Jess 152391, still under two years old, and Lad who was third in the Supreme Championship, won by T. W. Longton and Bess 101142. Lad was in the team again in 1989, and Alan was a team member in 1992 with Taff 172213, a son of Bwlch Taff 113243, Welsh National Champion in 1980 and 1981.

This is a remarkable record by any standard.

Alan Jones, Welsh Brace Champion, 1952, and W. F. Miles, Winner of the National

*(Left to right) E. N. Davies with Gwen 19455, A. Jones with Roy 15393
and Glen 17251, F. Morgan with Moss 14902 and Lad 14110*

Born 24/11/59   Black, white & tan   A. Jones, Pontllyfni

Awards

International Brace Champion with ROY 15393, 1964
Brace Aggregate Championship with ROY 15393, 1964
Welsh Farmers' Champion 1962
Welsh Brace Champion with ROY 15393, 1962 & 1964

```
                         ┌─ CAP 7594, J. Walker        ┌─ GLEN 3957, S. Banks
                         │                             └─ TIB 4458, S. Banks
  CRAIG 14766, J. Kirk   │
                         │                             ┌─ BILL 9040, J. Kirk
                         └─ NELL 10398, J. Walker      └─ MIST 6815, J. Kirk


                         ┌─ BOB 12684, J. Gilchrist    ┌─ SPOT 7320, J. Gilchrist
                         │                             └─ NELL 10141, G. Hunter
FLY 13632, G. McCormack  │
                         │                             ┌─ JOSS 6618, A. Rogerson
                         └─ MEG 11371, J. Gilchrist    └─ JED 9925, J. Robertson
```

BILL 9040   *International Supreme Champion 1955*
            International Farmers' Champion 1955
            International Aggregate Championship 1955
            Scottish Aggregate Championship 1955
            Exported to America, where he won the North American Championship in 1958
JOSS 6618   *English Shepherds' Aggregate Championship 1953 & 1954*
            English Shepherds' Champion 1953 & 1954

Born 20/12/58   Brown, white & tan   S. Jones, FFestiniog

Awards

Welsh Farmers' Champion 1963
Welsh Brace Champion with SPOT 24432, 1965

JIM 15024, D. McI. Robertson	**NUMBER 6152, D. Murray**	⎡VIC 4368, D. Murray ⎣NELL 4328, W. Jenkins
	QUEEN 6960, D. Murray	⎡VIC 4368, D. Murray ⎣NAN 6349, D. Murray
MEG 13378, A. Logan	**MIRK 10209, J. Robertson**	⎡MIRK 4438, J. M. Wilson ⎣MEG 4966, R. Balderstone
	QUEEN 6143, L. Coltherd	⎡SPOT 3032, A. Storie ⎣LASSIE 4707, A. Short

NUMBER 6152   *International Brace Champion 1953, 1954 & 1955*
Brace Aggregate Championship 1951, 1953 & 1955
Scottish Brace Champion 1951, 1952, 1953 & 1954

VIC 4368   *International Brace Champion 1953, 1954 & 1955*
International Driving Champion 1951
Brace Aggregate Championship 1951, 1953 & 1955
Scottish National Champion 1952
Scottish Brace Champion 1947, 1951, 1952, 1953 & 1954
Scottish Driving Champion 1950, 1951 & 1952

MIRK 4438   *International Supreme Champion 1950*
International Aggregate Championship 1950
Scottish Aggregate Championship 1950
Scottish National Champion 1950

GWEN 19455

Born 22/4/59   Black & white   E. N. Davies, Yspytty

Awards
Welsh Shepherds' Aggregate Championship 1961 & 1962
Welsh Shepherds' Champion 1961
Welsh Farmers' Champion 1964
Welsh Driving Champion 1962
Challis Shield 1964

	┌MOSS 8307, E. N. Davies	┌MOSS 6811, A. Jones └FLY 8037, A. Jones
KEN 11575, E. N. Davies	│	
	└SPY 8308, E. Holland	┌GLEN 6456, S. Roberts └CHARM 6233, S. Roberts
	┌PATCH 6531, T. S. Roberts	┌SWEEP 4702, G. Pugh └JESS 5177, T. S. Roberts
SUE 19434, E. Jones	│	
	└BET 9584, R. J. Davies	┌CAP 6602, J. Jones └JUNO 4869, R. J. Davies

MOSS 6811   *International Aggregate Championship 1952*
         Welsh Aggregate Championship 1950 & 1952
         Welsh Brace Champion 1952
SWEEP 4702   *Welsh Aggregate Championship 1948*
JUNO 4869   *Challis Shield 1957*

(Left to right) Jaff I, Jaff II, Nip 17278 and Jaff III

Born 18/4/60   Black, white & mottled   E. W. Edwards, Cefn Goch

Awards

Welsh Aggregate Championship 1965
Welsh Farmers' Champion 1965
Challis Shield 1965

PATCH 6531, T. S. Roberts	SWEEP 4702, G. Pugh	BOY 3890, W. Little FLY 3794, G. Redpath
	JESS 5177, T. S. Roberts	JAFF 4313, R. J. Hughes MEG 4386, G. Pugh
MEG 7817, G. T. Jones	JIM 5869, I. Jones	RON 5572, M. Roberts QUEEN 4477, W. B. Bagshaw
	DOVEY 6702, R. Williams	JEFF 4371, J. Jones DOVEY 4189, R. Davies

SWEEP 4702   *Welsh Aggregate Championship 1948*
JIM 5869   *Welsh Brace Champion 1954*
JAFF 4313   *International & Welsh Driving Champion 1946, 1947 & 1949*
       Welsh National Champion 1946 & 1948
       Welsh Brace Champion 1946
JEFF 4371   *Welsh Brace Champion 1949*

Born 2/3/57   Black, white & tan   W. H. Goodwin, Denbigh

Awards

Welsh Shepherds' Champion 1966

	┌ COON 8042, D. McLeod	┌ GARRY 3699, D. McLeod └ NAN 6094, D. McLeod
SAM 11326, W. Jones ┤		
	└ FLY 9248, A. McCormack	┌ RYE 4479, A. McCormack └ LARK 5806, J. Anderson
	┌ DAVE 9139, N. Manning	┌ MOSS 5176, J. M. Wilson └ QUEEN 6143, L. Coltherd
PEGGY 12463, T. Jones ┤		
	└ NELL 6916, N. Manning	┌ GLEN 3940, J. M. Wilson └ JOY 5290, K. Wood

GARRY 3699   *Scottish Shepherds' Aggregate Championship 1948*
International & Scottish Shepherds' Champion 1946

MOSS 5176 *International Aggregate Championship 1949*
Scottish Aggregate Championship 1949 & 1951
GLEN 3940 *International Supreme Champion 1946 & 1948*
International Farmers' Champion 1948
International Aggregate Championship 1946 & 1948
Scottish Aggregate Championship 1946 & 1948
Scottish National Champion 1946

W. Goodwin with Nap 18186

Born 9/3/60   Black, tan & white   H. J. Worthington, Abergavenny

Awards

International Supreme Champion 1963
International & Welsh Aggregate Championships 1963
Welsh Farmers' Champion 1967
Welsh Driving Champion 1964 & 1965

	┌ROY 7696, W. J. Evans	⌈MAC 5498, J. Evans ⌊MEG 6782, G. Jones
HEMP 13132, H. J. Worthington	└FLOSS 8582, H. J. Worthington	⌈LAD 6393, J. R. Millar ⌊BESS 6547, A. Lambie
	┌MOSS 4975, H. J. Worthington	⌈BEN 2812, J. Holmes ⌊MEG 4449, J. Holmes
FLY 12570, H. J. Worthington	└FLOSS 8582, H. J. Worthington	⌈LAD 6393, J. R. Millar ⌊BESS 6547, A. Lambie

HEMP 13132   *International Brace Champion 1960 & 1961*
               Brace Aggregate Championship 1960 & 1961
               Welsh Shepherds' Champion & Brace Champion 1959
FLY 12570   *International Shepherds' Champion 1959*
               International Brace Champion 1960 & 1961
               Brace Aggregate Championship 1960 & 1961

ROY 7696 *International Supreme Champion 1953*
·   *International Aggregate Championship 1953*
         International Brace Championship 1957
         Brace Aggregate Championship 1957
         Welsh Aggregate Championship 1953
         Welsh Brace Champion 1953
MOSS 4975 *International Shepherds' Champion 1951 & 1953*
         Welsh Shepherds' Aggregate Championship 1953 & 1954
         Welsh Shepherds' Champion 1949, 1951, 1953 & 1954

H. Worthington with Fly 12570 (left) and Hemp 13132 (right)

Herbert Worthington and his Dogs

Herbert Worthington's 1963 Supreme Champion, Juno 17815, was the first bitch to win the supreme accolade since W. J. Wallace's Jed I 1492 won the 1938 International. Juno, home-bred by Hemp 13132, out of Fly 12570, the 1959 International Shepherds' Champion, has not, perhaps, received the recognition she deserves, for her trial successes were impressive. She was Welsh National Champion in 1967; ninth in 1963; and second in the 1964, 1965, and 1969 Nationals. Her record in the Supreme Championship is equally impressive, for apart from her victory, she was tenth in 1964, seventh in 1965, and fourth in 1969. She also won the Welsh Driving Championships in 1964 and 1965.

Her sire, Hemp was 1959 Welsh Shepherds' Champion, gaining a place in the Welsh team, and was placed fifth in the Supreme Championship. Hemp was second to Fly in the 1959 International Shepherds' Championship, at which Fly won the Welsh Shepherds' Aggregate Championship. In partnership they were also Welsh Brace Champions, and won the 1960 and 1961 International Brace and Welsh Brace Aggregate Championships.

Both Fly and Hemp were out of Floss 8582, the former by Moss 4975, and Hemp by W. J. Evans' 1953 Supreme Champion, Roy 7696. Fly was in the 1960 team when Herbert, no longer employed as a shepherd, competed in the Farmers' Class, and the following year she was third in the Supreme Championship, won by Alan Jones and Roy 15393, son of W. J. Evans' Roy 7696.

Herbert Worthington's International Sheep Dog Trial successes began with Kep 4264, winning the 1946 Welsh Shepherds' Championship. Moss 4975 won the same award in 1949, 1951, 1953 and 1954, and was International Shepherds' Champion in 1951 and 1953, also winning the Welsh Shepherds' Aggregate Championship in 1953 and 1954

Maid 3677, a granddaughter of J. M. Wilson's Cap 3036, and also of Skeldon's Robbie 2743, was the 1950 Welsh Shepherds' Champion. Then Jaff 10855, a full brother to Fly, won the 1956 Welsh Shepherds', and Welsh Shepherds' Aggregate Championships, and was second in the International Shepherds' Championship.

In 1963 when Juno was Supreme Champion, Herbert Worthington won the Welsh Driving Championship with Hemp's son, Hemp II 24641, litter brother to Mrs Carpenter's Brocken Robbie 24636.

In 1970 Fly II 46113, daughter of Brocken Robbie, gained a team place and was Welsh Driving Champion.

Lad 54209, a grandson of J. Gilchrist's Scottish National Champion of 1965 and 1966, won the 1975 Welsh National, having been in the team in 1971, 1972 and 1974, going on to be eighth in the Supreme Championship in both 1971 and 1974, and winning the 1971 Welsh Aggregate Championship. Herbert was in the Welsh team in 1976 with Lad and, his daughter, Meg 78875.

ROY II 38227 R.O.M. Abergavenny

Jackie Baker with Roy

Born 7/4/63 Black, white & tan J. M. Baker, Cowbridge

Awards
Welsh Farmers' Champion 1968
Welsh Driving Champion 1966

ROY 14402, J. M. Baker	┌**ROY 7696, W. J. Evans**	┌**MAC 5498, J. Evans** └**MEG 6782, G. Jones**
	└**MERRY 11688, J. M. Baker**	┌**BEN 5592, D. Dickson** └**PHIL 6252, D. Dickson**
FAN N. R., R. Williams		

ROY 7696 *International Supreme Champion 1953*
International Aggregate Championship 1953
International Brace Champion 1957
Brace Aggregate Championship 1957
Welsh Aggregate Championship 1953
Welsh Brace Champion 1953

Born 1/12/63   Black, white, tan & mottled   L. R. Suter, Cross Keys

Awards

Welsh Farmers' Champion 1969

	WHITEHOPE NAP 8685, J. M. Wilson	GLEN 6123, W. McClure MEG 5141, W. McClure
SCOT 12017, L. R. Suter		
	JINTY 7481, W. Wardrop	TOSS 4059, J. Pollock NELL 5912, J. Drennan
FAN N. R., G. Edwards		

WHITEHOPE NAP 8685   *Scottish National Champion 1955*

Born 30/9/61   Black & white   M. R. Page, Llangadog

Awards

Welsh Farmers' Champion 1970

	┌ ROY 8993, J. J. Templeton	┌ ROY 4921, J. Purdie
		└ MOSS 5018, J. J. Templeton
ROY 16894, T. Swan		
	└ NELL 13595, T. Swan	┌ WHITEHOPE NAP 8685, J. M. Wilson
		└ NELL 9602, J. Anderson
	┌ CAP 9742, T. Swan	┌ CAP 3036, J. M. Wilson
		└ FAY 3961, J. Harvey
JILL 16896, T. Swan		
	└ MEG 10588, W. Wilson	┌ MOSS 5176, J. M. Wilson
		└ FLY 6141, J. McWhirter

ROY 8993   *International Aggregate Championship 1957—equal points with MOSS 11029*
           Scottish Aggregate Championship 1957 & 1959
           Scottish National Champion 1957
           Scottish Brace Champion 1958
WHITEHOPE NAP 8685   *Scottish National Champion 1955*
MOSS 5176   *International Aggregate Championship 1949*
           Scottish Aggregate Championship 1949 & 1951

Born 19/8/66   Black, white & tan   A. Jones, Pontllyfni

Awards

International Farmers' Champion 1973
Welsh Farmers' Champion 1971
Welsh Driving Champion 1969
Challis Shield 1971

	BROCKEN ROBBIE 24636, Mrs. E. B. Carpenter	HEMP 13132, H. Worthington BROCKEN MEG 13025, C. W. Carpenter
TAFFY 38314, T. J. Watkins		
	FLEECE 22145, T. J. Watkins	HEMP 13132, H. Worthington FLY 12570, H. Worthington
	HEMP 13132, H. Worthington	ROY 7696, W. J. Evans FLOSS 8582, H. Worthington
FLY 20919, R. E. Nicholls		
	PHIL 11264, A. T. Lloyd	MOSS 8754, J. M. Wilson NELL 10934, G. Anderson

HEMP 13132   *International Brace Champion 1960 & 1961*
               Brace Aggregate Championship 1960 & 1961
               Welsh Shepherds' & Welsh Brace Champion 1959

FLY 12570   *International Shepherds' Champion 1959*
               International Brace Champion 1960 & 1961
               Brace Aggregate Championship 1960 & 1961
               Welsh Shepherds' Aggregate Championship 1959
               Welsh Brace Champion 1959

ROY 7696   *International Supreme Champion 1953*
               International & Welsh Aggregate Championships 1953
               International Brace Champion 1957
               Brace Aggregate Championship 1957
               Welsh Brace Champion 1953

Born 9/1/66   Black, tan & white   R. E. Nicholls, Llandrindod Wells

Awards

Welsh Farmers' Champion 1972

BROCKEN ROBBIE 24636, Mrs. E. B. Carpenter	HEMP 13132, H. Worthington	ROY 7696, W. J. Evans FLOSS 8582, H. Worthington
	BROCKEN MEG 13025, C. W. Carpenter	BEN 9474, Miss E. B. Hirst LASSIE 9868, Miss E. B. Hirst
FLY 34035, J. James	ROY 15393, A. Jones	ROY 7696, W. J. Evans JILL 7742, W. J. Evans
	TOT 17564, J. James	ROY 12187, J. Roderick FLY 13970, T. Lloyd

HEMP 13132   *International Brace Champion 1960 & 1961*
Brace Aggregate Championship 1960 & 1961
Welsh Shepherds' & Welsh Brace Champion 1959

ROY 15393   *International Supreme Champion 1961*
International Farmers' Champion 1961
International Brace Champion 1964
International Aggregate & Welsh Aggregate Championships 1961
Brace Aggregate Championship 1964
Welsh National Champion 1959 & 1961
Welsh Farmers' & Driving Champion 1961
Welsh Brace Champion 1961, 1962 & 1964
Challis Shield 1959 & 1961

ROY 7696   *International Supreme Champion 1953*
International & Welsh Aggregate Championships 1953
International Brace Champion 1957
Brace Aggregate Championship 1957
Welsh Brace Champion 1953

E. B. CARPENTER

Born 16/10/70   Black, tan & white   M. R. Page, Llangadog

Awards

Welsh Shepherds' Aggregate Championship 1974 & 1978
Welsh Shepherds' Champion 1973, 1974 & 1978
Welsh Brace Champion with FLY 108143, 1980

ROY 45152, C. Storey	WISTON CAP 31154, J. Richardson	CAP 15839, J. Richardson FLY 25005, W. S. Hetherington
	JILL 33862, T. Anderton	ROB 21959, T. Longton MEG 24631, W. Miller
FLY 34035, J. James	ROY 15393, A. Jones	ROY 7696, W. J. Evans JILL 7742, W. J. Evans
	TOT 17564, J. James	ROY 12187, J. Roderick FLY 13970, T. Lloyd

WISTON CAP 31154 *International Supreme Champion 1965*
International Shepherds Champion 1966
Scottish Driving Champion 1969

ROY 15393 *International Supreme Champion 1961*
International Farmers' Champion 1961
International Brace Champion 1964
International Aggregate & Welsh Aggregate Championships 1961
Brace Aggregate Championship 1964
Welsh National Champion 1959 & 1961
Welsh Farmers' & Welsh Driving Champion 1961
Welsh Brace Champion 1961, 1962 & 1964
Challis Shield 1959 & 1961

ROB 21959 *International Brace Champion 1969*
Brace Aggregate Championship 1969
English Brace Champion 1968 & 1969

E. B. CARPENTER

Born 4/12/69   Black & white   A. G. Jones, Bryncroes

Awards

Welsh Farmers' Champion 1974
Challis Shield 1974

```
                          ┌SPOT 24981, J. Gilchrist   ┌BOB 12684, J. Gilchrist
CRAIG 47577, E. Griffith  │                           └WISTON NAN III 9896, P. McG. Hepburn
                          │
                          └MIST 39205, J. Bathgate    ┌ROCK 27425, J. Bathgate
                                                      └BUNT 20762, J. Cole

                           WISTON CAP 31154,          ┌CAP 15839, J. Richardson
FLY 49709, J. R. Griffith │ J. Richardson             └FLY 25005, W. S. Hetherington
                          │
                          └JESS 19648, J. Williams    ┌ROY 15393, A. Jones
                                                      └JESS 16713, R. Davies
```

SPOT 24981   *International Aggregate & Scottish Aggregate Championships 1966*
                 Scottish Shepherds' Aggregate Championship 1966
                 Scottish National & Scottish Shepherds' Champion 1965 & 1966
WISTON CAP 31154   *International Supreme Champion 1965*
                        International Shepherds' Champion 1966
                        Scottish Driving Champion 1969

ROY 15393 *International Supreme Champion 1961*
International Farmers' Champion 1961
International Brace Champion 1964
International Aggregate & Welsh Aggregate Championships 1961
Brace Aggregate Championship 1964
Welsh National Champion 1959 & 1961
Welsh Farmers' & Driving Champion 1961
Welsh Brace Champion 1961, 1962 & 1964
Challis Shield 1959 & 1961

Grant Jones and Tos 61152

236

E. B. CARPENTER

Born 14/8/68   Black & white   H. Worthington, Abergavenny

Awards

Welsh Farmers' Champion 1975
Challis Shield 1975

ROY 46408, D. I. Owen	SPOT 24981, J. Gilchrist	BOB 12684, J. Gilchrist
		WISTON NAN III 9896, P. McG. Hepburn
	BETT 29419, L. Morrison	BEN 19222, L. Morrison
		TIB 16764, L. Morrison
CORA 28589, S. P. Davies	JOCK 23439, S. P. Davies	SWEEP 18537, D. I. Owen
		KIM 19628, S. P. Davies
	FAN 23438, S. P. Davies	SWEEP 18537, D. I. Owen
		KIM 19628, S. P. Davies

SPOT 24981   *International Aggregate & Scottish Aggregate Championships 1966*
Scottish Shepherds' Aggregate Championship 1966
Scottish National & Scottish Shepherds' Champion 1965 & 1966

E. B. CARPENTER

Born 28/2/72   Black & white   A. Jones, Pontllyfni

Awards

International Farmers' Champion 1977 & 1979
International Brace Champion with SPOT 97015, 1980
International Driving Champion 1975 & 1976
Brace Aggregate Championship with SPOT 97015, 1980
Feedmobile Challenge Cup 1977
McDiarmid Trophy 1976 & 1977
Pedigree Chum Silver Salver 1979
Welsh Farmers' Champion 1976
Welsh Driving Champion 1975, 1976 & 1977
Challis Shield 1976

```
                          ┌ MOSS 41957, R. E. Nicholls    ┌ BROCKEN ROBBIE 24636, Mrs. E. B. Carpenter
                          │                               └ FLY 34035, J. James
MOSS 57707, A. Jones ─────┤
                          │                               ┌ ROY 21287, A. Jones
                          └ NELL 39432, R. G. Evans       └ NELL 30477, A. Jones

                          ┌ CRAIG 47577, E. Griffith      ┌ SPOT 24981, J. Gilchrist
                          │                               └ MIST 39205, J. Bathgate
NELL 61154, D. Owen ──────┤
                          │                               ┌ WISTON CAP 31154, J. Richardson
                          └ FLY 49709, J. R. Griffith     └ JESS 19648, J. Williams
```

MOSS 41957   *Welsh National & Welsh Farmers' Champion 1972*
SPOT 24981   *International Aggregate & Scottish Aggregate Championships 1966*
                 Scottish Shepherds' Aggregate Championship 1966
                 Scottish National & Scottish Shepherds' Champion 1965 & 1966
WISTON CAP 31154   *International Supreme Champion 1965*
                 International Shepherds' Champion 1966
                 Scottish Driving Champion 1969
NELL 61154 *is litter sister to Welsh National Champion, TOS 61152*

Born 18/12/69   Black & white   J. R. Thomas, Llandovery

Awards

International Supreme Champion 1977
International Shepherds' Champion 1976 & 1977
International Aggregate Championship 1976 & 1977
Welsh Shepherds' Aggregate Championship 1973, 1975, 1976 & 1977
Welsh Aggregate Championship 1976 & 1977
Captain Whittaker Outwork Cup 1977
R. Fortune Trophy 1977
Lord Mostyn Plate 1977
ISDS Blue Riband 1977
Pedigree Chum Supreme Championship Trophy 1977
Welsh Shepherds' Champion 1976 & 1977
Challis Shield 1977

CHIP 29946, L. Suter	┌ **BILL 16633, D. L. Evans**	┌ MOSS 4975, H. Worthington └ FLOSS 8582, H. Worthington
	└ **MEG 19713, R. H. Williams**	┌ ROY 14402, J. M. Baker └ MEG 16167, J. M. Baker
JILL 49652, H. Hawken	┌ **GARRY 19382, A. Chapman**	┌ CAP 7594, J. Walker └ NELL 15388, J. Kirk
	└ **JESS 37142, H. Hawken**	┌ CHIP 29946, L. Suter └ NELL 23235, H. Hawken

MOSS 4975   *International Shepherds' Champion 1951 & 1953*
Welsh Shepherds' Aggregate Championship 1953 & 1954
Welsh Shepherds' Champion 1949, 1951, 1953 & 1954

John Thomas' Craig 59425, the 1977 Supreme Champion and Welsh National Champion, became one of the modern key dogs of the breed. Craig was Welsh and International Shepherds' Champion in 1976 and 1977.

John moved across the Welsh Marshes to shepherd in England, and with Cap 91526, a son of Craig, he won the 1981 English and International Driving Championships, and was the 1982 English Shepherds' Champion. In the terrific gale that lashed the 1983 Aberystwyth International, Cap was second to the Supreme Champion, Tot Longton's Jess 88627, so close to emulating his sire's success.

Don 108889 was probably the best known son of Craig, and was himself a well proven stud dog.

His dam, D. Jones' Maid 97071, was by W. Welsh's 1978 Scottish Shepherds' Champion, Don 73710.

Don 108889 was English Shepherds' Champion in 1984, and he was paternal grandsire to R. Dalziel's 1989 and 1992 Supreme Champion, Wisp 161487.

John Thomas won the 1985, 1986 and 1989 Shepherds' Championships with Moss 127211, who was also English and International Driving Champion in 1986 and 1989; was ninth in the 1986 Supreme Championship; and was a team member again in 1990.

Craig's grandson, Joss 152124, was the 1988 English Shepherds' and Driving Champion; a team member the following year; and the English Shepherds' Champion in 1991 and 1992.

Craig 59425

240

CREATIVE PHOTOGRAPHERS

Born 20/11/73   **Black & white**   **E. N. Davies, Penmachno**

Awards

Welsh Farmers' Champion 1978
Challis Shield 1978

KEN 51524, Mrs. J. Davies	┌ ROY 15393, A. Jones	┌ ROY 7696, W. J. Evans └ JILL 7742, W. J. Evans
	└ SHAN 47523, E. N. Davies	┌ ROY 35976, E. N. Davies └ GWEN 19455, E. N. Davies
TESS 64075, Mrs. A. Edwards	┌ ROBIN 26091, E. Griffith	┌ SHEP 18504, T. Watson └ LASS 11655, J. Wood
	└ HEINI 33444, Mrs. A. Edwards	┌ ARAIL 17804, T. Edwards └ FFION 19623, T. Edwards

ROY 15393   *International Supreme Champion 1961*
                 International Farmers' Champion 1961
                 International Brace Champion 1964
                 International Aggregate & Welsh Aggregate Championships 1961
                 Brace Aggregate Championship 1964
                 Welsh National Champion 1959 & 1961
                 Welsh Farmers' & Driving Champion 1961
                 Welsh Brace Champion 1961, 1962 & 1964
                 Challis Shield 1959 & 1961

ROY 7696 *International Supreme Champion 1953*
International Aggregate & Welsh Aggregate Championships 1953
International Brace Champion 1957
Brace Aggregate Championship 1957
Welsh Brace Champion 1953

GWEN 19455 *Welsh Shepherds' Aggregate Championship 1961 & 1962*
Welsh Shepherds' Champion 1961
Welsh National & Farmers' Champion 1964
Welsh Driving Champion 1962
Challis Shield 1964

Cymro 82447

Born 23/5/71 Black & white M. Jones, Ruthin

Awards

International Brace Champion with BEN 105608, 1979
Brace Aggregate Championship with BEN 105608, 1979
Welsh Farmers' Champion 1979
Welsh Driving Champion 1979
Challis Shield 1979

CRAIG 47577, E. Griffith
— SPOT 24981, J. Gilchrist
— BOB 12684, J. Gilchrist
— WISTON NAN III 9896, P. McG. Hepburn
— MIST 39205, J. Bathgate
— ROCK 27425, J. Bathgate
— BUNT 20762, J. Cole

NELL 43755, W. T. Williams
— ROBIN 26091, E. Griffith
— SHEP 18504, T. Watson
— LASS 11655, J. Wood
— QUEEN 37247, D. T. Evans
— CRAIG 23995, W. King
— TESS 18268, W. King

SPOT 24981 *International Aggregate & Scottish Aggregate Championships 1966*
Scottish Shepherds' Aggregate Championship 1966
Scottish National & Scottish Shepherds' Champion 1965 & 1966

BWLCH TAFF 113243

AUSTIN BENNETT

Born 15/4/79   Black, white & tan   H. G. Jones, Bodfari

Awards

Captain Whittaker Outwork Cup 1982
Feedmobile Trophy 1982
McDiarmid Trophy 1982
Welsh Farmers' Champion 1980 & 1981
Challis Shield 1980 & 1981
W. J. Jones Trophy 1980, 1981 & 1982

GLEN 92091, H. G. Jones	GLEN 62253, D. MacDonald	GLEN 15845, J. Lothian FLOSS 58139, D. MacDonald
	LASS 62964, D. MacDonald	WISTON CAP 31154, J. Richardson BESS 25575, J. A. Cameron
BWLCH BRACKEN 74660, Mrs B. Jones	WISTON CAP 31154, J. Richardson	CAP 15839, J. Richardson FLY 25005, W. S. Hetherington
	SHEBA 33229, Mrs B. Jones	TWEED 12324, H. Rutter WENDY 23844, H. G. Jones

BWLCH BRACKEN 74660 *Welsh Brace Champion 1974*
WISTON CAP 31154 *International Supreme Champion 1965*
International Shepherds' Champion 1966
Scottish Driving Champion 1969
GLEN 62253 *Scottish National & Scottish Shepherds' Champion 1974*
Alexander Andrew Trophy 1974

Glyn Jones and His Dogs

It was perhaps fitting that the International Centenary Trial at Bala, close to the course on which the first sheepdog trial had been held in 1873, should be won by a Welshman. H. G. Jones was the victor, with Gel 63023. He had previously won the 1968 International Farmers' Championship with Hemp 36879, who was fourth in the Welsh National and qualified to compete in the Supreme Championship.

Glyn Jones and Gel were second in the 1975 Supreme Championship, won by R. C. MacPherson and Zac 66166; and Glen 92091 qualified to compete in the 1977 Supreme Championship. The following year Gel and Bwlch Bracken 74660, who were a superb partnership, were second in the International Brace Championship.

Young Bwlch Taff 113243, won the 1980 National, and having won the 1981 National, he was fifth in the Supreme Championship, won by E. W. Edwards and Bill 78263.

Cap 144844, a son of Bwlch Taff, qualified to compete in the 1990 Supreme Championship, and 1991 saw Taff 167290 gain fourth place in the Supreme Championship. In 1993 Cap and Taff competed in the International Brace Championship.

Born 22/2/78   Black, white & tan   M. R. Page, Brechfa

Awards

Welsh Shepherds' Aggregate Championship 1982
Welsh Shepherds' Champion 1982
Welsh Driving Champion 1982
Challis Shield 1982

	BROCKEN ROBBIE 24636, Mrs E. B. Carpenter	HEMP 13132, H. Worthington BROCKEN MEG 13025, C. W. Carpenter
ROBBIE 38315, T. J. Watkins	FLEECE 22145, T. J. Watkins	HEMP 13132, H. Worthington FLY 12570, H. Worthington
	ROY 45152, C. Storey	WISTON CAP 31154, J. Richardson JILL 33862, T. Anderson
NELL 65799, M. R. Page	FLY 34035, J. James	ROY 15393, A. Jones TOT 17564, J. James

NELL 65799 *Welsh Shepherds' Aggregate Championship 1974 & 1978*
Welsh National Champion 1973
Welsh Shepherds' Champion 1973, 1974 & 1978
Welsh Brace Champion 1980

HEMP 13132 *International Brace Champion 1960 & 1961*
Brace Aggregate Championship 1960 & 1961
Welsh Shepherds' & Welsh Brace Champion 1959

FLY 12570 *International Shepherds' Champion 1959*
International Brace Champion 1960 & 1961
Brace Aggregate Championship 1960 & 1961
Welsh Shepherds' Aggregate Championship 1959
Welsh Brace Champion 1959

WISTON CAP 31154 *International Supreme Champion 1965*
International Shepherds' Champion 1966
Scottish Driving Champion 1969

ROY 15393 *International Supreme Champion 1961*
International Farmers' Champion 1961
International Brace Champion 1964
International Aggregate & Welsh Aggregate Championships 1961
Brace Aggregate Championship 1964
Welsh National Champion 1959 & 1961
Welsh Farmers' & Welsh Driving Champion 1961
Welsh Brace Champion 1961, 1962 & 1964
Challis Shield 1959 & 1961

Mel Page and Nell 65799

M. R. Page's 1973 Welsh National and Shepherds' Champion, Nell 65799, a grand-daughter of Wiston Cap, proved herself to be an important brood bitch of the 1970s, in addition to her many trials successes. She was Welsh Shepherds' Champion in 1974 and 1978, and was in the Welsh Shepherds' Class in 1975. With her daughter, Fly 108143, she won the 1980 Welsh Brace Championship.

Cap 108145 – a litter brother to Fly, and sired by T. J. Watkins' Robbie 38315, who was litter brother to T. T. McKnight's Jaff 38313 – won the 1982 National and Driving Championships. He and Fly became a successful brace partnership

Mel Page's first National Champion was Sweep 23470, in 1970, a grandson of J. Templeton's Roy 8993, and in 1987 he was a team member with Joe 141919, a son of Dryden Joe 104626.

Born 10/11/77   Black & white   G. Williams, Mold

Awards

Welsh Farmers' Champion 1983
Challis Shield 1983

SPOT 97015, A, Jones
┌ MIRK 67258, J. Sandilands
│   ┌ MIRK 52844, J. Richardson
│   └ HOPE 46550, A. Kinloch
└ FLY N. R., J. M. Orr

JESS 102611, A. Owen
┌ CARLO 36705, R. G. Jones
│   ┌ MICK 19770, R. G. Jones
│   └ WENDY 33921, W. H. Jones
└ NELL N.R.

MIRK 52844   *International Shepherds' Champion 1975*
Scottish Shepherds' Aggregate Championship 1975
Scottish National & Scottish Driving Champion 1975
Scottish Shepherds' Champion 1973 & 1975
Alexander Andrew Trophy 1975
J. M. Wilson Challenge Shield 1975
CARLO 36705   *Welsh Shepherds' Aggregate Championship 1969*
MICK 19770   *Welsh Shepherds' Champion 1963*

G. Williams

Born 13/2/79   Black & white   J. P. Burke, Llandinam

Awards

Welsh Shepherds' Aggregate Championship 1984
Welsh Shepherds' Champion 1984
Welsh Driving Champion 1984
Challis Shield 1984

	┌ MOSS 64806, R. Short	┌ BEN 41202, R. Short └ MAID 25490, A. Reid
SWEEP 85943, P. Miller		
	└ JED 46647, R. Short	┌ TAM 21767, R. Short └ LIZ 37009, R. Wood
	┌ GLEN 76918, J. Dyson	┌ WISTON CAP 31154, J. Richardson └ SHIAN 63194, J. G. Jones
TOPSY 96503, J. P. Burke		
	└ JESS 74443, J. P. Burke	┌ MOSS 32667, J. Morgan └ JUDY 41114, J. P. Burke

SWEEP 85943 *English Farmers' Champion 1978*
GLEN 76918 *International Shepherds' Champion 1981*
Welsh Shepherds' Aggregate Championship 1981
Captain Whittaker Outwork Cup 1976
LIZ 37009 *International Shepherds' & Scottish Shepherds' Champion 1971*
Scottish Shepherds' Aggregate Championship 1971
Scottish Aggregate Championship 1974
Scottish Driving Champion 1974
WISTON CAP 31154 *International Supreme Champion 1965*
International Shepherds' Champion 1966
Scottish Driving Champion 1969

J. P. Burke with (left to right) Hemp 96504, Glen 113361 and
Jaff 123036

B. CARPENTER

Born 3/10/81   Black & white   A. Owen, Corwen

Awards

Welsh Aggregate Championship 1985
Welsh Farmers' Champion 1985
Challis Shield 1985
Welsh Driving Champion 1987

RHAIADR ZAC 94341, Miss A. Edwards	REX 78894, A. Jones	ROY 44716, J. G. Jones MEED 72955, J. G. Jones
	RHAIADR FLY 81521, E. Humphreys	WISTON CAP 31154, J. Richardson GAEL 63451, E. Humphreys
FAN 102412, R. Williams	MOSS 84044, S. Jones	WISTON CAP 31154, J. Richardson GYP 56601, T. Longton
	MEG 71772, W. Williams	CRAIG 47577, E. Griffith NELL 43755, W. T. Williams

WISTON CAP 31154   *International Supreme Champion 1965*
International Shepherd's Champion 1966
Scottish Driving Champion 1969
MEED 72955 *is litter sister to MEG 72953, granddam of SPOTAN 134842,*
1986 Welsh National Champion

AUSTIN BENNETT

Born 6/4/82   Black, white & tan   H. Owen, Caergeilliog

Awards

Welsh Shepherds' Aggregate Championship 1986
Welsh Shepherds' Champion 1986
Challis Shield 1986

DON 89257, J. G. Jones	ROY 44716, J. G. Jones	MOSS 37282, A. R. Williams / NELL 28340, H. Griffiths
	MEG 72953, J. G. Jones	WISTON CAP 31154, J. Richardson / SHIAN 63194, J. G. Jones
DOT 110512, H. Owen	MAC 70288, H. Davies	CRAIG 47577, E. Griffith / DOT 50036, H. Owen
	JILL 66841, O. Jones	ROBBIE 38315, R. T. Watkins / QUEENIE 50304, R. E. Nicholls

WISTON CAP 31154   *International Supreme Champion 1965*
International Shepherds' Champion 1966
Scottish Driving Champion 1969

Born 25/3/82   Black & white   G. Jones, Penmachno

Awards

International Supreme Champion 1990
International Farmers' Champion 1990
Captain Whittakers Outwork Cup 1990, equal points with DON 141536
Lord Mostyn Plate 1990
R. Fortune Plate 1990
International Aggregate Championship 1990
Welsh Aggregate Championship 1990
Blue Riband 1990
Rhwilas Cup 1990
Pedigree Chum Supreme Championship Trophy 1990
Pedigree Chum Silver Salver 1990
Welsh Driving Champion 1990
Welsh Farmers' Champion 1987
Challis Shield 1987

			CRAIG 47577, E. Griffith
		MOSS 72131, J. Millner	MEG 44766, T. J. Jones
LAD 91117, J. M. Evans			NAP 29213, C. Lloyd
	JUNNO 39329, J. M. Evans	NELL 26622, J. M. Evans
			MOSS 57707, A. Jones
JILL 110568, R. O. M., M. Knight	CRAIG 72737, A. Jones	NELL 61154, D. Owen
			VICK 74888, E. Griffith
	BONNY 96510, C. Lloyd	FLOSS 74698, D. E. Morgan

CRAIG 72737   *International Farmers' Champion 1977 & 1979*
International Brace Champion 1980
International Driving Champion 1975 & 1976
Brace Aggregate Championship 1980
Feedmobile Challenge Cup 1977
McDiarmid Trophy 1976 & 1977
Pedigree Chum Silver Salver 1979
Welsh National & Welsh Farmers' Champion 1976
Welsh Driving Champion 1975, 1976 & 1977
Challis Shield 1976

Gwyn Jones' Queen 152483, the 1990 Supreme Champion, represented Wales in 1986, and in 1987 when she was National Champion; in 1988, and 1990 when she was second to Hefin Jones' Meg 135659, National Champion both years; and also in 1992. Queen was fifth in the 1988 Supreme Championship won by Meirion Jones and Spot 152290, and Meg was third, and she was also third in the 1989 National, won by M. Owen and Rock 162204

Gwyn Jones is one of only three men to have won the Supreme Championship on three occasions. J. M. Wilson won nine Supreme Championships, three of them with Roy 1665, the only dog in all these years to have won so many times. Away back prior to World War I, Thomas Armstrong won the 1911 and 1914 Supreme Championship with Don 17, and the 1912 Championship with Sweep 21.

In 1974 Gwyn Jones' first Supreme Champion, Bill 51654, a son of Wiston Cap, was second in the Welsh National, won by Captain A. G. Jones and Tos 61152, and was Welsh and International Driving Champion. Bill was also in the 1976 Welsh team, when Shep 73360, became Supreme Champion. Shep was in the 1975 team, and was fourth in the 1978 Supreme Championship, won by R. Shennan and Mirk 67512, and he qualified to compete in the 1982 Supreme Championship.

Meg 12746, a granddaughter of J. Thomas' 1977 Supreme Champion, Craig 59425, was Gwyn Jones' next team dog, and she was fourth in the 1984 National. Gwyn was a team member with Davidson Kirk 153106, a son of D. Guild's Tweed 92756, in 1991.

Born 1/9/82   Black & white   H. W. Jones, Dollgellau

Awards

Welsh Farmers' Champion 1988 & 1990
Challis Shield 1988 & 1990

	┌MAC 74384, J. D. Jones	┌GLEN 62253, D. MacDonald └LASS 62964, D. MacDonald
PATCH 94433, I. Edwards	└NELL 74105, R. Bebb	┌ROY 59989, R. Bebb └NELL 59984, A. Jones
	┌ROY 88481, R. Brooks	┌JIM 73694, G. Lewis └FLEECE II 47535, R. G. Evans
JESS 105102, H. Humphreys	└JESS 92776, J. Ritchie	┌GLEN 73404, B. Bowden └TESS 85919, R. Bagley

GLEN 62253   *Scottish National & Scottish Shepherds' Champion 1974*
Alexander Andrew Trophy 1974
ROY 88481   *Welsh Driving Champion 1980*

ROCK 162204

1989   **ROCK 162204**   **Bala**

B. HAMER – COURTESY OF WSN

Born 16/5/86   Black, white & tan   D. I. Owen, Llanarthneg, Handler – M. Owen

Awards

Welsh Farmers' Champion 1989
W. J. Jones Trophy 1989

VIC 128240, J. Bathgate	ROY 114678, J. J. Templeton	MOSS 103923, J. J. Templeton / LASS 92191, T. Stevenson
	JEN 106069, J. Barr	HEMP 72301, A. J. Campbell / QUEEN 74047, H. Mackenzie
MIST 143619, A. Aitchison	DRYDEN JOE 104626, R. Dalziel	GLEN 75630, R. Fortune / DRYDEN QUEEN 70345, A. Macgregor
	MAID 120920, J. Keith	MOSS 103210, J. Murray / LASS 97910, D. McMillan

VIC 128240   *Scottish Shepherds' Aggregate Championship 1984*
                      Scottish Driving Champion 1984

256

ROY 114678 *International Farmers' Champion 1985, 1987 & 1989*
International Aggregate Championship 1985
Brace Aggregate Championship 1984
International Brace Champion 1984
International Driving & Scottish Driving Champion 1983 & 1987
Scottish Aggregate Championship 1981, 1982, 1983 & 1985
Feedmobile Trophy 1985 & 1989
McDiarmid Trophy 1981, 1985 & 1989
Captain Whittaker Outwork Cup 1987 & 1989
Pedigree Chum Silver Salver 1985 & 1987
Scottish National & Scottish Farmers' Champion 1982, 1983 & 1985
Scottish Brace Champion 1982, 1983 & 1984
Alexander Andrew Trophy 1982, 1983 & 1985
J. M. Wilson Challenge Shield 1982, 1983 & 1985

DRYDEN JOE 104626 *International Shepherds' Champion 1985*
Scottish Shepherds' Aggregate Championship 1985
Scottish National Champion 1986
Scottish Shepherds' Champion 1979 & 1986
Scottish Driving Champion 1986
Alexander Andrew Trophy 1986
J. M. Wilson Challenge Shield 1986

MOSS 103923 *Scottish Aggregate Championship 1979*
Feedmobile Challenge Cup 1979

HEMP 72301 *Scottish Driving Champion 1977*

GLEN 75630 *Scottish Brace Champion 1977*

ARVID PARRY JONES, COURTESY WSN

Born 1/11/83   Black & white   J. Lightfoot, Llandegla

Awards

Welsh Farmers' Champion 1991
Challis Shield 1991
Allison Award 1991

ELIAN JAFF 125519, R. Davies	┌ RISP 117139, E. N. Davies	┌ MOSS 91079, T. Bowey └ SPEY 99226, W. Ellwood
	└ NEL 98448, M. Hughes	┌ SWEEP 84612, D. Owen └ MEG II 73654, J. Ritchie
TESS 92026, R. Davies	┌ RHAIADR GEL 77261, R. Davies	┌ CAP 64980, E. Humphreys └ NAN 71652, E. Humphreys
	└ MEG 63296, K. Timson	┌ FLASH 53360, J. Roberts └ DOT 53295, R. Roberts

AUSTIN BENNETT

Born 17/4/86   Black & white   E. L. Daniel, Ystradgynlais

Awards

Welsh Farmers' Champion 1992
Challis Shield 1992

DRYDEN JOE 104626, R. Dalziel	**GLEN 75630,** R. Fortune	**CAP 67230, T. T. McKnight** / **SHELL 68768, T. T. McKnight**
	DRYDEN QUEEN 70345, A. McGregor	**SPOT 24981, J. Gilchrist** / **CHRIS 60920, A. McGregor**
NELL 127824, D. Jones	**MOSS 103210, J. Murray**	**GARRY II 72575, D. McTeir** / **FLY 93882, C. Napier**
	QUEEN 103721, D. McDougall	**DUFFY 69699, W. Stevenson** / **MIDGE 96931, W. Stevenson**

DRYDEN JOE 104626   *Scottish Shepherds' Champion 1979*
Scottish National Champion 1986
Scottish Shepherds' Champion 1986
Scottish Driving Champion 1986
Alexander Andrew Trophy 1986
J. M. Wilson Challenge Shield 1986

GLEN 75630 *Scottish Brace Champion with JILL 55741, 1977*
SPOT 24981 *International, Scottish & Scottish Shepherds' Aggregate Championships 1966*
Scottish National & Scottish Shepherds' Champion 1965 & 1966
GARRY II 72575 *Scottish Driving Champion 1980*

E. L. Daniel with Fly 163488

AUSTIN BENNETT

AUSTIN BENNETT

Born 17/10/88   Black, white & tan   B. Evans, Llanfarian

Awards

Welsh Shepherds' Aggregate Championship 1993
Welsh Shepherds' Champion 1993
Challis Shield 1993

CAP 157134, T. W. Japp	ROY 143966, W. Jones	MAC 116944, W. Jones
		JET 108199, R. Evans
	MEG 140531, E. Jones	BILL 120444, A. Jones
		GEM 100349, A. Jones
SIAN 160343, Mrs S. Gibson	ELIAN JAFF 125519, R. Davies	RISP 117139, E. N. Davies
		NEL 98448, M. Hughes
	JILL 136584, R. Jones	RHAIADR ZAC 94341, Miss A. Edwards
		JILL 118825, R. Davies

Irish National Winners

Irish Sheepdog Trials – The Early Years

Away back in 1888 a sheepdog trial was held in conjunction with a Dublin dog show, and ten years later a trial was held in Belfast, judged by Mr Piggin of Nottingham, who was involved in bench showing of collies. He owned show champion, and sheepdog trials winner, Ormskirk Charlie. In amongst the English competitors only one Irish dog was entered in this trial, but it did not actually compete.

A Northern Ireland Sheepdog Trial Society was formed in 1908 but there is no information about any of its trials. In 1923 the Clonmel Kennel Club invited Mr James Reid to advise on the promotion of sheepdog trials, and he and Alex Millar judged the first Clonmel Kennel Club trial in October 1924, when a dozen Irish competitors took part. The following year Mr Reid and Thomas Dickson judged, thirty-one Irish dogs competing, and demonstrations were given by T. Dickson with his famous dogs Hemp 153 and Foozle 350, Hemp having won the 1924 International Farmers' Championship and Foozle having won the same award the previous year.

Several other trials were held around this time, but it was in 1926 that the Clonmel K. C. inaugurated a meeting of interested parties from Eire and Northern Ireland, and under its auspices a third trial was held at Clonmel in September.

This was the beginning of the Irish trial circuit, which has gone from strength to strength. The Isle of Man enthusiasts compete in the Irish Nationals, though they hold their own Island Championship, and the 1970 Irish National was held on the Isle of Man.

Lionel Pennefather

The 'father' of Irish trials, G. L. Pennefather, was a spectator at the 1926 Clonmel trial, and has been involved with dogs and trials ever since. He has won the Irish National on five occasions, the first time in 1931 with Spy 1137, bred by J. B. Bagshaw. Spy accompanied Lionel Pennefather to South Africa in 1936, where he gave many demonstrations. Of the five dogs taken on this trip, only Spy was brought back to Ireland. In 1968 and again in 1980 Lionel Pennefather returned to South Africa, giving more of his popular demonstrations.

He won his second Irish National in 1938 with Ben, a son of Alex Millar's Ben 891. He initiated the moves for Northern Ireland's acceptance into the International Sheep Dog Society, which came about in 1961. This first affiliated National was won by J. McKee and Snip 10677, and three Irish dogs went forward to the International.

In 1962 Lionel Pennefather, J. McKee and E. Wright were elected as the first three Northern Ireland Directors of the International Sheep Dog Society, Lionel Pennefather being President. He won the Irish National that year with Bess 17145, who was also Irish National Champion in 1966 when the Irish National was first held in Eire, and twice reserve champion. She became the first Irish finalist to compete in the Supreme Championship.

Lionel Pennefather and E. Wright attended the 1964 Directors' meeting at Carlisle, following which the former was elected to the Council of the International Sheep Dog Society, and in 1965 the Republic of Ireland and Northern Ireland agreed to organise an annual Irish National trial, to be held alternately in each country.

Lionel Pennefather represented Ireland in the popular 'Daily Express' trials. In partnership with Snip 21772, Bess won the 1964 Irish Brace Championship, and she was 1963 Driving Champion, and Snip won the 1965 Driving Championship.

Fortunately, very few handlers work their dogs under fire, but Lionel Pennefather was working Maid at Killerton, Co Tyrone, when the field was straffed with gunfire from a passing car. Everyone, including Lionel Pennefather, flung themselves to the ground, but Maid, quite unconcerned by the flying bullets, stood calmly waiting for her master's commands. Shaken, he got up and carried on with his course, and was delighted when Maid was proclaimed the winner.

In 1983 the International Sheep Dog Society presented Lionel Pennefather with the Wilkinson Sword in honour of his tremendous contribution to sheepdog trials, particularly in Ireland. Now well into his eighties, this amazing man, who celebrated his eighty-second birthday by winning a trial with a home-bred bitch, still retains his interest in sheepdog matters, despite suffering with very bad eyesight.

1993 saw the Irish National 'come of age', the team consisting of fifteen competitors, in keeping with the other teams, sixty dogs running in the International Qualifying Trials.

L. Pennefather's Spy 1137

L. Pennefather's Ben

Lionel Pennefather receiving the Wilkinson Sword, 1983

MARJORIE QUARTON

Born 4/3/54   Black & white   J. W. McKee, Hillsborough

Awards

Irish Brace Champion with DAN 15485, 1962

LAD 9828, W. E. Dixon	┌ **BEN 7693, M. Moore**	┌ LAD 2036, C. Holmes └ JEAN 7648, J. Holmes
	└ **GUESS 5391, M. Moore**	┌ KEN 5337, M. Moore └ FLEECE 5338, M. Moore
SPY 9544, W. E. Dixon	┌ **CAP 6360, J. Relph**	┌ CAP 3036, J. M. Wilson └ GYP 4554, J. Relph
	└ **MERRIE 6880, J. Warwick**	┌ MOSS 4551, Capt. J. D. McPherson └ SNIP 4341, W. Jolly

MOSS 4551   *English Driving Champion 1947 & 1948*

After winning the first Irish National of 1961, with Snip 10677, Lyn McKee was second in the 1962 National with Whitehope Corrie 13706, won by Lionel Pennefather and Bess 17145. L. McKee also won the Brace Championship that year with Snip and Dan 15485. Whitehope Corrie, purchased from J. M. Wilson, was Irish National Champion in 1963, with Lionel Penne-father and Bess second. In 1966 Bess was Champion and Corrie was second, as he was also in 1967, and he was third in 1964.

Lyn McKee has been involved with the Irish and International Sheep Dog Society committees over many years, and he was once more a member of the Irish team in 1990, with Moss 139699.

BESS 17145

Born 4/12/58   Black & white   G. L. Pennefather, Ardmore

Awards

Irish Brace Champion with SNIP 21772, 1964
Irish Driving Champion 1963

MOSS 12265, G. Capstick	ROY 9518, W. Walters	TILLYOCHIE MOSS 7878, T. Bonella FLY 6864, T. Bonella
	MEG 8166, W. Walters	MOSS 4575, T. Mathias LASSIE 4799, T. Mathias
DOROTHY 14608, E. Metcalfe	LAD 11027, J. Chapman	SHEP 6107, J. K. Gorst LADY N. R., J. Baines
	SPY 9544, W. E. Dixon	CAP 6360, J. Relph MERRIE 6880, J. Warwick

LAD 11027   *International & English Driving Champion, 1957*
TILLYOCHIE MOSS 7878   *Scottish National Champion, 1956*

1963   # WHITEHOPE CORRIE 13706   Barenscourt

Born 26/5/56   Black & white   J. W. McKee, Dromore

GLEN 12917, H. Porter	┌JIM 5856, R. Swan	┌DRIFT 4380, J. R. Millar └MEG 5623, D. Young
	└FLO 5038, J. T. M. Thomson	┌ROVER 2308, W. Caig └MAID, J. T. M. Thomson
NELL 12916, H. Porter	┌GARRY 4915, J. Anderson	┌GLEN 3957, S. Banks └TIB 4458, S. Banks
	└NELL 6086, J. R. Hislop	┌NICKEY 3626, T. Watson └NELL 4100, T. Lothian

DRIFT 4380   *Scottish National Champion 1947*
Scottish Driving Champion 1946

E. B. CARPENTER

269

BUFF 23069

Born 9/8/60   Brown & white   J. Brady, Ballynure

Awards

Irish Driving Champion 1964, 1967 & 1968

WHITEHOPE CORRIE 13706, J. McKee	GLEN 12917, H. Porter	JIM 5856, R. Swan FLO 5038, J. T. M. Thomson
	NELL 12916, H. Porter	GARRY 4915, J. Anderson NELL 6086, J. R. Hislop
LASS 12974, J. Brady	KEP 8094, R. Dunn	MIRK 5444, J. McDonald CHRIS 4065, J. Cole
	JESS 7926, J. Brady	MICK 7039, J. Brady NELL 3854, F. Morten

WHITEHOPE CORRIE 13706   *Irish National Champion 1963*
MIRK 5444   *International Supreme Champion 1954*
Scottish Shepherds' Aggregate Championship 1952

The Bradys

In 1964 and 1967 Jim Brady won the Irish Nationals with Buff 23069, a red son of Whitehope Corrie, and again in 1970 with Buff's daughter Gyp 33128, who was fourth in 1968. Buff was Irish Driving Champion in 1964, 1967 and 1968, and was third in the 1963 team. J. Brady and Shane 57767, were in the 1971 and 1976 teams, and were second in 1978, and team members again in 1980 and 1981.

The 1972 and 1973 Nationals were won by J. Brady and Bosworth Jim 52007, a son of Bosworth Coon 34186, the 1968 Supreme Champion. Bosworth Jim, the first Irish dog to win an International award, was International Farmers' Champion in 1972, and seventh in the Supreme Championship; and International

Driving Champion in 1973, having won the Irish Driving Championships in both these years.

J. Brady's Risp 45699, a grandson of W. Hardisty's English National Champion Jim 12967, was second in the 1969 and 1970 Irish Nationals; 1970 Irish Driving Champion; fourth in the Supreme Championship at the Centenary International; and fifth in the 1976 Supreme Championship, where he was also International Farmers' Champion.

With Meg 99400, J. Brady competed in the 1979 National, and they were second in the 1980 National, his son David being third, just half a point behind, with Meg 81598, a daughter of J. Richardson's Scottish Shepherds' Champion, Sweep 39603. In 1982 Jim Brady represented Ireland with Eve 112604, and in 1985 with Jim 125956.

David Brady and Meg were in the 1974 and 1982 Irish teams, and he and Kris 94235, were also members of the 1974 team.

The family moved to Scotland in 1986 and now compete in the Scottish Nationals.

J. Brady with Buff 23069

Born 24/3/60   Black & white   J. F. Mullan, Co. Derry

GLEN 12917, H. Porter	⌈JIM 5856, R. Swan	⌈DRIFT 4380, J. R. Millar ⌊MEG 5623, D. Young
	⌊FLO 5038, J. T. M. Thomson	⌈ROVER 2308, W. Caig ⌊MAID J. T. M. Thomson
NELL 12916, H. Porter	⌈GARRY 4915, J. Anderson	⌈GLEN 3957, S. Banks ⌊TIB 4458, S. Banks
	⌊NELL 6086, J. R. Hislop	⌈NICKEY 3626, T. Watson ⌊NELL 4100, T. Lothian

DRIFT 4380   *Scottish National Champion 1947*
Scottish Driving Champion 1946

NELL 16949 *was full sister to WHITEHOPE CORRIE 13706,*
Irish National Champion 1963

The First 'All Ireland' Trial

Prior to 1965 the Irish National trials had been confined to handlers from Northern Ireland, but that year an 'All Ireland' trial was held, including handlers from Eire and the Isle of Man – henceforth a full Irish National – which was won by J. F. Mullan and Nell 16949. She was a full sister, from a later litter, to Whitehope Corrie, and was third in the 1966 and 1969 Nationals, and fourth in the 1967 National.

Born 28/3/66   White & black   J. H. Logan, Belfast

BUFF 23069, J. Brady	**WHITEHOPE CORRIE** **13706, J. McKee**	⌈GLEN 12917, H. Porter ⌊NELL 12916, H. Porter
	LASS 12974, J. Brady	⌈KEP 8094, R. Dunn ⌊JESS 7926, J. Brady
NELL 27847, P. O'Kane	ROY 17176, T. Brown	⌈TWEED 9601, W. J. Evans ⌊SNIP 10677, J. McKee
	SHEILA 15826, P. O'Kane	⌈SPOT 7321, J. Sharp ⌊MEG 10327, J. T. M. Thomson

BUFF 23069   *Irish National Champion 1964 & 1967*
    Irish Driving Champion 1964, 1967 & 1968
WHITEHOPE CORRIE 13706   *Irish National Champion 1963*
TWEED 9601   *International Supreme Champion 1958*
    International Aggregate Championship 1958
    English Aggregate Championship 1958
    English National Champion 1959
    English Driving Champion 1961
    English Brace Champion 1958 & 1960
SNIP 10677   *Irish National Champion 1961*
    Irish Brace Champion 1962

Born 9/2/62   Black & white   J. H. Logan, Belfast

Awards

Irish Brace Champion with JOCK II 16687, 1967
Irish Brace Champion with TRIM 52587, 1971
Irish Driving Champion 1966

(*continued*)

```
                              ┌DALE 15200, N. McKenzie      ┌SCOTT 11166, J. Anderson
                              │                             └TIB 11512, A. Beattie
DON 16475, N. McKenzie        │
                              └MOSSIE 11164, D. Guild       ┌MIRK 6084, J. Johnstone
                                                            └FLY 7081, D. Guild

                              ┌DICK 15431, A. Beattie       ┌CAP 7594, J. Walker
                              │                             └NELL 13205, R. Osborne
JEN 20501, H. Stewart         │
                              └TESS 17554, A. Paterson      ┌DAVE 12348, J. Fleming
                                                            └NELL 13934, A. McKie
```

1970   GYP 33128   Isle of Man

Born 1/3/64   Brown & white   J. Brady, Ballynure

```
                              WHITEHOPE CORRIE             ┌GLEN 12917, H. Porter
                              13706, J. McKee             └NELL 12916, H. Porter
BUFF 23069, J. Brady          │
                              └LASS 12974, J. Brady        ┌KEP 8094, R. Dunn
                                                           └JESS 7926, J. Brady

                              ┌JIM 12967, W. Hardisty      ┌LADDIE 8049, W. Goodfellow
                              │                            └MERRIE 6880, J. Warwick
JILL 22018, J. Brady          │
                              └MEG 19190, T. Harper        ┌FLINT 13049, G. L. Pennefather
                                                           └MISS 12765, G. L. Pennefather
```

BUFF 23069   *Irish National Champion 1964 & 1967*
Irish Driving Champion 1964, 1967 & 1968
WHITEHOPE CORRIE 13706   *Irish National Champion 1963*
JIM 12967   *English National Champion 1961*
J. H. Thorp Memorial Trophy 1961
LADDIE 8049   *Scottish National Champion 1958*

J. McSwiggan with (left to right) Spark
29370, Rock 36024, Flash 34399,
Tam 26504 and Lynn 28622

Born 25/1/65   Brown & white   J. McSwiggan, Gorticastle

Awards

Irish Brace Champion with LYNN 28622, 1969
Irish Brace Champion with CHAD 52621, 1972

TAM 26504, J. McSwiggan	┌JIM 17459, W. Barfoot	┌CRAIG 14766, J. Kirk └FLY 13632, G. McCormack
	└MEG 16984, A. Wilson	┌SAM 13329, J. Rutherford └QUEEN 9008, J. Harper
LYNN 28622, J. McSwiggan	┌WHITEHOPE CORRIE 13706, J. McKee	┌GLEN 12917, H. Porter └NELL 12916, H. Porter
	└BESS 17145, G. L. Pennefather	┌MOSS 12265, G. Capstick └DOROTHY 14608, E. Metcalfe

TAM 26504   *Irish Brace Champion 1965*
LYNN 28622   *Irish Brace Champion 1969*
WHITEHOPE CORRIE 13706   *Irish National Champion 1963*
BESS 17145   *Irish National Champion 1962 & 1966*
       Irish Brace Champion 1964
       Irish Driving Champion 1963

BOSWORTH JIM 52007 Clonmany
Onchan, I.O.M.

Born 23/5/68   Black, white, tan & mottle   J. Brady, Ballynure

Awards

International Farmers' Champion 1972
International Driving Champion 1973
Irish Driving Champion 1972 & 1973

BOSWORTH COON 34186, L. Evans	**BOSWORTH SCOT 22120,** L. Evans	BEN 13864, R. MacKay LASS 11713, D. Dickson
	FLY 13724, L. Evans	HAIG 9190, T. Jones FLY 9731, R. Davies
FLOSS 48501, L. Evans	**BROCKEN ROBBIE 24636,** Mrs E. B. Carpenter	HEMP 13132, H. Worthington BROCKEN MEG 13025, C. W. Carpenter
	FLY 34035, J. James	ROY 15393, A. Jones TOT 17564, J. James

BOSWORTH COON 34186 *International Supreme Champion 1968*
International Farmers' Champion 1969
International Aggregate Championship 1969
English Aggregate Championship 1968 & 1969
Captain Whittaker Outwork Cup 1968
English National & English Farmers' Champion 1969
J. H. Thorp Memorial Trophy 1969
BOSWORTH SCOT 22120 *International Driving Champion 1962*
HAIG 9190 *Welsh Driving Champion 1960*

HEMP 13132 *International Brace Champion 1960 & 1961*
Brace Aggregate Championship 1960 & 1961
Welsh Brace & Welsh Shepherds' Champion 1959
ROY 15393 *International Supreme Champion 1961*
International & Welsh Aggregate Championships 1961
International Brace Champion 1964
Brace Aggregate Championship 1964
International Farmers' Champion 1961
Welsh National Champion 1959 & 1961
Welsh Farmers' & Driving Champion 1961
Welsh Brace Champion 1961, 1962 & 1964
Challis Shield 1959 & 1961

J. Brady with Bosworth Jim

JIM 67676

MARC HENRIE

Born 23/2/71   Black & white   J. H. Logan, Newtonards

Awards

Irish Aggregate Championship 1977 & 1978
Irish Brace Champion with BILL 72574, 1975
Irish Driving Champion 1976

SCOT 28069, G. Young
┌ HEMP 21291, G. Wood ─┬ ROY 15393, A. Jones
│   └ QUEEN 12652, P. Jaffray
└ MIDGE 17786, G. Young ┬ BEN 7346, T. Parker
                        └ SPY 14256, H. Brierley

BESS 52738, R. Henderson
┌ SPOT 24981, J. Gilchrist ─┬ BOB 12684, J. Gilchrist
│   └ WISTON NAN III, 9896, P. McG. Hepburn
└ MEG 38447, R. Henderson ┬ SPOT 14469, W. King
                          └ JEAN 34467, R. Milne

SCOT 28069 *International & Scottish Shepherds' Champion 1969*
            Scottish Shepherds' Aggregate Championship 1969
SPOT 24981 *International Aggregate Championship 1966*
            Scottish Aggregate Championship 1966
            Scottish Shepherds' Aggregate Championship 1966
            Scottish National & Scottish Shepherds' Champion 1965 & 1966
ROY 15393   *International Supreme Champion 1961*
            International Farmers' & Welsh Farmers' Champion 1961
            International Brace Champion 1964
            International & Welsh Aggregate Championships 1961

Brace Aggregate Championship 1964
Welsh National Champion 1959 & 1961
Welsh Driving Champion 1961
Welsh Brace Champion 1961, 1962 & 1964
Challis Shield 1959 & 1961

MARC HENRIE

J. H. Logan with Jim 67676

Born 16/12/71   Black & white   T. Flood, Clonroche

Awards
Irish Brace Champion with NELL 71990, 1976 & 1977
Irish Driving Champion 1975, 1977 & 1979

	┌ RISP 45699, J. Brady	┌ SPOT 24981, J. Gilchrist └ SNIP 21772, J. J. Thompson
SCOT 57965, T. Flood		
	└ NELL 43414, M. O'Neill	┌ FLASH 19291, N. Deacon └ LASSIE 9971, M. Flood
	┌ SPOT 38147, N. Deacon	┌ BUFF 23069, J. Brady └ JILL 22018, J. Brady
COSY 55242, Miss M. Dixon		
	└ JESS 28004, N. Deacon	┌ SPOT 13823, H. Persse └ NELL 17994, N. Deacon

SCOT 57965   *Irish National Champion 1978*
                       Irish Driving Champion 1974 & 1978
                       Clonmany Trophy 1976 & 1977
RISP 45699   *Irish Driving Champion 1970*
NELL 43414   *Irish Aggregate Championship 1974*
                       Irish Driving Champion 1971

SPOT 24981 *International & Scottish Aggregate Championships 1966*
Scottish Shepherds' Aggregate Championship 1966
Scottish National & Scottish Shepherds' Champion 1965 & 1966
BUFF 23069 *Irish National Champion 1964 & 1967*
Irish Driving Champion 1964, 1967 & 1968

Tim Flood with Cosy 70560

1976 **GAY 69947** Peel, I.O.M.

Born 18/8/71 Black & white M. Graham, Ballamodha, I. O. M.

WISTON CAP 31154, J. Richardson	CAP 15839, J. Richardson	COON 10011, J. Richardson LYN 13707, R. Frame
	FLY 25005, W. S. Hetherington	BILL II 17937, J. M. Wilson LASSIE 19421, J. Hogarth
TESS 57400, W. Barnes	FLEET 38813, J. Cropper	ROCK 27425, J. Bathgate TRIM 26864, J. Bonella
	LIZ 37509, A. Todd	MOSS 12088, M. Illingworth MERLE 16232, R. Moore

WISTON CAP 31154   *International Supreme Champion 1965*
International Shepherds' Champion 1966
Scottish Driving Champion 1969
FLEET 38813   *International Brace Champion 1973*
Brace Aggregate Championship 1973
English Driving Champion 1968 & 1970
MOSS 12088   *International Brace Champion 1963*
Brace Aggregate Championship 1963

Born 20/3/69   Black, white & tan   T. Flood, Clonroche

Awards

Irish Driving Champion 1974 & 1978
Clonmany Trophy 1976 & 1977

RISP 45699, J. Brady	SPOT 24981, J. Gilchrist	BOB 12684, J. Gilchrist WISTON NAN III 9896, P. McG. Hepburn
	SNIP 21772, J. J. Thompson	JIM 12967, W. Hardisty FLY 11362, W, Hardisty
NELL 43414, M. O'Neil	FLASH 19291, N. Deacon	LAD 10676, H. Persse MEG 15613, H. Persse
	LASSIE 9971, M. Flood	JIM 6198, J. Evans NELL II 6199, J.Evans

RISP 45699   *Irish Driving Champion 1970*
NELL 43414   *Irish Aggregate Championship 1974*
                 Irish Driving Champion 1971
SPOT 24981   *International & Scottish Aggregate Championship 1966*
                 Scottish Shepherds' Aggregate Championship 1966
                 Scottish National & Scottish Shepherds' Champion 1965 & 1966
JIM 12967   *English National Champion 1961*
                 J. H. Thorp Memorial Trophy 1961
FLY 11362   *English Brace Champion 1957*

FRANK MOYES

T. Flood and Flash with Eric Halsall

Born 16/2/75   Black, white & tan   T. Flood, Clonroche

Awards
Irish Aggregate Championship 1980
Royal Dublin Society Trophy 1980

SCOT 57965, T. Flood	RISP 45699, J. Brady	SPOT 24981, J. Gilchrist SNIP 21772, J. J. Thompson
	NELL 43414, M. O'Neill	FLASH 19291, N. Deacon LASSIE 9971, M. Flood
SUE 83787, T. Flood	ROY 58455, T. Flood	FLASH 19291, N. Deacon LASSIE 9971, M. Flood
	MEG 72167, T. Flood	MOSS 41957, R. E. Nicholls MEG 60360, R. E. Nicholls

SCOT 57965   *Irish National Champion 1978*
                     Irish Driving Champion 1974 & 1978
                     Clonmany Trophy 1976 & 1977
RISP 45699   *Irish Driving Champion 1970'*
NELL 43414   *Irish Aggregate Championship 1974*
                     Irish Driving Champion 1971
SPOT 24981   *International & Scottish Aggregate Championships 1966*
                     Scottish Shepherds' Aggregate Championship 1966
                     Scottish National & Scottish Shepherds' Champion 1965 & 1966
MOSS 41957   *Welsh National & Welsh Farmers' Champion 1972*

Tim Flood with (left to right) Cosy 70560, Pip 124578, Scot 57965 and Flash 106580

Born 18/7/74   Black & white   J. H. Logan, Belfast

Awards

International Driving Champion 1980

GLEN 59859, J. T. Jack	⌐ MOSS 50511, A. Shennan	⌐DON 30938, A. Ainslie └MIDGE 28849, W. Douglas
	└ JILL 52713, A. Grant	⌐SWEEP 39603, J. Richardson └JILL 24285, J. Turner
NELL 56224, J. T. Jack	⌐ WISTON CAP 31154, J. Richardson	⌐CAP 15839, J. Richardson └FLY 25005, W. S. Hetherington
	└ KIM 40213, W. Reid	⌐GLEN 28714, G. Griffiths └KIM 26717, G. Griffiths

WISTON CAP 31154   *International Supreme Champion 1965*
International Shepherds' Champion 1966
Scottish Driving Champion 1969
SWEEP 39603   *International & Scottish Driving Champion 1968*
Scottish Shepherds' Champion 1968

286

Harford Logan

J. H. Logan began his long and successful trials career in International trials with Nell 10656 coming third in the 1962 Irish National, and Nell and Pete 18591 winning the Irish Brace Championship the following year. He won his first National in 1968 with Moy 42363, a daughter of Buff 23069. In 1966 Cap 24328 was second in the National, and was Driving Champion; his kennelmate, Jack II 16687, was also in the team. These two dogs were the 1967 Brace Champions, and in 1969 Cap won the Irish National.

J. H. Logan was in the 1971 team with Trim 52587, a daughter of Risp 45699; and Jim 67676, a grandson of J. Gilchrist's Scottish National Champion, Spot 24981, won the 1974 and 1977 Irish Nationals, and was a member of the teams in 1975, 1978 and 1979. Sweep 87666, a grandson of Wiston Cap, was the 1980 Irish National Champion, and also International Driving Champion.

Harford Logan 'emigrated' to Scotland in 1980, and promptly won the 1981 Scottish National with Star 109497, also gaining a team place with Sweep (the Irish Champion of the previous year), who qualified to compete in the Supreme Championship, coming in ninth position. Star was in the 1982 Scottish team, and qualified to compete in the Supreme Championship.

Residing again in Ireland, J. H. Logan was in the 1992 and 1993 Irish teams with Dick 174159, who was eighth in the 1992 Supreme Championship.

J. H. Logan with Jim and Sweep 87666

DEREK JOHNSON

FRANK MOYES

Born 23/7/76   Black & white   D. O'Sullivan, Clogheen

Awards

Irish Driving Champion 1981
Royal Dublin Society Trophy 1981

SCOT 57965, T. Flood	┌ **RISP 45699, J. Brady**	┌ SPOT 24981, J. Gilchrist └ SNIP 21772, J. J. Thompson
	└ **NELL 43414, M. O'Neill**	┌ FLASH 19291, N. Deacon └ LASSIE 9971, M. Flood
NAN 90121, J. McConnell	┌ **CAP 47822, J. Jack**	┌ MOSS 16138, D. Young └ NELL 22932, J. Jack
	└ **DOT 63999, J. Jack**	┌ DRIFT 51202, T. T. McKnight └ FLY 56678, J. Jack

SCOT 57965   *Irish National Champion 1978*
   Irish Driving Champion 1974 & 1978
   Clonmany Trophy 1976 & 1977
RISP 45699   *Irish Driving Champion 1970*
NELL 43414   *Irish Aggregate Championship 1974*
   Irish Driving Champion 1971
SPOT 24981   *International & Scottish Aggregate Championships 1966*
   Scottish Shepherds' Aggregate Championship 1966
   Scottish National & Scottish Shepherds' Champion 1965 & 1966
DRIFT 51202   *International & Scottish Driving Champion 1970*

Born 10/8/78   Black & white   G. Lutton, Portadown

Awards
Royal Dublin Society Trophy 1982

CHIP 77779, J. McSwiggan
┌ DALE 55615, S. O'Leary
│   ┌ JAFF 38313, T. T. McKnight
│   └ NAN 47878, T. Blacklock
└ LYNN 28622, J. McSwiggan
    ┌ WHITEHOPE CORRIE 13706, J. McKee
    └ BESS 17145, G. L. Pennefather

MOY 75295, W. Watt
┌ MOSS 40688, G. L. Pennefather
│   ┌ GLEN 27311, E. Powles
│   └ ITHON GWENNO 26885, E. Powles
└ MEG 66065, P. Watters
    ┌ SHANE 57767, J. Brady
    └ FLY 61222, P. Watters

CHIP 77779 *International Brace Champion 1977*
Brace Aggregate Championship 1977
Irish Brace Champion 1980
DALE 55615 *Clonmany Trophy 1974*
LYNN 28622 *Irish Brace Champion 1969*
JAFF 38313 *Scottish Brace Champion 1969*
WHITEHOPE CORRIE 13706 *Irish National Champion 1963*
BESS 17145 *Irish National Champion 1962 & 1966*
Irish Brace Champion 1964
Irish Driving Champion 1963

George Lutton with Glen 109694

FRANK MOYES

Born 26/5/78 Black & white J. Irvine, Carrick Fergus

Awards

Irish Driving Champion 1983
Royal Dublin Society Trophy 1983

SHANE 71700, J. Brady	┌ **SPORT 69607, G. Stevenson, R. O. M.**	┌ Unknown └ Unknown
	└ **FLY 61222, P. Watters**	┌ **BEN 19887, A. Martin** └ **FLOW 41412, A. Martin**
MEG 81598, J. Brady	┌ **SWEEP 39603, J. Richardson**	┌ **WISTON CAP 31154, J. Richardson** └ **LASSIE 23501, J. McDonald**
	└ **GALE 64174, J. Wallace**	┌ **MIRK 50347, A. Buist** └ **JEN 56912, A. Buist**

SWEEP 39603 *International Driving Champion 1968*
Scottish Shepherds' Champion 1968
Scottish Driving Champion 1968
WISTON CAP 31154 *International Supreme Champion 1965*
International Shepherds' Champion 1966
Scottish Driving Champion 1969

1984	**PIP 124578**	**Mahon Bridge**
1988		**Castlewellan**
1989		**Cashel**

Born 15/9/80   Black, white & tan   T. Flood, Clonroche

Awards

International & Irish Brace Champion with FLASH 149178, 1989
International & Irish Driving Champion 1988
International Aggregate Championship 1984
Irish Aggregate Championship 1984
Feedmobile Challenge Cup 1984
Irish Driving Champion 1989
Royal Dublin Society Trophy 1984, 1988 & 1989

SCOT 57965, T. Flood
    ┌ RISP 45699, J. Brady
            ┌ SPOT 24981, J. Gilchrist
            └ SNIP 21772, J. J. Thompson
    └ NELL 43414, M. O'Neill
            ┌ FLASH 19291, N. Deacon
            └ LASSIE 9971, M. Flood

MIDGE 99535, T. Flood
    ┌ ROY 58455, T. Flood
            ┌ FLASH 19291, N. Deacon
            └ LASSIE 9971, M. Flood
    └ MEG 72167, T. Flood
            ┌ MOSS 41957, R. E. Nicholls
            └ MEG 60360, R. E. Nicholls

SCOT 57965	*Irish National Champion 1978*
	Irish Driving Champion 1974 & 1978
	Clonmany Trophy 1976 & 1977
RISP 45699	*Irish Driving Champion 1970*
NELL 43414	*Irish Aggregate Championship 1974*
	Irish Driving Champion 1971
SPOT 24981	*International & Scottish Aggregate Championships 1966*
	Scottish Shepherds' Aggregate Championship 1966
	Scottish National & Scottish Shepherds' Champion 1965 & 1966
MOSS 41957	*Welsh National & Welsh Farmers' Champion 1972*

Tim Flood

One of Ireland's most successful handlers is Tim Flood, who, with home-bred dogs, has been a team member for many years. His famous dog Scot 57965, a grandson of J. Gilchrist's Scottish National Champion, Spot 24981, sired many of Ireland's successful trial dogs, five of his off-spring having won Irish Nationals.

In 1972, 1974 and in 1975, Scot, a son of J. Brady's Risp 45699, and M. O'Neill's Nell 43414, was third in the Nationals. Scot, aged nine, was entered in the 1978 National instead of Cosy 70560, who was lame with arthritis, and after several previous placings won the Irish National Championship, and went on to be ninth in the Supreme Championship. He won the 1974 and 1978 Irish Driving Championships.

Cosy, a daughter of Scot, won the 1975 National, and was Driving Champion in 1975, 1977 and 1979, and she and Nell 71990, were Irish Brace Champions in 1976 and 1977. Cosy was second in the 1977 National, and a member of the 1979 and 1980 teams.

Flash 10658, a son of Scot, won the 1979 National and was a member of the 1980 team, coming eighth in the Supreme Championship. Craig 108412, was a team member in 1981, 1982 and 1983.

Tim Flood then won the 1984, 1988 and 1989 Nationals with Pip 124578, another son of Scot, and he was reserve to the 1984 Supreme Champion, W. Reed's Turk 118169. Pip was second in the 1985 National, and was the Driving Champion in 1988 and 1989.

With Pip and Flash, Tim Flood won the 1989 Irish and International Brace Championships. To continue this 'family's' successes, Dun 163303, a son of Pip, was fourth in the 1991 National.

Tim Flood, a quiet, cheery man, was an All Ireland Hurler of great distinction before he became interested in the sheepdog trials, at which he has certainly gained distinction.

1985   **EVE 112604**   **Douglas, I.O.M.**

Born 20/1/79   Black & white   D. Birchall, Dunlavin

Awards

Irish Aggregate Championship 1982, 1987 & 1989
Royal Dublin Society Trophy 1985

SCOT 57965, T. Flood	┌ RISP 45699, J. Brady	┌ SPOT 24981, J. Gilchrist └ SNIP 21772, J. J. Thompson
	└ NELL 43414, M. O'Neill	┌ FLASH 19291, N. Deacon └ LASSIE 9971, M. Flood
NELL 109735, W. Hallinan	┌ ROY 76015, A. Quinsey	┌ LADDIE 52423, T. Kealy └ NELL 49704, T. Kealy
	└ EVE 68978, S. O'Leary	┌ DALE 55615, T. Blacklock └ BET 59306, T. Blacklock

SCOT 57965   *Irish National Champion 1978*
               Irish Driving Champion 1974 & 1978
               Clonmany Trophy 1976 & 1977
RISP 45699   *Irish Driving Champion 1970*
NELL 43414   *Irish Aggregate Championship 1974*
               Irish Driving Champion 1971
SPOT 24981   *International & Scottish Aggregate Championships 1966*
               Scottish Shepherds' Aggregate Championship 1966
               Scottish National & Scottish Shepherds' Champion 1965 & 1966

Dennis Birchall

Dennis Birchall has been very successful in Irish Nationals, with three particular dogs, since he first gained a place with Kate 101410, in the 1981 team. She was equal second with Tim Flood's Pip, in the 1985 National, won by her kennelmate, Eve 112604, all three dogs sired by Tim Flood's Scot. Kate was placed ninth in the Supreme Championship, and partnered by Mist 109678, won the International Brace Championship. These two were Irish Brace Champions in 1982, 1983 and 1985.

Eve was a sister to John Templeton's Max 110507, who was third in the 1980 Supreme Championship, and later was sold to a handler in the USA. Eve was second in the 1982 and 1983 Nationals; third in 1988 and 1989, and fourth in 1987, and qualified to compete in the 1989 Supreme Championship.

Mist was a team member in 1983 as well as winning the Brace Championship. D. Birchall competed in the 1991 and 1992 teams with Jan 188256, a daughter of Mist.

D. Birchall with Eve 112604

J. Brennan with Meg 126291 (left) and Jet 122421 (right)

Born 14/11/80   Black & white   J. Brennan, Templemore

Awards

Irish Driving Champion 1986

BOUY 69273, R. Potter	⌐**LADDIE 40729, E. F. Morgan**	⌐**LADDIE 31172, P. Wilson** └**JEAN 17607, C. Bright**
	└**NELL 38711, W. Beaton**	⌐**ROY 16206, W. Cuthbert** └**TESS 23793, W. Cuthbert**
FAWSLEY BECK 76744, **R. Potter**	⌐**BRIGHT 57274, E. F. Morgan**	⌐**MIRK 43493, S. B. Price** └**JEAN 17607, C. Bright**
	└**FLY 37136, F. Collins**	⌐**LADDIE 14110, E. F. Morgan** └**GWEN 32695, R. Fitch**

LADDIE 40729   *English Shepherds' Champion 1969*
LADDIE 14110   *International Shepherds' & English Shepherds' Champion 1961*
                      English Shepherds' Aggregate Championship 1961

Born 22/11/79   Black & white   E. Feeney, Grange

Awards

Royal Dublin Society Trophy 1987

CRAIG 72737, A. Jones	┌**MOSS 57707, A. Jones**	┌**MOSS 41957, R. E. Nicholls** └**NELL 39432, R. G. Evans**
	└**NELL 61154, D. Owen**	┌**CRAIG 47577, E. Griffith** └**FLY 49709, J. R. Griffith**
NELL 87092, J. P. Leonard	┌**MIRK 43230, A. MacPherson**	┌**BEN 15884, R. C. MacPherson** └**LADY 15484, R. C. Tulip**
	└**MAID 73859, W. Cormack**	┌**BILL 43389 W. Cormack** └**JUNE 59734, W. Cormack**

CRAIG 72737	*International Farmers' Champion 1977 & 1979*
	International Brace Champion 1980
	International Driving Champion 1975 & 1976
	Brace Aggregate Championship 1980
	Feedmobile Challenge Cup 1977
	McDiarmid Trophy 1976 & 1977
	Pedigree Chum Silver Salver 1979
	Welsh National & Welsh Farmers' Champion 1976
	Welsh Driving Champion 1975, 1976 & 1977
	Challis Shield 1976
MOSS 41957	*Welsh National & Welsh Farmers' Champion 1972*
JUNE 59734	*Scottish National & Scottish Farmers' Champion 1973*
	Alexander Andrew Trophy 1973
NELL 61154	*is litter sister to Welsh National Champion, TOS 61152*

Born 22/12/83   Black, white, tan & mottle   T. Lambe, Enniscorthy

Awards

Irish Aggregate Championship 1990
Royal Dublin Society Trophy 1990

ROY 124575, J. Lambe	┌ SCOT 57965, T. Flood	┌ RISP 45699, J. Brady └ NELL 43414, M. O'Neill
	└ MIDGE 99535, T. Flood	┌ ROY 58455, T. Flood └ MEG 72167, T. Flood
FLY 135863, D. Duggan	┌ GLEN 74392, W. Hanbidge	┌ JAFF 59516, W. Hanbidge └ NELL 46463, R. Sheane
	└ GYP 94198, W. Hanbidge	┌ MOSS 75344, J. W. McKee └ PATCH 78426, J. W. McKee

SCOT 57965   *Irish National Champion 1978*
Irish Driving Champion 1974 & 1978
Clonmany Trophy 1976 & 1977
RISP 45699   *Irish Driving Champion 1970*
NELL 43414   *Irish Aggregate Championship 1974*
Irish Driving Champion 1971

The Watt Trio

As there are certain 'families' of dogs that are successful in the trial world, so there are human families in which the art of successful sheepdog handling continues through the generations. One such family in Ireland is the shepherding Watt trio – father William, and sons Gordon and Barton.

William Watt was third in the 1978 National with Moy 75295, who was fourth in the 1979 team, when fifteen-year-old Gordon was second with Chum 93897, a son of his father's Moy. Gordon was the youngest Irish competitor to compete at an International, and he won the Irish Young Handlers' Award for six consecutive years, the first award being in 1978. In 1985 and 1986 his younger brother, Barton, won this award, competing at his first National when sixteen years old, with Moy 128083, a daughter of his father's Moy. In the 1986 National, Barton and Moy were second, and she was also in the 1987 National team.

Gordon Watt was the Irish Shepherds' Champion in 1981 and 1982 with Rose 99231, a daughter of Lad 80955 and Moy 75295, and Rose was the 1982 Driving Champion. With Chip 122248, Gordon was second in the 1989 National.

William Watt won the 1980 and 1985 Irish Shepherds' Championship with Lad 80955, and Chip 130670 respectively. Chip, a son of Lad, was also Irish and International Driving Champion, and Lad and his son Craig 99232, won the 1981 Irish Brace Championship.

George Lutton's 1982 Irish National Champion, Glen 109694, was a son of William Watt's Moy 75295, and Glen was a team member in 1985 and 1987, and Ben 196195, his son, was in the 1993 team, and was the Irish Driving Champion.

The Byrnnes, Junior and Senior

Father and son, Pat Byrnne senior and Pat Byrnne junior, have both been regular members of the Irish teams, Pat Byrnne senior, competing with Nip 159288 in 1989 and also in the 1991, 1992 and 1993 teams. With Dot 151515, a daughter of J. Templeton's Roy 114678, Pat Byrnne junior was second in the 1988 and 1993

Nationals, Dot being tenth in the 1988 Supreme Championship. She was also in the team on several other occasions. In partnership with Star 166276, Dot won the 1990 Irish Brace Championship.

Teenage Handlers

Ireland seems to produce numerous teenage handlers, capable of creditable performances in the Nationals. The youngest competitor so far has been twelve-year-old Alistair Lyttle with two-and-a-half-year-old Kate, in 1987, and they represented Ireland in the International Young Handlers' Trial.

Toddy Lambe proved his early potential by winning the 1990 Irish National Championship with Nell 146196, a granddaughter of Tim Flood's Scot, when only twenty-one, and became the youngest competitor to ever compete in the Supreme Championship. His first appearance on the trial field was in 1983, and in 1984 he represented Ireland in the International Young Handlers' Trial with Susie 138200, a daughter of Tim Flood's Cosy 70560. Nell represented Ireland on several occasions.

Irish-bred Dogs

As the interest in Irish sheepdog trials has increased over the years, so too has the standard of competition improved, and many of the modern trial dogs are Irish-bred for several generations, and distinct 'families' are being formed. Many present-day handlers are regular team members, often competing for several years with the same dogs – to mention a few – J. P. McFadden with Glen 127946 and Lyn 168527; J. Brennan with Meg 126291 and Del 166557; J. Irvine with Shep 109351, son of J. Brady's Shane and David Brady's black Meg; and G. Lutton with Glen 109694. Meanwhile the competitive strength of the Irish teams is increasing year by year.

The Irish National and the Isle of Man

Handlers from the Isle of Man compete in the Irish Nationals, though the Manx National is an annual event, consisting of a qualifying trial in which the six highest-pointed dogs compete in a double fetch for the Championship. A Brace Class is also included.

Many Manx competitors have represented Ireland: R. Kinrade has regularly been an Irish team member from the early 1970's to the present day; D. Little was in the 1986 and 1987 teams, and J. Chadwick with Asterton Nell 160690, a daughter of Sidney Price's Davy 131049, was in the 1993 team.

The Irish National was held in the Isle of Man in 1970 and 1973, and in 1976 when M. Graham and Gay 69947, a daughter of Wiston Cap, won the Irish National Championship. They also won the Isle of Man Championship that year. In 1985 the Isle of Man was once again the venue for the Irish National.

The first handler from the Isle of Man to compete at an International was G. Quirk in the Brace Championship in 1968, having won the Irish Brace Championship with Chum 47289 and Teresa 47290. Both he and T. Quayle, were very successful competitors in the Isle of Man Brace Championships, the latter winning the Irish Brace Class with Bob 40131 and Gyp 40132, in 1970. The 1973 Irish Brace Championship was won by G. Quirk with Chum and Clive 70727, and D. Little won the 1984 award with Mirk 111004 and Ben 145915.

J. Brady with Shane 57767

FRANK MOYES

CHRISTINE WALKER

Born 10/4/87   Black, white & tan   R. Goligher, Eglington

Awards
Allison Award 1991

GLEN 137661, J. Gordon	┌ **JIM. N. R., E. Russell**	┌ unknown └ unknown
	└ **GYP 55308, W. Ellwood**	┌ **SWEEP 22666, R. Wood** └ **TIB 45308, J. Wilson**
FAY 155922, Miss P. Beddows	┌ **DAVY 131049, S. B. Price**	┌ **BOBBY 119815, T. Bowey** └ **SANDY 122755, J. Wilson**
	└ **BETT 117901, D. Jordan**	┌ **DON 97066, C. Starkey** └ **JESS 66448, W. Lloyd**

DAVY 131049 *International Supreme Champion 1987*
I. S. D. S. Blue Riband 1987
English Aggregate Championship 1987
R. Fortune Trophy 1987
Lord Mostyn Plate 1987
Pedigree Chum Supreme Championship Trophy 1987
Lang's Scotch Whisky Quaiche 1987
Sun Alliance Salver 1987
Rhiwlas Trophy 1987
English National Champion 1987
English Farmers' Champion 1987
Ivy Parry Trophy 1987
SWEEP 22666   *Scottish Shepherds' Aggregate Championship 1968*

1992   **FLASH II 180639**   **Baronscourt**

Born 7/2/89   Black & white   M. O'Neill, Summerhill

Awards
Royal Dublin Society Trophy 1992

WATTIE 162693, J. R. Welsh	YORK 127630, J. Paterson	GLEN 75630, R. Fortune DOT 99192, T. Hutchinson
	DI 126147, J. Paterson	MOSS 103923, J. Templeton LADY 83624, J. McNeil
JET 157747, M. O'Boyle	JIM 125956, J. Brady	DON 73710, W. Welsh GAIL 104391, W. Welsh
	GEM 114639, M. O'Boyle	SHANE 71700, J. Brady MEG 81598, D. Brady

GLEN 75630   *Scottish Brace Champion with JILL 55741, 1977*
MOSS 103923   *Scottish Aggregate Championship 1979*
           Feedmobile Trophy 1979
DON 73710   *International Shepherds' Champion 1979*
           Scottish Shepherds' Aggregate Championship 1979
           Scottish Shepherds' Champion 1978
SHANE 71700   *Irish Aggregate Championship 1981*

Martin O'Neill

Martin O'Neill, who is renowned for his great sportsmanship, and one of Ireland's best handlers, has been a team member on many occasions since 1968, when Nell 43414 was third. In 1970 she was fourth. She was second in the 1972 and 1973 teams, and a member again in 1974, and she was the 1971 Irish Driving Champion. Nell, dam of Tim Flood's Scot, was the first dog from Eire to qualify to compete in the Supreme Championship in 1972.

With Risp 61527, Martin O'Neill competed in the 1973, 1976 and 1977 Nationals; with Scott 103933, in 1981, and after an absence of a few years, he competed with Laddie 174762, in the 1991 team.

It was a very popular win when he and Flash II 180639, secured the 1992 Irish National – an award that had for so long eluded him.

M. O'Neill with Risp 61527 (left) and Scott 103933 (right)

Born 13/6/87   Black, tan & white   J. P. McFadden, Ballymena

Awards
Brace Aggregate Championship 1992
Irish Brace Champion with DON 177381, 1992

YORK 127630, J. Paterson	┌**GLEN 75630, R. Fortune**	┌**CAP 67230, T. T. McKnight** └**SHELL 68768, T. T. McKnight**
	└**DOT 99192, T. M. Hutchinson**	┌**DON 73710, W. Welsh** └**MAUD 80584, T. M. Hutchinson**
DI 137205, J. Porteous	┌**MOSS 103923, J. Templeton**	┌**HEMP 72301, A. J. Campbell** └**QUEEN 74047, H. MacKenzie**
	└**LASSIE 80703, D. Porteous**	┌**BEN 56646, D. McTeir** └**CREE 57459, J. Porteous**

GLEN 75630   *Scottish Brace Champion with JILL 55741, 1977*
MOSS 103923   *Scottish Aggregate Championship 1979*
                  Feedmobile Trophy 1979
DON 73710   *International Shepherds' Champion 1979*
                Scottish Shepherds' Aggregate Championship 1979
                Scottish Shepherds' Champion 1978
HEMP 72301   *Scottish Driving Champion 1977*
BEN 56646   *International Shepherds' Champion 1972*
                Scottish Shepherds' Aggregate Championship 1972
                Scottish National & Shepherds' Champion 1972
                Alexander Andrew Trophy 1972

Appendices

Further Reading

Viv Billingham (1984), *One Woman and Her Dog*, Patrick Stephens Ltd.

Iris Combe (1978), *Border Collies*, Faber & Faber Ltd.

Iris Combe (1983) *Shepherds, Sheep and Sheepdogs*, Dalesman Books

Roy Goutté (1990), *The Principal Lines*, Vols 1 & 2, Alresford Press Ltd.

Roy Goutté (1994), *The Principal Lines*, Vol 3, Pembroke & Canine Press

Sheila Grew (revised 1993), *Key Dogs of the Border Collie Family*, Vols 1 & 2, Heritage Farms Publishing Company

Eric Halsall (1980), *Sheepdogs, My Faithful Friends*, Patrick Stephens Ltd.

Eric Halsall (1982), *Sheepdog Trials*, Patrick Stephens Ltd.

Eric Halsall (1992), *British Sheepdogs*, International Sheep Dog Society

John Holmes (1960), *The Farmer's Dog*, Popular Dogs Publishing Co. Ltd.

Tony Iley (1978), *Sheepdogs at Work*, Dalesman Books

H. Glyn Jones & Barbara Collins (1978), *A Way of Life*, Farming Press Books

R. B. Kelly (1942), *Sheepdogs*, Angus & Robertson, Australia

Tim Longton & Edward Hart (1976), *The Sheepdog, Its Work and Training*, David & Charles

J. H. McCulloch (1938), *Sheepdogs and Their Masters*, The Moray Press

J. H. McCulloch (1952), *Border Collie Studies*, The Pentland Press

S. Moorehouse (1950), *The British Sheepdog*, H. F. & G. Witherby Ltd.

Matt Mundell (1981), *Country Diary*, Gordon Wright Publishing

Marjorie Quarton (1986), *All about the Working Collie*, Pelham Books

Peidje Vidler (1983), *The Border Collie in Australasia*, Gotrah Enterprises

J. Wentworth-Day (1952), *The Wisest Dogs in the World*, Longshaw Sheepdog Trials Association

Working Sheepdog News a bi-monthly magazine published by Delia Sturgeon, 4 Mountain Road, Conwy, Gwynedd, North Wales LL32 8PU

International Sheep Dog Society Awards

National Trophies

England

Sentinel Rylock Trophy (National Champion)
Macclesfield Shepherds' Cup
John A. Sanderson Challenge Cup (Farmers' Champion)
J. A. Thorp Memorial Cup (Highest-pointed English-bred dog or bitch)
J. H. Whittingham Trophy (Breeders)
Ivy Parry Trophy (Highest points in outrun, lift and fetch)
John E. Roebuck Brace Cup (Brace Champion)
Arthur Grounds Trophy (Driving Champion)

Scotland

The Rainie National Shield (National)
A. A. Armstrong Shepherds' Cup
J. W. McNaughton Cup (Farmers' Champion)
Drumlog Cup (Youngest Handler)
A. Andrew Trophy (Highest-pointed Scottish-bred dog or bitch)
J. M. Wilson Challenge Shield (National Champion)
Warnock Trophy (Highest-pointed dog or bitch on 1st day)
Jack Fraser Trophy (Best Sportsman)
Helensburgh Trophy (Brace)
Tom Gilholm Trophy (Driving)

Wales

The Pritchard's Cup (National Champion)
The Long Farmers' Cup
Ceredigion Jubilee Cup (Shepherds' Champion)
Challis Shield (Highest-pointed Welsh-bred dog or bitch)
W. J. Jones Trophy (Highest-pointed young dog or bitch up to three years at January 1st)
Borth & Ynyslas Trophy (Youngest Handler)
The Fenwick Cup (Brace)
D. W. Davies Cup (Driving)

Ireland

The Rainie National Cup
The Brace Cup
Charmichael Driving Championship

The Clonmany Trophy (Singles Reserve Team Member)
S. O'Leary Trophy (Youngest Handler)
Royal Dublin Society Trophy (Highest-pointed Irish-bred dog or bitch)
Rumivite Cup (Highest-pointed dog or bitch handled by a shepherd)
David Forsythe Trophy (Best Sportsman)

International Awards

Sun Alliance Shepherds' Trophy
Duchess of Devonshire Farmer Trophy
Stirling Team Shield
C.E.H. Yates English Shepherds' Aggregate Cup
Lord Mostyn Scottish Aggregate Cup
J. E. Roebuck Welsh Shepherds' Aggregate Cup
Omagh Marts Irish Shepherds' Aggregate Cup
Wilsons Rose Bowl (Brace Champion)
David Stone Brace Aggregate Trophy
Supreme Championship 3rd Challenge Shield
Capt. Whittaker Rosebowl (Highest Outwork)
Lord Mostyn Plate (Supreme Champion)
R. Fortune Trophy (Supreme Champion)
Ernest Broadley Cup (Breeder of Winner)
Roberthill Trophy (Sire of Winner)
Gwilliam Goblet (Breeder of Winner)
Feedmobile Challenge Cup (Runner up to Supreme Champion)
McDiarmid Trophy (Bred/handled by Competitor)
Clara Roebuck Cup (Highest Aggregate National & International)
W. R. Seward English Aggregate Trophy (National and International)
J. S. Gray Scottish Aggregate Trophy (National and International)
C. D. Fenwick Welsh Aggregate Trophy (National and International)
G. L. Pennefather Irish Aggregate Trophy (National and International
The Edinburgh Trophy (Oldest Competitor)
The Donaldson Cup (Youngest Competitor)
J. B. Bagshaw Trophy (Driving Champion)
Ashton Priestley Silver Salver (Best Sportsman)
Blue Riband (Supreme Champion's Collar)
The Rhiwlas Trophy (Society's Oldest Trophy)

Specials

Pedigree Chum Supreme Championship Trophy

Pedigree Chum Silver Salver (Qualifier)

Eden Valley Mineral Water Co. Crystal Carafe (Highest Scoring English Entrant)

Wilkinson Sword

The Wilkinson Sword is awarded annually to a member of the Society who the council feel has given great service to the collie and to sheepdog trials.

The necessary points for acceptance in a National are dependent on the 'scores' of dogs seeking the opportunity to compete. From the 150 required entrants, those with the highest number of points are selected.

Points are obtained from first to sixth place in open trials in which at least 25 dogs compete. Points gained over the three years prior to the relevant National are combined for the dog's total score.

Details of International Sheep Dog Society membership and rules can be obtained from the secretary:

Mr A. Philip Hendry C.B.E.
The International Sheep Dog Society
Chesham House, 47 Bromham Road
Bedford MK40 2AA
Telephone: 0234 352672

Dog Registration

Numbers following each dog's name refer to its registration number in the International Sheep Dog Society Stud book. Pedigrees can be traced through the stud books to the dogs first registered in the early 1900s. Puppies have to be registered by the age of six months, and their parents must be registered. Certificates are issued to the puppies' owners.

It is advisable to have all puppies eye-tested for the presence of collie eye anomaly (CEA) between the ages of six to ten weeks.

All three-year-old dogs must be certified clear of progressive retinal atrophy (PRA) and clear of CEA. This testing is carried out by specialist vets from the British Veterinary Association Eye Panel.

To be registered on merit (R.O.M.) the dog must prove its working ability to the satisfaction of an International Sheep Dog Society Director, if it does not compete in sheepdog trials.

A dog that competes at trials must have won a first prize, or two second placings, or a second and a third placing, in open trials in which at least twenty-five dogs competed. A fee of £60 has then to be paid to the International Sheep Dog Society.

Only members of the International Sheep Dog Society are eligible to register dogs. Likewise, only members can compete in the National and International trials. Handlers compete in the country in which they reside, regardless of nationality.

National and International Championship Courses

(Reproduced by kind permission of the ISDS)

National Championships and International Qualifying Trials

(1) *Course* – The Course, Scale of Points and Time Limit now fixed by the Directors are set out below and the responsibility for laying out the Course in accordance with the Rules rests with the Trials Committee and the Course Director.

(2) *Gathering 400 yards* – In the outrun the dog may be directed on either side. A straight fetch from the lift to the handler, through a centre gate (7 yards wide) 150 yards from the handler. No re-try at the gate is allowed. The handler will remain at the post from the commencement of the outrun and at the end of the fetch he will pass the sheep behind him.

(3) *Driving* – The handler will stand at the post and direct his dog to drive the sheep 450 yards over a triangular course through two sets of gates 7 yards wide, a second attempt at either gate is NOT allowed. The drive ends when the sheep enter the shedding ring. The handler will remain at the post until the sheep are in the shedding ring. In the case of a short course, when the fetch is less than 400 yards, the drive will be lengthened when possible so that the total length of the fetch and drive is 850 yards, or as near to the length as is reasonably practicable. The drive may be either to left or right and shall be decided by the Trials Committee immediately prior to the Trial.

(4) *Shedding* – Two unmarked sheep to be shed within a ring 40 yards in diameter. The dog must be in full control of the two sheep shed (in or outside the ring) otherwise the shed will not be deemed satisfactory. On completion of the shed the handler shall reunite his sheep before proceeding to pen.

(5) *Penning* – The pen will be 8 feet by 9 feet with a gate 8 feet wide to which is secured a rope 6 feet long. On completion of shedding, the handler must proceed to the pen, leaving his dog to bring the sheep to the pen. The handler is forbidden to assist the dog to drive the sheep to the pen. The handler will stand at the gate holding the rope and must not let go of the rope while the dog works the sheep into the pen. The handler will close the gate. After releasing the sheep, the handler will close and fasten the gate.

(6) *Single sheep* – The handler will proceed to the shedding ring leaving the dog to bring the sheep from the pen to the ring. One of two marked sheep will be shed off within the ring and thereafter worn (in or outside the ring) to the judges' satisfaction. Handlers are forbidden to assist the dog in driving off, or attempting to drive off the single any distance or by forcing it on the dog.

SCALE OF POINTS – Outrun 20; Lifting 10; Fetching 20; Driving 30; Shedding 10; Penning 10; Single 10. **Total 110** per Judge (Aggregate 440)

TIME LIMIT – 15 minutes. No extension.

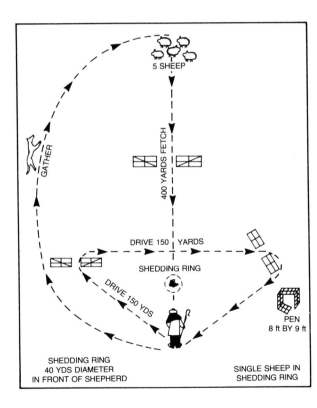

310

National and International Brace Championship

Course –

(1) Gathering – There will be 10 or such number of sheep as the Committee decide upon, in one lot in the centre of the field at a distance of approximately 800 yards. Both dogs will start at the same time. Crossing at the completion of the outrun is permissible but dogs should remain on the side to which they have crossed and they should not recross. The fetch should be straight through a gate (9 yards wide) in the centre of the field. Should the gate be missed no re-try is allowed. Each dog will keep to its own side and the handler will remain at the post and at the end of the fetch will pass the sheep behind him.

(2) Driving – The handler stands at the post and directs his two dogs to drive the sheep 600 yards over a triangular course through two sets of gates (9 yards wide), back to the handler. No re-try is allowed at either gate.

Each dog is to keep to its own side and handler must remain at the post until the end of the drive. The drive is finished when the sheep enter the shedding ring.

(3) Shedding – The sheep will be divided into two equal lots by either dog inside the shedding ring; one lot will be driven off and left in charge of one dog – the other lot will be penned in a diamond shaped pen with an entrance of 5 feet and no gate. This dog will be left in charge while the other lot are penned by the other dog in similar pen approximately 50 yards away.

SCALE OF POINTS – Gathering 80 (Outrun 2 × 20 = 40; Lifting 20 and Fetching 20); Driving 30; Shedding 10; Penning (2 × 10) 20. **Total 140** per Judge (Aggregate 560).

TIME LIMIT – 25 minutes. No extension.

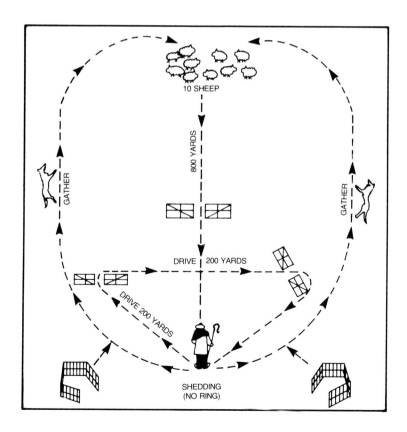

311

International Supreme Championship

(Restricted to 15 highest pointed dogs in Qualifying Trials irrespective of country or class)

SCALE OF POINTS – Gathering 100 (each Out-run 20; each Lift 10; each Fetch 20); Driving 40; Shedding 20; Penning 10. **Total 170.** (Aggregate 680)

TIME LIMIT – 30 minutes. No extension.

COURSE –

(1) *Gathering* – Distance about 800 yards for one lot of 10 sheep (if possible unseen by the dog) which should be brought through the gate (9 yards wide) in the centre of the field to a post fixed 20 yards through the gate; the dog having reached the post will then be re-directed for another lot of sheep (if possible unseen by the dog) which should also be brought through the gate and united with the first lot. The first run to be right or left as decided by the Trials Committee before the Trial and all competitors will run on that side, the second run to be on the other side. Should the gate be missed no re-try is allowed. Both the dog and the first lot of sheep must be past the gate to the post 20 yards inside the gate before the dog is re-directed for the second lot. At the end of the fetch the handler shall pass the sheep behind him.

(2) *Driving* – The drive shall be for 600 yards from where the handler stands in a triangular course through two gate obstacles (9 yards wide), back to the handler. The drive may be right or left as directed. Should the gates be missed no re-try is permitted at either gate. The drive should be in straight lines and ends when the sheep enter the shedding ring. The handler will remain at the post until the drive is finished.

(3) *Shedding* – The fifteen unmarked sheep to be shed off within a ring 40 yards in diameter. In shedding the sheep will be passed between the handler and his dog and the dog brought in to stop and turn back the marked sheep. Manoeuvring for 'cuts' is not allowed. Should any marked sheep leave the shedding ring and join any unmarked sheep already shed off the unmarked sheep with which the marked sheep has joined will be brought into the ring and shedding re-started. Until the fifteen unmarked sheep are shed off penning will not be permitted.

(4) *Penning* – The five marked sheep must be penned and the gate shut. The pen will be 8 feet by 9 feet with a gate 6 feet wide, to which is secured a rope 8 feet long. On completion of shedding, the handler must proceed to the pen, leaving the dog to bring the sheep to the pen. The handler is forbidden to assist his dog in driving the sheep to the pen. The handler will stand at the gate holding the rope and must not let go of the rope, while the dog works the sheep into the pen. The handler must close the gate. After releasing the sheep, the handler will close and fasten the gate.

(5) *General* – No points will be awarded for work done in the shedding ring or at the pen when either of these phases of the work has not been completed within the prescribed time limit.

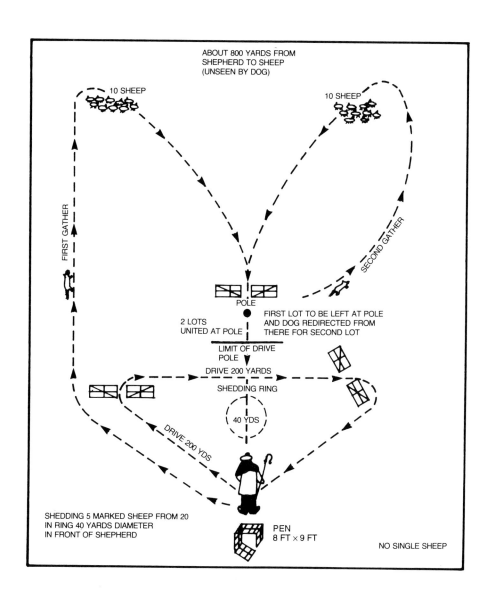

ABOUT 800 YARDS FROM
SHEPHERD TO SHEEP
(UNSEEN BY DOG)

10 SHEEP

10 SHEEP

FIRST GATHER

SECOND GATHER

POLE

2 LOTS
UNITED AT POLE

FIRST LOT TO BE LEFT AT POLE
AND DOG REDIRECTED FROM
THERE FOR SECOND LOT

LIMIT OF DRIVE
POLE

DRIVE 200 YARDS

SHEDDING RING

DRIVE 200 YDS

40 YDS

SHEDDING 5 MARKED SHEEP FROM 20
IN RING 40 YARDS DIAMETER
IN FRONT OF SHEPHERD

PEN
8 FT × 9 FT

NO SINGLE SHEEP

313

Pedigree Charts Showing Breeding Lines of International Sheep Dog Society Supreme Champions to 1993

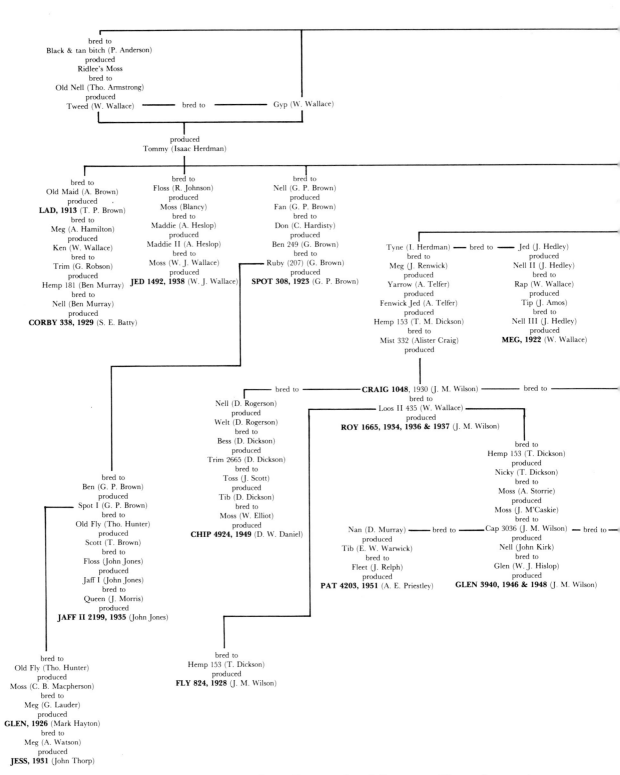

bred to
Black & tan bitch (P. Anderson)
produced
Ridlee's Moss
bred to
Old Nell (Tho. Armstrong)
produced
Tweed (W. Wallace) ——— bred to ——— Gyp (W. Wallace)

produced
Tommy (Isaac Herdman)

bred to
Old Maid (A. Brown)
produced
LAD, 1913 (T. P. Brown)
bred to
Meg (A. Hamilton)
produced
Ken (W. Wallace)
bred to
Trim (G. Robson)
produced
Hemp 181 (Ben Murray)
bred to
Nell (Ben Murray)
produced
CORBY 338, 1929 (S. E. Batty)

bred to
Floss (R. Johnson)
produced
Moss (Blancy)
bred to
Maddie (A. Heslop)
produced
Maddie II (A. Heslop)
bred to
Moss (W. J. Wallace)
produced
JED 1492, 1938 (W. J. Wallace)

bred to
Nell (G. P. Brown)
produced
Fan (G. P. Brown)
bred to
Don (C. Hardisty)
produced
Ben 249 (G. Brown)
bred to
Ruby (207) (G. Brown)
produced
SPOT 308, 1923 (G. P. Brown)

Tyne (I. Herdman) ——— bred to ——— Jed (J. Hedley)
produced
Meg (J. Renwick)   Nell II (J. Hedley)
produced   bred to
Yarrow (A. Telfer)   Rap (W. Wallace)
produced   produced
Fenwick Jed (A. Telfer)   Tip (J. Amos)
produced   bred to
Hemp 153 (T. M. Dickson)   Nell III (J. Hedley)
bred to   produced
Mist 332 (Alister Craig)   **MEG, 1922** (W. Wallace)
produced

bred to ——— **CRAIG 1048**, 1930 (J. M. Wilson) ——— bred to ———
                    bred to
Nell (D. Rogerson)   Loos II 435 (W. Wallace)
produced   produced
Welt (D. Rogerson) **ROY 1665, 1934, 1936 & 1937** (J. M. Wilson)
bred to
Bess (D. Dickson)
produced   bred to
Trim 2665 (D. Dickson)   Hemp 153 (T. Dickson)
bred to   produced
Toss (J. Scott)   Nicky (T. Dickson)
produced   bred to
Tib (D. Dickson)   Moss (A. Storrie)
bred to   produced
Moss (W. Elliot)   Moss (J. M'Caskie)
produced   bred to
CHIP 4924, 1949 (D. W. Daniel)

bred to
Ben (G. P. Brown)
produced
Spot I (G. P. Brown)
bred to
Old Fly (Tho. Hunter)
produced
Scott (T. Brown)
bred to
Floss (John Jones)
produced
Jaff I (John Jones)
bred to
Queen (J. Morris)
produced
JAFF II 2199, 1935 (John Jones)

Nan (D. Murray) ——— bred to ——— Cap 3036 (J. M. Wilson) — bred to —
produced   produced
Tib (E. W. Warwick)   Nell (John Kirk)
bred to   bred to
Fleet (J. Relph)   Glen (W. J. Hislop)
produced   produced
PAT 4203, 1951 (A. E. Priestley)   **GLEN 3940, 1946 & 1948** (J. M. Wilson)

bred to
Old Fly (Tho. Hunter)
produced
Moss (C. B. Macpherson)
bred to
Meg (G. Lauder)
produced
GLEN, 1926 (Mark Hayton)
bred to
Meg (A. Watson)
produced
JESS, 1931 (John Thorp)

bred to
Hemp 153 (T. Dickson)
produced
FLY 824, 1928 (J. M. Wilson)

Names in bold capitals indicate International Supreme Champions

316

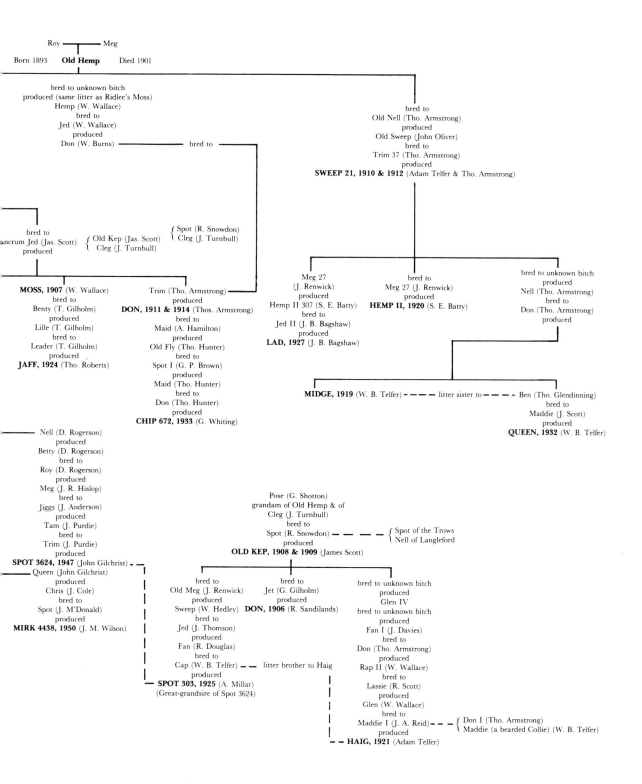

Supreme Champions to 1951*

* Adapted from the pedigree chart given in *Border Collie Studies* by J. H. McCulloch

Supreme Champions 1952 to 1993

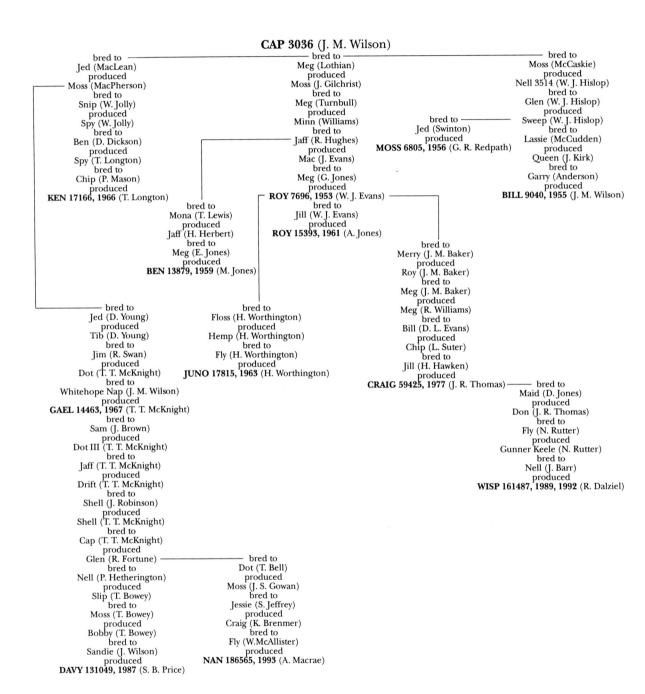

CAP 3036 (J. M. Wilson)

bred to
Jed (MacLean)
produced
Moss (MacPherson)
bred to
Snip (W. Jolly)
produced
Spy (W. Jolly)
bred to
Ben (D. Dickson)
produced
Spy (T. Longton)
bred to
Chip (P. Mason)
produced
KEN 17166, 1966 (T. Longton)

bred to
Meg (Lothian)
produced
Moss (J. Gilchrist)
bred to
Meg (Turnbull)
produced
Minn (Williams)
bred to
Jaff (R. Hughes)
produced
Mac (J. Evans)
bred to
Meg (G. Jones)
produced
ROY 7696, 1953 (W. J. Evans)
bred to
Jill (W. J. Evans)
produced
ROY 15393, 1961 (A. Jones)

bred to ———
Jed (Swinton)
produced
MOSS 6805, 1956 (G. R. Redpath)

bred to
Moss (McCaskie)
produced
Nell 3514 (W. J. Hislop)
bred to
Glen (W. J. Hislop)
produced
Sweep (W. J. Hislop)
bred to
Lassie (McCudden)
produced
Queen (J. Kirk)
bred to
Garry (Anderson)
produced
BILL 9040, 1955 (J. M. Wilson)

bred to
Mona (T. Lewis)
produced
Jaff (H. Herbert)
bred to
Meg (E. Jones)
produced
BEN 13879, 1959 (M. Jones)

bred to
Merry (J. M. Baker)
produced
Roy (J. M. Baker)
bred to
Meg (J. M. Baker)
produced
Meg (R. Williams)
bred to
Bill (D. L. Evans)
produced
Chip (L. Suter)
bred to
Jill (H. Hawken)
produced
CRAIG 59425, 1977 (J. R. Thomas) ———

bred to
Maid (D. Jones)
produced
Don (J. R. Thomas)
bred to
Fly (N. Rutter)
produced
Gunner Keele (N. Rutter)
bred to
Nell (J. Barr)
produced
WISP 161487, 1989, 1992 (R. Dalziel)

bred to
Jed (D. Young)
produced
Tib (D. Young)
bred to
Jim (R. Swan)
produced
Dot (T. T. McKnight)
bred to
Whitehope Nap (J. M. Wilson)
produced
GAEL 14463, 1967 (T. T. McKnight)
bred to
Sam (J. Brown)
produced
Dot III (T. T. McKnight)
bred to
Jaff (T. T. McKnight)
produced
Drift (T. T. McKnight)
bred to
Shell (J. Robinson)
produced
Shell (T. T. McKnight)
bred to
Cap (T. T. McKnight)
produced
Glen (R. Fortune) ———
bred to
Nell (P. Hetherington)
produced
Slip (T. Bowey)
bred to
Moss (T. Bowey)
produced
Bobby (T. Bowey)
bred to
Sandie (J. Wilson)
produced
DAVY 131049, 1987 (S. B. Price)

bred to
Floss (H. Worthington)
produced
Hemp (H. Worthington)
bred to
Fly (H. Worthington)
produced
JUNO 17815, 1963 (H. Worthington)

bred to
Dot (T. Bell)
produced
Moss (J. S. Gowan)
bred to
Jessie (S. Jeffrey)
produced
Craig (K. Brenmer)
bred to
Fly (W.McAllister)
produced
NAN 186565, 1993 (A. Macrae)

MEG 306, 1922 (W. Wallace)
bred to
Nap (Herdman)
produced
Moss IV (W. Wallace)
bred to
Maddie II (Hislop)
produced
Fly (W. J. Wallace)
bred to
Roger (W. Wallace)
produced
Foch (W. J. Wallace)
bred to
Betty (Cowan)
produced
Madge (Cowan)
bred to
Reed (Corbet)
produced
MIRK 5444, 1954 (J. McDonald)

bred to ———— **GLEN 3940, 1946, 1948** (J. M. Wilson)———— bred to
Jed (J. Purdie)   Meg (Kirkland)
produced   produced
Sweep (W. J. Evans)   Glen (J. Richardson)
bred to   bred to
Jed (W. James)   Meg (R. Hunter)
produced   produced
Glen (H. Greenslade)   Coon (J. Richardson)
bred to   bred to
Floss (C. Cook)   Lyn (R. Frame)
produced   produced
CRAIG 15445, 1964 (L. Suter)   Cap (J. Richardson)
                                                                        bred to
                                                                        Fly (W. S. Hetherington)
                                                                        produced
                                              WISTON CAP 31154, 1965 (J. Richardson)

CHIP 4924, 1949, 1952 (D. W. Daniel)
bred to ——————————————————— bred to
Floss (D. W. Daniel)   Floss (D. W. Daniel)
produced   produced
KEN 13306, 1960 (E. L. Daniel)   Nell (A. T. Lloyd)
                                                        bred to
                                    Garry (H. Greenslade) ———————————— bred to
                                                        produced   Nell (R. Brooks)
                               GARRY 17690, 1962 (A. T. Lloyd)   produced
                                                                                                Sweep (W. D. Reed)
                                                                                                bred to
                                                                                                Fly (R. Barrel)
                                                                                                produced
                                                                                                Jasper (W. D. Reed)
                                                                                                bred to
                                                                                                Meg (H. Lewis)
                                                                                                produced
                                                                              TURK 118169, 1984 (W. D. Reed)

319

MIRK 4438, 1950 (J. M. Wilson)

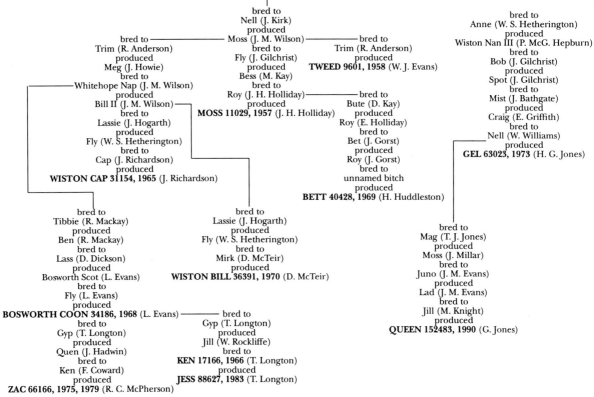

bred to
Nell (J. Kirk)
produced

bred to ———— Moss (J. M. Wilson) ———— bred to
Trim (R. Anderson)   bred to   Trim (R. Anderson)
produced   Fly (J. Gilchrist)   produced
Meg (J. Howie)   produced   **TWEED 9601, 1958** (W. J. Evans)
bred to   Bess (M. Kay)
Whitehope Nap (J. M. Wilson)   bred to
produced   Roy (J. H. Holliday) ———— bred to
Bill II (J. M. Wilson) ———   produced   Bute (D. Kay)
bred to   **MOSS 11029, 1957** (J. H. Holliday)   produced
Lassie (J. Hogarth)   Roy (E. Holliday)
produced   bred to
Fly (W. S. Hetherington)   Bet (J. Gorst)
bred to   produced
Cap (J. Richardson)   Roy (J. Gorst)
produced   bred to
WISTON CAP 31154, 1965 (J. Richardson)   unnamed bitch
produced
BETT 40428, 1969 (H. Huddleston)

bred to
Anne (W. S. Hetherington)
produced
Wiston Nan III (P. McG. Hepburn)
bred to
Bob (J. Gilchrist)
produced
Spot (J. Gilchrist)
bred to
Mist (J. Bathgate)
produced
Craig (E. Griffith)
bred to
Nell (W. Williams)
produced
GEL 63023, 1973 (H. G. Jones)

bred to   bred to
Tibbie (R. Mackay)   Lassie (J. Hogarth)
produced   produced
Ben (R. Mackay)   Fly (W. S. Hetherington)
bred to   bred to
Lass (D. Dickson)   Mirk (D. McTeir)
produced   produced
Bosworth Scot (L. Evans)   **WISTON BILL 36391, 1970** (D. McTeir)
bred to
Fly (L. Evans)
produced
BOSWORTH COON 34186, 1968 (L. Evans) ——— bred to
bred to   Gyp (T. Longton)
Gyp (T. Longton)   produced
produced   Jill (W. Rockliffe)
Quen (J. Hadwin)   bred to
bred to   **KEN 17166, 1966** (T. Longton)
Ken (F. Coward)   produced
produced   **JESS 88627, 1983** (T. Longton)
ZAC 66166, 1975, 1979 (R. C. McPherson)

bred to
Mag (T. J. Jones)
produced
Moss (J. Millar)
bred to
Juno (J. M. Evans)
produced
Lad (J. M. Evans)
bred to
Jill (M. Knight)
produced
QUEEN 152483, 1990 (G. Jones)

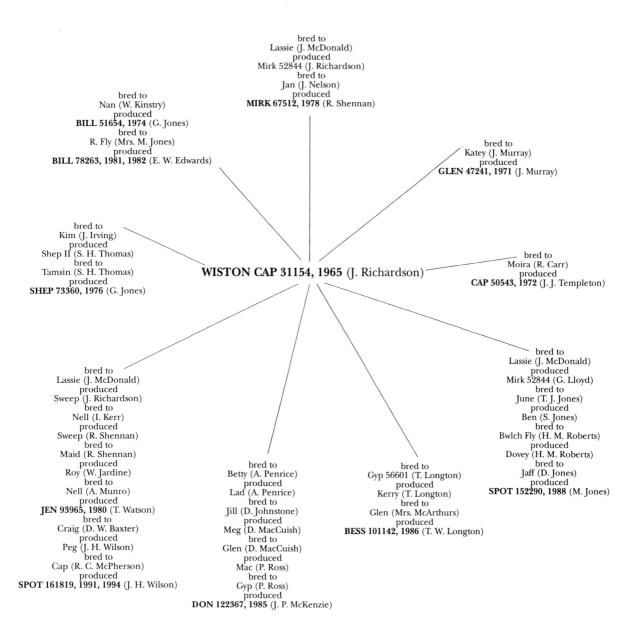

bred to
Lassie (J. McDonald)
produced
Mirk 52844 (J. Richardson)
bred to
Jan (J. Nelson)
produced
MIRK 67512, 1978 (R. Shennan)

bred to
Nan (W. Kinstry)
produced
BILL 51654, 1974 (G. Jones)
bred to
R. Fly (Mrs. M. Jones)
produced
BILL 78263, 1981, 1982 (E. W. Edwards)

bred to
Katey (J. Murray)
produced
GLEN 47241, 1971 (J. Murray)

bred to
Kim (J. Irving)
produced
Shep II (S. H. Thomas)
bred to
Tamsin (S. H. Thomas)
produced
SHEP 73360, 1976 (G. Jones)

WISTON CAP 31154, 1965 (J. Richardson)

bred to
Moira (R. Carr)
produced
CAP 50543, 1972 (J. J. Templeton)

bred to
Lassie (J. McDonald)
produced
Sweep (J. Richardson)
bred to
Nell (I. Kerr)
produced
Sweep (R. Shennan)
bred to
Maid (R. Shennan)
produced
Roy (W. Jardine)
bred to
Nell (A. Munro)
produced
JEN 93965, 1980 (T. Watson)
bred to
Craig (D. W. Baxter)
produced
Peg (J. H. Wilson)
bred to
Cap (R. C. McPherson)
produced
SPOT 161819, 1991, 1994 (J. H. Wilson)

bred to
Betty (A. Penrice)
produced
Lad (A. Penrice)
bred to
Jill (D. Johnstone)
produced
Meg (D. MacCuish)
bred to
Glen (D. MacCuish)
produced
Mac (P. Ross)
bred to
Gyp (P. Ross)
produced
DON 122367, 1985 (J. P. McKenzie)

bred to
Gyp 56601 (T. Longton)
produced
Kerry (T. Longton)
bred to
Glen (Mrs. McArthurs)
produced
BESS 101142, 1986 (T. W. Longton)

bred to
Lassie (J. McDonald)
produced
Mirk 52844 (G. Lloyd)
bred to
June (T. J. Jones)
produced
Ben (S. Jones)
bred to
Bwlch Fly (H. M. Roberts)
produced
Dovey (H. M. Roberts)
bred to
Jaff (D. Jones)
produced
SPOT 152290, 1988 (M. Jones)

National Champion Handlers and Dogs

J. B. Bagshaw	1925 English	LAD 305
J. B. Bagshaw	1931 English	MOSS 569
W. B. Bagshaw	1928, 1932 English	JESS 818
W. B. Bagshaw	1946 English	MAC 4418
J. M. Baker	1968 Welsh	ROY II 38227
D. Birchall	1985 Irish	EVE 112604
T. Bonella	1956 Scottish	TILLYOCHIE MOSS 7878
T. Bonella	1962 Scottish	BEN 16449
J. Brady	1964, 1967 Irish	BUFF 23069
J. Brady	1970 Irish	GYP 33128
J. Brady	1972, 1973 Irish	BOSWORTH JIM 52007
K. Brehmer	1978 English	BEN 92094
J. Brennan	1986 Irish	MEG 126291
G. P. Brown	1923 Scottish	SPOT 308
T. Brownrigg	1991 English	NAP 131097
J. P. Burke	1984 Welsh	GLEN 113361
W. M. Cook	1967 English	MAID 28779
W. Cormack	1973 Scottish	JUNE 59734
J. Cropper	1986 English	CAP 142018
R. Dalziel	1986 Scottish	DRYDEN JOE 104626
R. Dalziel	1992 Scottish	WISP 161487
E. L. Daniel	1992 Welsh	FLY 163488
S. Davidson	1980 Scottish	BEN 88284
S. L. Davidson	1988 Scottish	MOSS 138632
S. L. Davidson	1989 Scottish	CHIEF (CRAIG) 120006
D. W. Davies	1936 Welsh	NETT 989
E. N. Davies	1964 Welsh	GWEN 19455
E. N. Davies	1978 Welsh	CYMRO 82447
J. Denniff	1954 English	SWEEP 5594
Mrs J. Deptford	1991 Scottish	GWEN 160435
B. Dodd	1988 English	LADDIE 151099
E. W. Edwards	1965 Welsh	NIP 17278
A. Elliott	1984 English	MOSS 131207
T. E. Elliott	1973 English	BILL 39521
B. Evans	1993 Welsh	TAFF 177576
L. Evans	1969 English	BOSWORTH COON 34186
L. Evans	1976 English	CHIP 62102
W. J. Evans	1949 Welsh	SWEEP 4204
W. J. Evans	1958 English	MOSS 7971
W. J. Evans	1959 English	TWEED 9601
W. J. Evans	1962 English	DON 13392
W. J. Evans	1963 English	BEN 12953
E. Feeney	1987 Irish	CRAIG 118161
T. Flood	1975 Irish	COSY 70560
T. Flood	1978 Irish	SCOT 57965
T. Flood	1979 Irish	FLASH 106580
T. Flood	1984, 1988, 1989 Irish	PIP 124578
A. Foster	1980 English	DART 92163

J. Gilchrist	1965, 1966 Scottish	SPOT 24981
R. Goligher	1991 Irish	MAID 169072
W. Goodfellow	1958 Scottish	LADDIE 8049
W. H. Goodwin	1966 Welsh	NAP 18186
J. K. Gorst	1953 English	BETT 6260
J. K. Gorst	1957 English	QUEEN 8810
M. Graham	1976 Irish	GAY 69947
H. Greenslade	1955, 1956 Welsh	GLEN 7690
Miss J. Hardisty	1977 English	FLASH 79000
W. Hardisty	1961 English	JIM 12967
W. Harris	1950 Welsh	SWEEP 5096
J. Harrison	1990 English	CRAIG 148254
A. Hayton	1947 English	BARNEY 4365
M. Hayton	1937 English	PAT 2219
P. Hetherington	1970 Scottish	NELL 53708
W. J. Hislop	1948 Scottish	SWEEP 3834
W. J. Hislop	1959 Scottish	SWEEP 13146
W. J. Hislop	1961 Scottish	JIM 12572
J. Hogarth	1963 Scottish	LADDIE 13204
J. H. Holliday	1951 English	ROY II 5406
J. H. Holliday	1968 English	MOSS II 28996
C. Holmes	1952 English	LAD 4453
H. Huddleston	1972 English	UDALE SIM 52690
H. Huddleston	1989 English	JIM 150661
R. J. Hughes	1928 Welsh	LADDIE 867
R. J. Hughes	1946, 1948 Welsh	JAFF 4313
L. J. Humphreys	1929, 1930 Welsh	TOSS 464
L. J. Humphreys	1931, 1934 Welsh	LAD 990
L. J. Humphreys	1933, 1939 Welsh	MOSS 2206
J. Irvine	1983 Irish	SHEP 109351
J. James	1975 English	MIRK 68102
A. Jones	1959, 1961 Welsh	ROY 15393
A. Jones	1962 Welsh	GLEN 17251
A. Jones	1971 Welsh	LAD 44675
A. Jones	1976 Welsh	CRAIG 72737
A. G. Jones	1974 Welsh	TOS 61152
G. Jones	1987 Welsh	QUEEN 152483
H. G. Jones	1980, 1981 Welsh	BWLCH TAFF 113243
H. W. Jones	1988, 1990 Welsh	MEG 135659
J. Jones	1932 Welsh	BLACKIE 1635
J. Jones	1935 Welsh	FLY 1574
W. Jones	1958 Welsh	BEN 11401
M. Jones	1979 Welsh	CRAIG 67343
S. Jones	1963 Welsh	VICKEY 15968
J. Kerr	1968 Scottish	QUEEN 24078
T. Lambe	1990 Irish	NELL 146196
J. Lightfoot	1991 Welsh	BLACK 144068
A. G. Little	1934, 1936 English	FLY 1764
W. R. Little	1954 Scottish	SPOT 6775
D. W. Lloyd	1983 English	JIM 103518
H. Loates	1979 English	WISTON JILL 79096
J. H. Logan	1968 Irish	MOY 42363
J. H. Logan	1969 Irish	CAP 24328
J. H. Logan	1974, 1977 Irish	JIM 67676

J. H. Logan	1980 Irish	SWEEP 87666
J. H. Logan	1981 Scottish	STAR 109497
Tim Longton	1949 English	DOT 4844
Tim Longton	1965 English	SNIP 16879
Tim Longton	1966 English	KEN 17166
Tim Longton	1970 English	GLEN II 48637
Tim Longton	1974 English	ROY 54175
Tim Longton	1981 English	TWEED 96630
Tom Longton	1950, 1956 English	MOSSIE 6235
T. W. Longton	1985 English	BESS 101142
T. W. Longton	1992 English	GEM 147666
G. Lutton	1982 Irish	GLEN 109694
W. F. Miles	1938 Welsh	KATE 2601
W. F. Miles	1952 Welsh	WALLY 4361
A. Millar	1922, 1925, 1926, 1927 Scottish	SPOT 303
A. Millar	1924 Scottish	TOT 155
A. Millar	1928, 1929 Scottish	MIRK 836
A. Millar	1930 Scottish	BEN 891
A. Millar	1934 Scottish	KEN 1477
J. R. Millar	1947 Scottish	DRIFT 4380
J. R. Millar	1949 Scottish	BEN 4931
J. R. Millar	1953 Scottish	TAM 7032
J. R. Millar	1969 Scottish	KEN II 18754
E. F. Morgan	1964 English	MOSS 14902
E. Morris	1926, 1927 Welsh	SPOT 615
J. F. Mullan	1965 Irish	NELL 16949
D. Murray	1938 Scottish	SWEEP 1962
D. Murray	1952 Scottish	VIC 4368
D. MacDonald	1974 Scottish	GLEN 62253
J. P. McFadden	1993 Irish	LYN 168527
J. W. McKee	1961 Irish	SNIP 10677
J. W. McKee	1963 Irish	WHITEHOPE CORRIE 13706
T. T. McKnight	1964 Scottish	GAEL 14463
T. T. McKnight	1971 Scottish	MIRK 28776
A. McMillan	1967 Scottish	JOCK 21994
R. C. MacPherson	1971 English	NAP 43986
A. S. Macrae	1984 Scottish	MIRK 96612
J. McRobert	1990 Scottish	GLEN 143941
J. McSwiggan	1971 Irish	ROCK 36024
D. McTeir	1972 Scottish	BEN 56646
R. E. Nicholls	1972 Welsh	MOSS 41957
M. O'Neill	1992 Irish	FLASH II 180639
D. O'Sullivan	1981 Irish	NELL 99019
A. Owen	1985 Welsh	BEN 129820
G. Owen	1954 Welsh	NELL 8739
H. Owen	1986 Welsh	SPOTAN 134842
M. Owen	1989 Welsh	ROCK 162204
M. R. Page	1970 Welsh	SWEEP 23470
M. R. Page	1973 Welsh	NELL 65799
M. R. Page	1982 Welsh	CAP 108145
G. L. Pennefather	1962, 1966 Irish	BESS 17145
S. B. Price	1987 English	DAVY 131049
E. Priestley	1922, 1923 English	MOSS 233
E. Priestley	1930 English	HEMP 1006

E. A. Priestley	1955 English	JIM 10071
E. A. Priestley	1960 English	SWEEP 11115
E. Pritchard	1925 Welsh	JUNO 618
J. Pritchard	1922 Welsh	LADDIE 406
G. Pugh	1951 Welsh	DON 6644
G. Pugh	1953 Welsh	LADDIE 4362
W. Rae	1977 Scottish	CONNIE 84203
J. Renwick	1935, 1938 English	KEP 1654
W. Renwick	1939 English	BET 2398
J. Richardson	1975 Scottish	MIRK 52844
T. Roberts	1923, 1924 Welsh	JAFF 379
D. Shennan	1976 Scottish	MEG 63230
D. Shennan	1978 Scottish	NAN 85606
R. Shennan	1979 Scottish	MIRK 67512
R. Short	1960 Scottish	NELL 12743
L. R. Suter	1969 Welsh	SALLY 46413
A. Telfer	1924 English	HAIG 252
W. B. Telfer	1926, 1927, 1929 English	QUEEN 533
J. J. Templeton	1957 Scottish	ROY 8993
J. J. Templeton	1982, 1983, 1985 Scottish	ROY 114678
J. R. Thomas	1977 Welsh	CRAIG 59425
S. H. Thomas	1982 English	PENPELL BESS 107127
W. J. Thomas	1957, 1960 Welsh	GLEN 7395
J. Thorp	1948 English	FAN 4424
P. Turnbull	1993 English	NAP 188631
W. J. Wallace	1933 English	JED 1492
J. R. Welsh	1987 Scottish	JEN 134760
G. Williams	1983 Welsh	DON 106096
R. H. Williams	1937 Welsh	JAFF 2598
R. O. Williams	1947 Welsh	LAD 3091
J. Wilson	1993 Scottish	SAM 192693
J. M. Wilson	1931, 1932 Scottish	CRAIG 1048
J. M. Wilson	1933 Scottish	NICKEY 1823
J. M. Wilson	1935, 1936, 1939 Scottish	NELL 1627
J. M. Wilson	1937 Scottish	ROY 1665
J. M. Wilson	1946 Scottish	GLEN 3940
J. M. Wilson	1950 Scottish	MIRK 4438
J. M. Wilson	1951 Scottish	WHITEHOPE TIB 6903
J. M. Wilson	1955 Scottish	WHITEHOPE NAP 8685
H. J. Worthington	1967 Welsh	JUNO 17815
H. J. Worthington	1975 Welsh	LAD 54209

Indexes

General Index

National Championship years for handlers are given, followed by the page numbers in brackets. Other page numbers are general and family references.

A
'All Ireland' Trial, first, 272
American World Championship, 8
Armstrong, T., 108
Armstrong, Thomas, 10, 100, 254
Ashton, Ellis, 7

B
Bagshaw, J. B., 1925 (14), 1931 (18), 23, 104, 188, 264
Bagshaw, W. B., 1928 (16), 1932 (16), 1946 (27), 104
Baker, J. M., 1968 (229)
Batty, S. E., 23
Benn, Belinda, 69
Billingham, Viv, 69
Birchall, Dennis., 1985 (294), 295
Blue Riband award, 4
Bonella, T., 1956 (127), 1962 (133)
Border Collie, film, 104
Bousefield, Jean, *see* Hardisty, Jean
Boveagh line, 100
Brady, David, 271, 299
Brady, Jim, 142, 270–271, 293, 299, 1964 (270), 1967 (270), 1970 (274), 1972 (276), 1973 (276)
Brehmer, K., 1978 (72), 168
Brennan, J., 1986 (296), 299
Brown, Andrew, 10, 23, 101
Brown, G. P., 10, 100, 101–102, 186, 200, 1923 (106)
Brown, J., 136
Brown, T. P., 100, 101
Brownrigg, T., 1991 (92)
Burke, J. P., 145, 212, 1984 (249)
Byrness in Redesdale, 3
Byrnne, Pat junior, 299
Byrnne, Pat senior, 299

C
Caig, G., 58
Capstick, T., 7
Carlton, D., 52
Carnwath, Scotland's first official trial, 3
Carpenter, Mrs E. B., 228
Chadwick, J., 299
Chapman, J., 58
Coggan, R., 53
Coggin, J., 52
Coltherd, A., 23
Cook, M., 52, 136
Cook, M. W., 1967 (49)
Cormack, W., 1973 (150)
Cricceith Sheepdog Society, 4

Cropper, J., 1986 (83)
Cropper, Katy, 69

D
Dalziel, R. (Bobby), 52, 69, 166, 168, 170, 212, 240, 1986 (169), 1992 (180)
Daniel, D. W., 103, 212, 217
Daniel, E. L., 69, 1992 (259)
Davidson, S. L., 69, 165, 170, 1980 (160), 1988 (172), 173, 1989 (174)
Davies, D. W., 1936 (195)
Davies, E. N., 218, 1964 (222), 1978 (241)
Denniff, Joe, 1954 (35), 200
Deptford, Julie, 69, 170, 1991 (178)
Dickson, D., 52
Dickson, Thomas, 264
Dodd, Brian, 62, 145, 1988 (86)
Dovedale, 2

E
Edwards, E. W., 144, 165, 200, 245, 1965 (223)
Edwards, Rhos, 69
Elliott, A., 1984 (80)
Elliott, T. E., 1973 (63)
English Brace Class, 7
Evans, B., 1993 (261)
Evans, E. J., 52
Evans, Llyr, 1969 (51), 53, 1976 (67), 212
Evans, W. J., 1949 (202), 1958 (38), 1959 (39), 1962 (42), 1963 (44), 58, 104, 186, 200, 202, 217, 228

F
Feeney, E., 1987 (297)
Ferguson, T., 58
Fish, children's T. V. serial, 104
Flash the Sheepdog, film, 104
Flemish Farm film, 104
Flood, Tim, 165, 293, 295, 299, 1975 (280), 1978 (283), 1979 (284), 1984 (292), 1988 (292), 1989 (292)
Foster, A., 1980 (75)

G
Gael, poem by Joe Johnstone, 136–137
Gardner, James, 3
Gilchrist, J., 23, 58, 103, 165, 173, 228, 287, 293, 1965 (138), 1966 (138)
Gilchrist, James, 139
Gilchrist, John, 139
Gilholm, T., 58

Goligher, R., 1991 (301)
Goodfellow, W., 23, 69, 1958 (129)
Goodwin, W. H., 1966 (224)
Gorst, J. K., 58, 60, 1953 (34), 1957 (37)
Graham, M., 145, 300, 1976 (282)
Greenslade, Harry, 1955 (211), 1956 (211), 212
Griffith, Elwyn, 139
Guild, D., 254
Gwilliam, R., 53, 78
Gwilliam, Richard, 53

H
Haddington, 4
Hardisty, Jean (later Bousefield), 69, 1977 (71)
Hardisty, W., 69, 271, 1961 (41)
Harris, W., 1950 (203)
Harrison, J., 8, 1990 (90)
Hastie, J., 52
Hayton, Arthur, 1947 (28), 104
Hayton, Mark, 1937 (24), 100, 104, 200
Hetherington, Peter, 137, 1970 (146)
Hetherington, W. S., 139, 144
Hettrick, John, 136
Hislop, W., 157, 200
Hislop, W. J., 103, 1948 (119), 1959 (130), 1961 (132)
Hogarth, J., 144, 1963 (134)
Holliday, J. H., 165, 1951 (32), 1968 (50)
Holmes, Cecil, 1952 (33), 200
Huddleston, E., 58, 59
Huddleston, H., 52, 1972 (57)
Huddleston, Harry (Arkholme), 58, 60, 1989 (88)
Huddleston, William, 58
Hughes, R. J., 200, 1928 (190), 1946 (199), 1948 (199)
Humphreys, L. J., 1929 (191), 1930 (191), 1931 (192), 1934 (192), 1933 (194), 1939 (194)
Hunter, T., 23, 100, 101, 186, 188
Hutton, George, 136

I
Iley, T., 52
International Brace Championship, 7
International Sheep Dog Society
    centenary trial to Bala, 2
    history, 4
International Sheep Dog Society Trials, development
    1873–1906, 2–3
    1906–present, 4
Irish-bred dogs, 299
Irish National, 4
Irish National and the Isle of Man, 300
Irish Sheepdog Trials, early years, 264, 265
Irvine, J., 145, 299, 1983 (291)
Isle of Man, 299
Isle of Man Championships, 264
Isle of Man and the Irish National, 300

J
James, John, 53, 145, 1975 (65)
Jones, A. G., 139, 145, 254, 1974 (235)
Jones, Alan, 69, 139, 145, 200, 217, 228, 1959 (216), 1961 (216), 1962 (219), 1971 (232), 1976 (238)
Jones, D., 240
Jones, G., 78, 136, 144, 157, 168, 254, 1987 (253)
Jones, Glyn, 3, 245
Jones, Hefin, 254
Jones, H. G., 52, 145, 1980 (244), 1981 (244)
Jones, H. W., 1988 (255), 1990 (255)
Jones, John (Corwen), 186, 188
Jones, John (Trawsfynydd), 186, 1932 (193), 1935 (194)
Jones, M., 165, 173, 1979 (243)
Jones, Meirion, 165, 173, 186, 254, 1979 (243)
Jones, Selwyn, 142, 1963 (221)
Jones, W., 1958 (215)
Jones-Jarrett, Mr, 4

K
Kerr, John, 1968 (141), 142
Kinrade, R., 299
Kirk, J., 103, 136

L
Lambe, T. (Toddy), 1990 (298), 299
Lauder, G., 197, 200
Liddle, A. G., 1934 (20), 1936 (20)
Lightfoot, J., 1991 (258)
Lilico, James, 10, 100, 108
Little, D., 299, 300
Little, W. R., 1954 (125)
Llangollen, 2
Lloyd, A. T., 165, 212, 217
Lloyd, D. W., 145, 1983 (79)
Lloyd-Price
    first official sheepdog trial, 2
    grandson, 3
Loates, H., 145, 1979 (73)
Logan, J. Harford, 145, 165, 287, 1968 (273), 1969 (273), 1974 (278), 1977 (278), 1980 (286), 1981 (161)
Longshaw, 2, 7
Longton, Jack (brother to Tot), 60
Longton, T., 58
Longton, Thomas (son of Tot), 52, 60, 62
Longton, Thomas (Tot) (son of Tim), 52, 60, 165, 240, 1950 (31), 1956 (31)
Longton, Tim Jnr (brother to Tot), 53, 58, 60, 61, 62, 136, 139, 142, 145, 1949 (30), 1965 (47), 1966 (48), 1970 (55), 1974 (64), 1981 (76)
Longton, Tim Snr, 60
Longton, Timothy (son of Tim Jnr), 60
Longton, T. W., 1985 (81), 1992 (93), 144, 218
Loyal Heart, film, 104
Lucas, E., 58
Lutton, George, 1982 (289), 299

Lyttle, Alistair, 299

M
McCormack, Mrs Annie, 69
MacDonald, D., 1974 (151)
McDonald, J., 60, 145
McFadden, J. P., 299, 1993 (304)
McGregor Hepburn, P. G., 139
McKee, J. W., 264, 1961 (267), 1963 (269)
McKenzie, J., 165
McKnight, T. T., 52, 136, 137, 157, 173, 247, 1964 (135), 1971 (148)
McMillan, A., 1967 (140)
McMillan, Fiona, 69
MacPherson, C. B., 99, 100, 104, 197, 200
McPherson, J. D., 197
MacPherson, Raymond C., 7, 7–8, 52, 137, 165, 245, 1971 (56)
Macrae, Alasdair S., 69, 145, 166, 168, 1984 (167)
McRobert, J. F., 168, 1990 (176)
McSwiggan, J., 142, 1971 (275)
McTeir, D., 145, 157, 1972 (149)
Martindale, T. C., 58
Mason, Jean, 69
Metcalf, Philip, 58
Miles, W. F. (Bill), 197, 1938 (198), 1952 (206)
Millar, Alex, 3, 103, 108, 264, 1922 (105), 1924 (107), 1925 (105), 1926 (105), 1927 (105), 1928 (109), 1929 (109), 1930 (110), 1934 (113)
Millar, J. R. (son of Alex), 108, 157, 1947 (118), 1949 (120), 1953 (124), 1969 (143)
Moore, James, 100
Morgan, E. F., 1964 (45)
Morris, Edward, 188, 1926 (189), 1927 (189)
Mostyn, E. L. Hon. (later Lord), 4
Mullan, J. F., 272, 1965 (272)
Murray, David, 100, 103, 1938 (116), 1952 (123)
Murray, David (son of David), 104
Murray, J., 53, 60, 144
Murray, Jean, 103–104
My Dog, Number, film, 103–104

N
New Cumnock, 3
Nicholls, R. E., 218, 1972 (233)
Northern Ireland
    amalgamating with Republic of Eire, 4
    first competing, 4
Northern Ireland Sheepdog Trial Society, 264

O
Ollerenshaw, R., 53, 59
O'Neill, Martin, 293, 1992 (302), 303
O'Sullivan, D., 1981 (288)
Owd Bob, film, 104
Owen, A., 145, 1985 (251)
Owen, D. I., 1989 (256)
Owen, Gwilliam, 200, 1954 (209)
Owen, H., 145, 1986 (252)

Owen, M., 254, 256
Owen, O. J., 200

P
Page, M. R., 145, 212, 247, 1970 (231), 1973 (234), 1982 (246)
Pennefather, G. L. (Lionel), 58, 264–265, 1962 (268), 1966 (268)
Perrings, Mike, 137
Piggin, Mr, 2, 264
Price, Sidney B., 165, 300, 1987 (85)
Priestley, E. A., 7, 58, 1955 (36), 1960 (40)
Priestley, Ernest, 7, 1922 (6), 1923 (6), 1930 (17), 23
Priestley, Malcolm, 7
Pritchard, E., 1925 (187)
Pritchard, John, 1922 (184), 188
Pugh, G. (Griff), 200, 1951 (204), 1953 (208)
Purdie, J., 108, 139

Q
Quayle, T., 300
Quirk, G., 300

R
Rae, W., 145, 1977 (155)
Redpath, G., 139, 200
Reed, G., 52
Reed, W., 293
Registration system, 4
Reid, James A., 4, 99–100, 264
Relph, Joe, 104, 202
Renwick, Adam, 23, 101
Renwick, James, 1935 (21), 1938 (21), 23
Renwick, John, father of James and William, 23
Renwick, W., 58, 139
Renwick, William, 23, 1939 (26)
Republic of Eire, 4
Richardson, J., 53, 78, 145, 271, 1975 (152)
Rigby, W., 2
Roberts, T. (Tom), 1923 (185), 1924 (185), 186, 188
Russell, J., 53

S
Sandiland, R., 23
Scotland, early trials, 3
Scott, James, 10, 23
Scottish Brace Championship, 7
Shennan, David, 137, 145, 157, 1976 (153), 1978 (156)
Shennan, Robert, 144, 145, 157, 218, 254, 1979 (158)
Shepherd of the Hills, film, 104
Shepherds' class abolished, 4
Short, R., 165, 1960 (131)
Smith, John, 200
Song of the Plough, film, 104
Stoddart, Sam, 100
Stud book, 4
Supreme Champion trophy, 3
Suter, L. R., 53, 136, 1969 (230)
Sykes, Barbara, 69

Sykes, Vickie, 69

T
Teenage handlers, 299–300
Telfer, Adam, 58, 99, 1924 (9)
Telfer, Adam Jnr, 10
Telfer, Adam Snr, bred Old Hemp 9, 3, 10, 10–11
Telfer, Adam Stewart, great-great-grandson, 11
Telfer, Jean Ayre, 10
Telfer, John, 10, 11
    great-grandson, 11
Telfer, Walter, 3, 10, 11, 108, 188
Telfer, W. B., 1926 (15), 1927 (15), 1929 (15)
Templeton, J. G. (son of John), 166
Templeton, John J., 7, 52, 59, 144, 173, 247, 295, 299,
    1957 (128), 1982 (163), 1983 (163), 1985 (163)
Thomas, J. R., 52, 60, 217, 240, 254, 1977 (239)
Thomas, S. H., 53, 78, 145, 1982 (77)
Thomas, W. J., 1957 (214), 1960 (214)
Thomson, James, 2, 3
Thomson, Jean, 69
Thorp, J., 1948 (29)
Turnbull, Paul, 69, 1993 (95)

U
Udale Sim, poem, 60

W
Wales, first trials, 4
Wallace, William, father of W. J. Wallace, 4, 10, 53, 99,
    100

Wallace, W. J., 53, 228, 1933 (19), 53
Watson, T., 52, 157, 165, 247
Watt, Barton (son of William), 299
Watt, Gordon (son of William), 299
Watt, William, 299
Welsh, J. R., 165
    for T. Hutchinson, 1987 (171)
Welsh, W., 240
Whiting, George, 186
Whittaker, Captain, 4
Williams, G., 1983 (248)
Williams, J. C., 200
Williams, R. H., 186, 1937 (196)
Williams, R. O., 1947 (201)
Williams, Robert, 200
Wilson, David, father of J. M. Wilson, 3
Wilson, J., 1993 (182)
Wilson, J. M., 23, 52, 53, 99, 102–103, 108, 144, 157,
    165, 170, 197, 200, 202, 212, 228, 254, 1931
    (111), 1932 (111), 1933 (112), 1935 (114), 1936
    (114), 1937 (115), 1939 (114), 1946 (117), 1950
    (121), 1951 (122), 1955 (126)
Wiston 'line', 144–145
Worthington, Herbert J., 200, 217, 228, 1975 (237),
    1967 (226)
Wright, E., 264

Y
Young, D., 136
Youngs, H., 53

Dog Index

Index to National Champions, etc. and their occurrences in pedigrees; main references in bold.

A
Allan 12085, 212
Ancrum Jed, 10
Anne 4545, 138, 139
Asterton Nell 160690, 300

B
Barney 4365, **28**
Ben 891, 108, **110**, 113, 264
Ben 2481, 23
Ben 4333, 200
Ben 4931, 108, **120**, 124, 143
Ben 5714, 139
Ben 9474, 103
Ben 11401 R.O.M., 200, **215**
Ben 12262, 94, 108, 143
Ben 12953, 44, 202
Ben 13879, 165, 186
Ben 16449, **133**
Ben 56646, 145, **149**, 161, 167, 304
Ben 88284, 91, **160**, 172, 173, 175, 177
Ben 92094, **72**
Ben 119873, 165, 166, 181
Ben 129820, 145, **251**
Ben 145915, 300
Ben 196195, 299
Bess 6338, 104
Bess 17145, 58, 64, 264, 267, **268**, 275, 290
Bess 89022, 61
Bess 101142, 52, 60, **81**, 93, 144, 218
Bess 107127, 145
Bess 161886, 69
Bet 2398, 23, **26**
Bet 4353, 200
Bet 6260, **34**, 58, 60
Bett 49428, 58
Bett 40428, 52, 58, 60
Bill 9040, 103, 220
Bill 13243, 7
Bill 39521, **63**
Bill 51654, 136, 144, 254
Bill 78263, 144, 165, 245
Bill 177773, 157
Bill II 17937, 52, 144
Bill II 18890, 157
Black 144068, **258**
Blackie 1635, 186, **193**
Bob, 2
Bob 12684, 139
Bob 40131, 300

Bob 79686, 139
Border Boss, 53, 100
Bosworth Coon 34186, 7, **51**, 52, 53, 60, 68, 74, 78, 82, 94, 212, 270, 276
Bosworth Jim 52007, 270, **276**
Bosworth Moss 16054, 52
Bosworth Scot 22120, 51, 52, 68, 74, 276
Brocken Glen 105526, 52
Brocken Robbie 24636, 228
Bruce, 3
Buff 23069, 142, **270**, 273, 274, 280, 287
Bute 178106, 168
Bwlch Bracken 74660, 245
Bwlch Taff 113243, 52, 145, 218, **244**, 245

C
Caley (of Thornhill), 100, 188
Cap, 60, 188
Cap 237, 10, 108
Cap 3036, 53, 103, 165, 200, 212, 228
Cap 6360, 104
Cap 13274, 136
Cap 13733, 157
Cap 15839, 78
Cap 24328, **273**, 287
Cap 50543, 7, 52, 59, 144, 157, 165
Cap 67711, 61
Cap 78525, 78
Cap 91526, 179, 240
Cap 108145, 145, 212, **246**, 247
Cap 142018, **83**
Cap 144844, 245
Cap 161769, 61
Carlo 36705, 248
Chance, 116
Chief 120006 (working name Craig), 173, **174**
Chip 672, 186
Chip 4924, 103, 212, 217
Chip 22797, 212
Chip 62102, 52, 53, **67**
Chip 77779, 182, 290
Chip 130670, 299
Chum 47289, 300
Chum 93897, 299
Cleg, 10
Clive 70727, 300
Clun Gael 95727, 53
Connie 84203, 145, **155**
Coon 1608, 200
Coon 5701, 202

Coon 9077, 200
Corrie 182846, 168
Cosy 70560, **280**, 293, 299
Craig, 197
Craig 1048, 99, **111**, 112, 115, 116, 120, 123, 205, 208
Craig 15445, 53, 66, 68, 136
Craig 47577, 139
Craig 59425, 52, 89, 179, 181, 217, **239**, 240, 254
Craig 67343, 186, **243**
Craig 72737, 139, 145, 217, **238**, 254, 297
Craig 99232, 299
Craig 108412, 293
Craig 118161, **297**
Craig 120006, 69
Craig 148254, **90**
Cymro 82447, 218, **241**

D
Dale 55615, 290
Dan 15485, 267
Dart 92163, **75**
Davy 131049, **85**, 165, 300, 301
Del 166557, 299
Dick 174159, 287
Don 11, 15, 23
Don 17, 15, 100, 106, 107, 108, 110, 254
Don 6644, 200, **204**
Don 13392, **42**, 202
Don 73710, 89, 171, 240, 302, 304
Don 106096, **248**
Don 108889, 60, 88, 181, 182, 240
Don 122367, 165
Don 142576, 69
Don I 17, 191
Dot 4844, **30**, 60
Dot 11228, 136
Dot 151515, 299
Dot III 18925, 136, 137, 154
Drift 4380, 108, **118**, 136, 210, 269, 272
◄Drift 51202, 80, 154, 156, 157, 170, 288
Dryden Joe 104626, 83, **169**, 212, 247, 257, 259
Duke 6017, 58, 61
Dun 163303, 293
Dusk 18923, 136

E
Elwyn Glen 190830, 168
Eve 112604, 271, **294**, 295

F
Fan 2401, 58
Fan 4424, **29**, 31
Fan 4442, 31
Fan 6938, 52
Fenwick Jed, 10, 33, 114
Fingland Loos 435, 99–100
Flash 106580, **284**, 293
Flash 79000, 69, **71**
Flash II 180639, **302**, 303

Fleece 11049, 64
Fleet, 7
Fleet 203, 58
Fleet 37588, 165
Fleet 38813, 84, 282
Fleet 4555, 104, 202
Floss 8582, 228
Floss 11400, 212
Fly, 58
Fly 165, 58, 100, 101, 186
Fly 824, 99, 102
Fly 1574, 186, **194**
Fly 1764, **20**
Fly 8899, 141
Fly 11362, 69, 71, 283
Fly 12570, 226, 228, 232, 247
Fly 23160, 157
Fly 25005, 144
Fly 33034, 53
Fly 73340, 157
Fly 108143, 247
Fly 163448, 212, **259**
Fly II 46113, 228
Foch 2344, 53
Foozle 350, 264
Frisk, 108

G
Gael 14463, 49, 52, **135**, 136, 147, 148, 154
Gael 63582, 78
Gael 134686, 69
Garry 3699, 46, 224
Garry 11742, 212
Garry 17690, 165, 212, 217
Garry 49864, 157
Garry 98341, 69
Garry II 72575, 260
Gay 69947, 145, **282**, 300
Gel 63023, 3, 245
Gel 124181, 61
Gem 147666, 52, 61, 62, **93**
Glen, 104
Glen 698, 29, 100, 104, 200
Glen 2213, 58
Glen 3940, 41, 103, 108, **117**, 119, 120, 124, 125, 129,
    157, 202, 209, 211, 212, 214, 225
Glen 3957, 125
Glen 4339, 58
Glen 5107, 23
Glen 6425, 139
Glen 7395, **214**
Glen 7690, **211**, 212
Glen 12063, 103
Glen 17251, 217, 218, **219**
Glen 29405, 55
Glen 47241, 53, 60, 144
◄Glen 62253, **151**, 245, 255
Glen 75630, 83, 85, 91, 95, 164, 170, 257, 260, 302,
    304

Glen 76918, 250
Glen 92091, 245
Glen 109694, **289**, 299
Glen 113361, 145, 212, **249**
Glen 124915, 69
Glen 127946, 299
Glen 143941, 168, **176**
Glen II 48637, **55**
Glyn, 104
Goss 91940, 52
Gwen 19455, **222**, 242
Gwen 160435, 69, **178**
Gyp, 7
Gyp 33128, 142, 270, **274**
Gyp 38336, 52, 60, 82, 94
Gyp 40132, 300
Gyp 56601, 52, 60

H
Hadwin's Quen 56602, 52
Haig 252, **9**, 10, 58, 186, 190, 195
Haig 9190, 51, 68, 276
Heaplaw Moss 4420, 23
Hemp 153, 6, 7, 17, 20, 58, 99, 108, 109, 111, 112, 114,
    115, 116, 191, 194, 195, 264
Hemp 1006, 7, **17**
Hemp 4504, 53
Hemp 13132, 200, 226, 228, 232, 233, 247, 276
Hemp 36879, 245
Hemp 59856, 137
Hemp 72301, 91, 161, 164, 177, 257, 304
Hemp II 307, 14, 23, 26
Hemp II 24641, 228
Holly 160182, 69
Hope 7029, 50
Hope 9943, 165
Hope 158875, 173

J
Jace 62098, 52
Jack II 16687, 287
Jaff 379, 16, **185**, 186, 188, 194
Jaff 2598, 126, 186, **196**
Jaff 2885, 202
Jaff 4313, 43, **199**, 200, 210, 215, 217, 223
Jaff 10855, 228
Jaff 38313, 137, 147, 154, 160, 172, 173, 175, 247, 290
Jaff I 379, 196
Jaff II 2011, 33, 196
Jaff II 2199, 186, 201
Jan 188256, 295
Jasper 79280, 179
Jed 358, 7
Jed 1492, **19**, 53, 228
Jed 4047, 211
Jed 4941, 139
Jeff, 104
Jeff 4371, 223
Jeff 14422, 152

Jen 93965, 52, 165
Jen 134760, 165, **171**
Jenny, 110
Jess 818, **16**
Jess 1007, 29
Jess 88627, 60, 165, 240
Jess 152391, 218
Jess II 2852, 29
Jet 352, 57
Jet 607, 7
Jill 2735, 203
Jim 5869, 223
Jim 10071, **36**
Jim 12572, **132**
Jim 12967, **41**, 57, 69, 71, 271, 274, 283
Jim 67676, **278**, 287
Jim 103518, **79**, 145
Jim 125956, 271
Jim 150661, 60, **88**
Jix, 102
Jock 2029, 28
Jock 21994, **140**
Joe 141919, 247
Joss 6618, 220
Joss 152124, 240
June 59734, 95, **150**, 297
Juno 618, **187**
Juno 4869, 36, 38, 40, 51, 222
Juno 17815, **226**, 228

K
Kate 2601, 197, **198**
Kate 101410, 295
Kay 12084, 197
Ken 1194, 58
Ken 1477, 108, **113**, 122
Ken 5015, 197
Ken 13306, 69, 212
Ken 17166, **48**, 53, 58, 61, 74, 139
Ken 47974, 53, 59
Ken 101980, 212
Ken II 18754, 108, **143**, 157
Kep 13, 10, 16, 23, 58, 59, 100, 185–186
Kep 1654, **21**, 23
Kep 4264, 228
Kep 13954, 58
Kerry 84042, 52
Kirk 153106, 254
Kris 94235, 271
Kyle 47050, 137

L
Lad Junior, 102
Lad 19, 58, 100, 101
Lad 305, **14**, 23, 26, 188, 192
Lad 859, 7
Lad 990, **192**
Lad 3091, **201**
Lad 4453, **33**, 200

Lad 11027, 58, 268
Lad 37094, 147
Lad 41928, 60
Lad 44675, 217, 218, **232**
Lad 54209, 217, 228, **237**
Lad 64612, 53
Lad 80955, 299
Lad 130299, 218
Laddie 406, **184**, 187, 188
Laddie 867, **190**
Laddie 4362, **208**
Laddie 8049, 23, 41, 69, **129**, 274
Laddie 13204, **134**
Laddie 14110, 296
Laddie 40729, 296
Laddie 151099, 62, **86**, 145
Laddie 174762, 303
Lark 9679, 7
Lass 11713, 52
Lassie, 23
Lassie 518, 57
Lassie 9868, 103, 104
Lassie 12694, 150
Lassie 19421, 144
Lassie 23501, 145
Lassie 71318, 78
Lassie 91601, 61
Lille 26, 58
Liz 37009, 250
Loos II 435, 99–100, 112, 114, 115, 120, 194, 205
Lyn 168527, 299, **304**
Lynn 28622, 182, 275, 290

M
Mac 4418, **27**
Mac 8133, 7
Maddie 2656, 58
Maddie 4337, 34, 37, 58
Maddie III 10992, 58
Maggie 140478, 61
Maid, 264
Maid 209, 58
Maid 3677, 228
Maid 14173, 165
Maid 169072, **301**
Maid 28779, **49**, 52, 136, 148
Maid 51269, 157
Maid 97071, 240
Max 110507, 165, 295
Max 166230, 69
Meg, 116, 299
    dam of Old Hemp 10
Meg 27, 23
Meg 57, 197, 198, 199
Meg 306, 4, 19, 53
Meg 12625, 165
Meg 12746, 254
Meg 17826, 141, 142
Meg 63230, 137, 145, **153**, 156, 157

Meg 78875, 228
Meg 81598, 271
Meg 96043, 212
Meg 99400, 271
Meg 115981, 69
Meg 126291, **296**, 299
Meg 135659, 254, **255**
Meg II 4348, 124, 143
Mick 19770, 248
Midge 152, 10
Mindrum Nell 11106, 75
Minn 3387, 43, 200, 210, 217
Mirk 836, 108, **109**
Mirk 4438, 36, 39, 103, **121**, 122, 130, 138, 217, 221
Mirk 5444, 60, 270
Mirk 12283, 23
Mirk 13296, 63
Mirk 28776, 84, 136, **148**
Mirk 47857, 139
Mirk 52844, 53, 66, 79, 87, 95, 145, **152**, 159, 162, 164,
    173, 175, 177, 248
Mirk 67512, 144, 145, 157, **158**, 218, 254
Mirk 68102, 53, **65**, 145
Mirk 96612, 145, **167**, 168
Mirk 111004, 300
Mirk II 80772, 157
Mirk II 120673, 168
Mist 332, 108
Mist 109678, 295
Moss 22, 10, 53, 100
Moss 233, **6**, 7, 17, 23, 26
Moss 454, 100, 104, 188, 197, 198, 199, 200
Moss 569, **18**
Moss 12088, 282
Moss 2032, 104
Moss 2206, **194**
Moss 4551, 38, 41, 48, 127, 136, 197, 267
Moss 4975, 227, 228, 239
Moss 5018, 165
Moss 5176, 36, 39, 40, 46, 47, 103, 130, 133, 134, 138,
    217, 225, 231
Moss 6805, 45, 139, 200
Moss 6811, 43, 217, 222
Moss 7971, 36, **38**, 202
Moss 8754, 23
Moss 11029, 50, 165
Moss 14902, **45**
Moss 41957, 79, 82, 218, **233**, 238, 285, 293, 297
Moss 57707, 218
Moss 103923, 91, 161, 164, 165, 181, 257, 302, 304
Moss 127211, 240
Moss 131207, **80**
Moss 137368, 69
Moss 138632, 165, **172**, 173
Moss 139699, 267
Moss II 28996, **50**
Moss III 28, 184
Mossie, 58, 59
Mossie 6235, **31**, 60

Moy 42363, **273**, 287
Moy 75295, 299
Moy 128083, 299

N
Nan 490, 101
Nan 85606, **156**, 157
Nan 186565, 69, 166, 168
Nancy 242, 107, 108
Nap 11691, 141
Nap 16043, 141
Nap 17605, 165
Nap 18186, **224**
Nap 28777, 136
Nap 43986, 7, **56**
Nap 131097, **92**
Nap 148436, 168
Nap 188631, 69, **95**
Nell, 58
Nell 205, 10, 101
Nell 1627, 99, 102, 103, **114**
Nell 3514, 103, 136
Nell 6879, 42, 63, 202, 217
Nell 7077, 61
Nell 8739, 200, **209**
Nell 10656, 287
Nell 112637, 157
Nell 12743, **131**
Nell 16024, 212
Nell 16949, **272**
Nell 43414, 280, 283, 285, 288, 293, 294, 298, 303
Nell 53708, 85, 137, **146**
Nell 61154, 139, 238
Nell 65799, 92, 145, **234**, 247
Nell 71990, 293
Nell 99019, **288**
Nell 127436, 165
Nell 129513, 166
Nell 146196, **298**, 299
Nell 170326, 69
Nell 173962, 166
Ness 14695, 69
Nett 989, **195**
Nickey 1823, 99, **112**, 117, 119
Nickey 4698, 131
Nip, 58
Nip 16878, 31154, 87
Nip 17278, 200, **223**
Nip 68389, 136
Nip 159288, 299
Nobel, 53
Number 6152, 103, 221

O
Old Hemp 9, 3, 10, 11, 188
Old Maid 1, 10, 23, 101
Old Trim 39, 57
Ormskirk Charlie, 2, 7

P
Paddy 4364, 28
Pal Glen, 104
Pat 2219, **24**, 27, 28, 104
Pat 4203, 7, 58, 104
Patch of Thornby 59392, 52
Pattie 1515, 24, 27, 104
Penpell Bess 107127, 53, **77**, 78
Pete 18591, 287
Pip 124578, **292**, 293, 295
Pose, 10

Q
Queen, 62, 104
Queen 533, 10, **15**, 188
Queen 3113, 139
Queen 8810, 37, 58
Queen 24078, **141**, 142, 171
Queen 152483, 168, **253**, 254
Queenie, 58

R
Rap, 52
Risp 45699, 271, 280, 283, 285, 287, 288, 293, 294, 298
Risp 61527, 303
Rob 21959, 55, 60, 74, 75, 234
Robbie 2743, 228
Robbie 38315, 247
Robin 5499, 56, 217
Rock 1285, 197
Rock 1321, 207
Rock 36024, 142, **275**
Rock 162204, 254, **256**
Roos, 188
Rose 99231, 299
Roy, sire to Old Hemp 9, 10
Roy 1665, 99, 100, 102, **115**, 204, 254
Roy 2028, 23
Roy 5323, 139
Roy 5406, 50
Roy 7696, 42, 58, 200, 202, 217, 227, 228, 229, 232, 233, 242
Roy 7729, 60
Roy 8993, **128**, 140, 150, 165, 231, 247
Roy 14152, 60
Roy 14746, 156, 157
Roy 15393, 69, 200, **216**, 217, 228, 233, 234, 236, 241, 247, 277, 278
Roy 54175, 61, **64**, 136
Roy 88481, 255
Roy 114678, 90, **163**, 165, 257, 299
Roy II 5406, **32**
Roy II 16894, 165
Roy II 38227 R.O.M., **229**
Ruby 207, 100

S
Sally 46413 R.O.M., **230**

Sam 16555, 136
Sam 192693, **182**
Scot 545, 58
Scot 564, 186
Scot 28069, 164, 168, 170, 278
Scot 57965, 165, 280, **283**, 285, 288, 293, 294, 298, 299
Scott 103933, 303
Shane, 299
Shane 57767, 270
Shane 71700, 302
Shawsholm Fly 20080, 165
Shep 6107, 57
Shep 73360, 78, 144, 157, 254
Shep 80763, 173
Shep 109351, 145, **291**, 299
Shep II 49061, 78
Shona 62645, 136
Slade 141825, 69
Snip 10677, 264, **267**, 273
Snip 11496, 69
Snip 16879, **47**
Snip 21772, 264
Speed 4382, 51, 108, 130, 143
Spot 303, 10, 99, **105**, 108
Spot 308, 57, 100, 101, **106**, 186, 188, 189, 190, 192, 193, 194, 196, 200
Spot 615, 188, **189**, 196
Spot 3624, 23, 43, 58, 108, 139, 209, 214
Spot 7320, 139
Spot 9476, 56, 217
Spot 24981, 8, 71, 76, 84, 87, 103, **138**, 139, 150, 154, 160, 165, 170, 173, 175, 235, 237, 238, 243, 260, 278, 281, 283, 285, 287, 288, 293, 294
Spot 97015, 218
Spot 152290, 173, 186, 254
Spot 182249, 166
Spot II 604, 101
Spot II 6775, 39, **125**
Spotan, 188
Spotan 134842, 145, **252**
Spottie 37430, 53
Spottie 46442, 52, 53
Spy, 3
Spy 1137, 264
Spy 4553, 104
Star 109497, 145, **161**, 165, 287
Star 166276, 299
Sue 52445, 53
Susan 4046, 53
Susan 42639, 53, 78
Susie 138200, 299
Swan 8233, 69
Sweep 21, 10, 14, 100, 254
Sweep 164, 7, 17, 22, 23, 101, 184, 187, 188, 191, 192, 195
Sweep 1962, 103, **116**, 123
Sweep 3834, 35, 46, 103, **119**, 132, 157, 200, 204
Sweep 4204, **202**, 211

Sweep 4702, 40, 215, 222, 223
Sweep 5096, **203**
Sweep 5594, **35**, 200
Sweep 11115, 7, **40**
Sweep 13146, **130**
Sweep 16216, 197
Sweep 22666, 301
Sweep 23470, **231**, 247
Sweep 39603, 80, 145, 155, 167, 271, 286, 291
Sweep 51651, 157
Sweep 85943, 250
Sweep 87666, 145, **286**, 287

T
Taff 9248, 217
Taff 20938, 218
Taff 80135, 139
Taff 91192, 69
Taff 167290, 168, 245
Taff 172213, 218
Taff 177576, **261**
Tam, 108
Tam 1489, 31
Tam 3465, 139
Tam 7032, 108, **124**, 143
Tam 25605, 139
Tam 26504, 275
Tamsin 66472, 78
Teresa 47290, 300
Tess, 101
Tibbie 11113, 186
Tillyochie Moss 7878, **127**, 212, 268
Tommy 16, 10, 53, 99, 100, 101, 188
Tony 66922, 52
Tos 61152, 139, 145, **235**, 254
Toss 151, 10
Toss 464, **191**
Toss 3001, 100, 103
Tot 155, 18, **107**, 108, 110, 113
Trim, 139
Trim 37, 10, 100
Trim 52587, 287
Trim 157047, 69
Turk, 2, 104
Turk 118169, 293
Tweed, 2
Tweed 9601, **39**, 133, 140, 141, 186, 202, 273
Tweed 29403, 157
Tweed 62901, 8
Tweed 92756, 89, 254
Tweed 96630, 61, **76**, 87, 142, 145
Tweed 140476, 61
Tweedhope Glen 169258, 69
Tyne 145, 10

U
Udale Sim 52690, **57**, 59, 92

V

Vic 4368, 56, 103, **123**, 221
Vic 117838, 218
Vic 128240, 256
Vickey 15968, 142, **221**
Vim 685, 108, 110
Vim 1984, 207

W

Wally 4361, 197, **206**
Wattie 37429, 53
White 2182, 201
Whitehope Corrie 13706, 47, 64, 142, 267, **269**, 270, 272, 273, 274, 275, 290
Whitehope Nap 8685, 7, 44, 49, 51, 55, 56, 60, 103, **126**, 133, 136, 147, 148, 151, 202, 230, 231
Whitehope Tib 6903, **122**

Wisp 161487, 52, 69, 165, 166, 168, **180**, 240
Wiston Bill 36391, 144, 157
Wiston Cap 31154, 4, 52, 53, 55, 60, 66, 68, 74, 76, 78, 79, 82, 87, 94, 136, 144, 144–145, 147, 149, 152, 154, 155, 159, 162, 165, 168, 177, 234, 235, 238, 245, 247, 250, 251, 252, 282, 286, 287, 291
Wiston Jill 79096, **73**, 145
Wiston Nan III 9896, 139
Wullie 111993, 69
Wylie 1184, 7

Y

Yarrow, 10

Z

Zac 66166, 7, 52, 137, 165, 245

FARMING PRESS BOOKS & VIDEOS

Below is a sample of the wide range of agricultural and veterinary books and videos published by Farming Press. For more information or for a free illustrated catalogue of all our publications please contact:

**Farming Press Books & Videos, Wharfedale Road,
Ipswich IP1 4LG, United Kingdom
Telephone (0473) 241122   Fax (0473) 240501**

BOOKS

A Way of Life: Sheepdog Training, Handling and Trialling
H. GLYN JONES AND BARBARA C. COLLINS
A complete guide to sheepdog work and trialling, in which Glyn Jones' life is presented as an integral part of his tested and proven methods.

Dog Ailments   EDDIE STRAITON
How to diagnose and treat the common dog ailments and conditions.

One Dog, His Man & His Trials
MARJORIE QUARTON
Shep's tales of a sheepdog's life in Ireland with its rogues, adventures and humorous encounters, canine and human.

A Guide to Sheepdog Trials in Britain and Ireland   BARBARA C. COLLINS
Full details on over 400 trials for competitors as well as spectators.

VHS COLOUR VIDEOS

Come Bye! and Away!   H. GLYN JONES
Glyn Jones demonstrates the basic sheepdog training techniques, focusing on the moment when a young dog is first let off the leash in a field of sheep and learns to obey the four commands.

That'll Do!   H. GLYN JONES
Sequel to the first video, in which Glyn Jones teaches more specific commands and then reduces command contact.

Farming Press Books & Videos is part of the Morgan-Grampian Farming Press Group which publishes a range of farming magazines: *Arable Farming*, *Dairy Farmer*, *Farming News*, *Pig Farming*, *What's New in Farming*. For a specimen copy of any of these please contact the address above.